THE TEACHING OF DEVELOPMENT ECONOMICS

THE TEACHING OF DEVELOPMENT ECONOMICS

Its Position in the Present State of Knowledge

THE PROCEEDINGS OF THE
MANCHESTER CONFERENCE ON TEACHING
ECONOMIC DEVELOPMENT, APRIL 1964

Edited by
Kurt Martin & John Knapp

FRANK CASS & CO. LTD.
1967

First published in 1967 by
FRANK CASS AND COMPANY LIMITED
67 Great Russell Street, London, WC1

Printed in Great Britain by
Billing & Sons Limited, Guildford and London

CONTENTS

Part Two: Oral Discussion

PART A: THE STATE OF KNOWLEDGE. EDITED BY JOHN KNAPP

PART B: TEACHING ECONOMIC DEVELOPMENT. EDITED BY KURT MARTIN

ACKNOWLEDGEMENTS

THE organizers of the Conference wish to place on record their appreciation of the excellent hospitality dispensed to our visitors by the Warden and staff of Woolton Hall, University of Manchester. The Conference could not have taken place without the finance which it was possible to make available from funds granted to the Faculty of Economic and Social Studies, University of Manchester, by the Ford Foundation. Thanks are due to the Editors and Publishers of the *Bulletin* of the University of Oxford Institute of Economics and Statistics for permission to reproduce the article: "The Limitations of the Special Case", by D. Seers, from the issue of the *Bulletin* for May, 1963. The Conference was held under the auspices of the Centre of Development Studies, University of Manchester.

INTRODUCTION

I

THE project of a Conference on Problems of Teaching Development Economics[1] was first proposed by the junior editor of the present volume as a result of the stimulus provided by Mr. Dudley Seers's article on "The Limitations of the Special Case". This article was referred to in the invitations we issued, and is reprinted, with permission, at the head of this volume. The acceptance of invitations to attend on the part of a large number of distinguished British economists, and the arrival of eminent economists who had travelled from overseas for the purpose, showed, we think, that there existed a widespread feeling that Mr. Seers had a case that needed to be discussed. There was also the circumstance that, in a number of British universities, new courses in development economics had either recently been, or were about to be, launched. The Conference offered an opportunity to compare experiences and plans.

It was decided in advance that the oral proceedings of the Conference (which were recorded on tape) should be divided into a first session concerned with The State of Knowledge and a second, to be concerned with Teaching. The papers submitted to the Conference were similarly grouped. Inevitably, and in our view rightly, the actual consideration of these two topics, which took place in the course of a highly spontaneous oral discussion, was not kept altogether separate throughout. We have seen no good reason to attempt to alter the actual sequence of oral contributions in the course of editing them.

1. The Conference was held during the Easter vacation of 1964. The passage of time since then, together with the tendency for ideas to develop and change rapidly in the fast-growing field of development economics, makes it more than usually necessary to point out that some of the positions taken up at the Conference by the contributors to these proceedings many no longer reflect their present views. In addition, a number of the contributors to the volume were subsequently appointed to whole-time or part-time posts in H.M. Civil Service. It should be understood that their contributions reflected only their views in their capacity as scholars, and that their expressions of them preceded their entry into Government service.

II

The discussion of the *State of Knowledge* was dominated by the question of its degree of "adequacy", concerning which Mr. Seers had submitted "Some Leading Questions" to the Conference, along the lines of his 1963 paper. Some of the apparent disagreement over this topic turned out to be purely semantic in character.

There was general if somewhat belated agreement at the Conference that *differences in circumstances* may often call for significant departures from some of the factual assumptions habitually made in Anglo-Saxon economic theories, with corresponding changes both in the results of analysis and in its application in diagnosis and policy formulation. In econometric language, the foregoing amounts to saying that the estimated structure of a given theory may be expected to vary with differences in the economic and social environment. This proposition needs only to be clearly stated to command general assent.

In his succinct review paper on "Economic Theory and the Underdeveloped Countries"[1] Mr. Myint distinguished the foregoing issue, which he labelled the issue of "realism" (and which had loomed rather large in what Mr. Seers had been arguing), very sharply from another, more important issue which was also involved in Mr. Seers's argument, namely, the question of the "relevance", as Mr. Myint called it, of western economic theory. In econometric language, the issue here is the degree of adequacy, or otherwise, of the structure of our models of development.[2] On this issue, differences among the participants appeared to be both large and persistent. Agreement was confined to recognition of the fact that the development theories we now possess do not enable us to explain the variations in the wealth of nations which we observe.

Attitudes varied widely in the face of this situation. At one extreme, there was the qualified orthodoxy of Professor Hagen, who, in discussion, regarded the bulk of our existing body of analysis as being, within its limits, everywhere relevant, excepting only most of the elements of the "new orthodoxy" of development theories which have appeared on the scene since World War II. Professor Hagen was severely critical of the latter in his paper on "What We

1. Since published in the *Journal of Political Economy*, October, 1965.
2. It is of some interest to note a further semantic fact: we are informed that the issue referred to by Mr. Myint as that of "realism" would be described by econometricians as the question of "relevance", while they would use the word "realism" where Mr. Myint uses "relevance".

do not know about the Economics of Development in Low Income Societies". Against this, there was the radicalism of a number of others—e.g. Mrs. Robinson, Mr. Balogh, Mr. Streeten, Mr. Seers, and Mr. Knapp—who denied that conventional textbook analysis was relevant for development *anywhere*, western countries included. Professor Hagen's explanation of the failure of economic theory to account for variations in the wealth of nations is that the key to these variations lies in differences in "the amount of creative energy which flows into technological advance" (and this) "is largely determined by factors concerning which economics has nothing to say". This position amounts to saying that conventional economics is all right, but unimportant for development. By contrast, Mr. Streeten's paper on "The Use and Abuse of Models in Development Planning", represents, in part, an attempt to provide a fairly comprehensive classificatory survey of the multifarious sources of error and bias in the models of development which have been used as points of departure for the economic planning activities of recent years. This discussion, together with Mr. Streeten's sketch of a model of development and his suggestions for reformulations of existing concepts, as well as his oral contributions, clearly signified his conviction, which appeared to be shared by a number of people, that while present-day development economics is very far indeed from being adequately relevant, there are nevertheless no grounds for thinking that it has reached the end of its tether in terms of its future possibilities.

Mr. Balogh's paper, on "The Economics of Educational Planning" can be regarded as an illustration, in a fashionable but nevertheless important field, of the manner in which a number of the types of misuse of economic analysis distinguished by Mr. Streeten operate.

Mr. Myint's paper, as well as the sizeable part of Miss Ady's paper on "Teaching Development Economics" which dealt with the relevance of parts of conventional micro- and macro-analysis to the history and actual functioning of low-income economies, appeared to be occupying intermediate positions in this debate. In particular, Mr. Myint, while admitting the existence of a "need to develop a new dynamic approach to the underdeveloped countries", nevertheless put up a stout defence of the "orthodox static theory of allocation of scarce resources", asserting that this "remains as relevant to these countries as any other part of economic theory so long as they suffer from serious misallocations of resources which they can ill afford". Miss Ady, on the other hand, concluded her account of the uses to which certain parts of orthodox economic theory can be put by "leaving open the issues so much still in dispute as to the functioning of the allocative mechanism".

A leading part was taken in the oral discussion of the state of knowledge by Mr. Nicholas Kaldor. He first argued that the general trend of the discussion had started by being excessively negative and pessimistic. He conceded the present inability of economists to provide explanations for variations in the wealth of nations. He also associated himself with the more radical critics of the contents of academic texts on both general economics and on development economics, saying that they were mostly of little or no use from the point of view of understanding development, and could indeed be harmful in the hands of unimaginative people having influence on policy formation in low income countries. He maintained, nevertheless, that one could not deny that "economics does something". His experience as an adviser in low-income countries convinced him that inability to give useful advice was not, in practice, the difficulty. Although this view of the usefulness of economists in the field commanded a considerable measure of support at the Conference—this was expressed by Mr. Jackson, Mr. Cassen, Mr. Rado and Mr. Hanson—there remained a strong current of unease in the face of this argument of Mr. Kaldor's. Professor Kahn, in particular, gave voice to comments which implied that it did not say much for the relevance of an academic discipline to claim that, when entrusted to "first-rate minds", it could yield useful fruit. The Conference, he said, was considering the state of knowledge in the context of its suitability for teaching to people the bulk of whom could not be assumed to be the possessors of first-rate minds. Mr. Kaldor's reply to this came towards the end of the Conference, during the session on teaching, in the form of a statement of the outlines of what a book on development economics suitable for teaching to students would have to be like. This was joined with what seemed to many of those present a quite brilliantly worded discourse on the history of economic thought in relation to the central preoccupations of economists. The recent basic work in abstract theory of von Neumann and Sraffa represented, he said, revivals and resolutions of approaches and problems first posed and discussed by the "classical" school, i.e. the eighteenth-century physiocrats, Adam Smith, Ricardo, Karl Marx, and J. S. Mill. His own work and that of Mrs. Robinson had close affinities to that of the classics, although they both started from a Keynesian position. Mr. Kaldor said that it was possible to envisage an entirely general first approach to understanding development. This would consist of a simplified version of the von Neumann model, which could then be elaborated in such a way as to enable one to illuminate the characteristics of particular types of societies and situations, as special cases.

The theory would be of a macro-economic character, making use of strategic aggregates, e.g. social classes, agriculture and industry, the investment and consumption sectors. These were much used in classical theory, but were formalized out of existence in neo-classical theory.

Mr. Kaldor's hopeful concluding estimate of the prospects for advance was made the more valuable by the fact that it seemed to place into perspective a number of issues concerning the best way forward, which had, perhaps inevitably, been discussed in somewhat disjointed fashion at the Conference.

The question of the prospects for arriving at a *general* theory of economic development, and of obtaining from this something in the nature of a general development strategy for policy use in different parts of the world, had been raised by Mr. Seers in his "Leading Questions". He also followed this up at the conference with a plea for regarding the analysis of the available empirical materials on the world economy as a subject suitable, in its own right, for teaching as well as for research into the relevance of theory.

Before Mr. Kaldor had spoken, Mr. Seers's ambitions on the score of developing a general theory had been supported, in principle at least, by Mr. Myint, Mr. Streeten and Mr. Knapp, but there were also a number of sceptics, led by Mr. Worswick.

Another, related, issue had been the question of how far it might be possible to incorporate important "non-economic" variables into development models. A strong plea for this had been made by Professor Nove and Mr. Eshag as well as by Mr. Streeten, but the latter had also insisted that this kind of extension of the frontiers of the subject must not be made into an excuse, or a substitute for improving on the conceptual relevance of strictly economic models. A number of speakers, notably Mr. Hanson, Professor Gluckman, and Mr. Kaldor, made fascinating comments on the importance of administrative, social and political conditions as constraints on the activities of advisers in low-income countries.

Some mention must also be made of a series of exchanges which took place on the subject of the usefulness or otherwise of mathematical techniques and of econometrics. In terms of its relevance to the state of knowledge, this debate led to the predictable conclusion that, if these techniques were to be useful, they must not be misused.

The role of these techniques for teaching purposes is referred to in the next section.

III

The discussion on Teaching was based on three papers submitted to the Conference. Miss Ady's paper, to which reference has already been made, dealt mainly with the possibility of utilizing the tools of economic analysis on the subject matter of courses in development economics. Professor Zimmerman's paper, describing "Teaching Economic Planning at the Institute of Social Studies, The Hague", and Dr. Martin's on "Teaching Economic Development at Manchester", are reports on the activities of two of the earliest established centres of specialized teaching in this field. During the oral discussion accounts were also given of the organization of teaching in development economics, or plans for this, at Oxford (Mr. Jackson and Mr. Beckett), London (Mrs. Penrose), Cambridge (Mr. Berrill and Miss Deane), Edinburgh (Mr. Stewart), Glasgow (Professor Wilson), Leeds (Mr. Hanson), and Belfast (Professor Parkinson). Professor Munthe of the University of Oslo gave information about the work of his department in this field.[1]

It was noted at the Conference that development economics is now an established subject in the teaching curricula of most British universities, in the sense that undergraduates can take a paper in it as one of their optional subjects. However, the attention of the Conference was mainly focused on the problems of running courses of study in subjects relevant to development within some framework specially designed for the purpose.

The problems of organizing such courses which were discussed at the Conference concerned the length of courses, the type of students for which they would cater, the qualifications and standards required for admission and successful completion of courses, and so on.

No uniformity exists, partly because the courses have different aims, and partly because these courses of training are everywhere still in an experimental stage. The principal problems which arose under these various headings were summarized and discussed by Mr. Worswick at the request of the organizers of the Conference, and were also commented upon by Mr. Morris of the then Department of Technical Co-operation.

1. Where possible, postscripts have been added to the text, giving information about new developments which have taken place in the above institutions since the Conference. It will be noted that this list does not include all of the University teaching centres in development to be found in the United Kingdom.

The discussion of the content of courses was, in the nature of things, an extension of the discussion on the state of knowledge. Apart from the issues already referred to in the previous section, the balance of instruction between macro- and micro-economics, the place of mathematics and econometrics, the question of the desirability of linking the study of economics with studies in administration, languages (in connection with area studies), political science, sociology or even engineering, the merits of methods like case studies, workshops and training in field work, were all discussed.

Readers will find reflections on these matters in the contributions of Mr. Jackson, Mrs. Penrose, Mr. Balogh, Professor Wilson, Mr. Seers, Mr. Cassen, Mr. Hanson and Professor Parkinson, among others.

K. MARTIN.
J. KNAPP.

The Limitations of the Special Case[1]

DUDLEY SEERS

THIS paper is the reaction of an economist who, after several years of work overseas on problems of economic development, has had an opportunity to reflect on the usefulness of his subject. If the tone is rather sharp in places, I must ask the reader to understand that close personal contact with the problems of backward countries instils, for many reasons, a sense of urgency and some impatience. Economics seems very slow in adapting itself to the requirements of the main task of the day—the elimination of acute poverty in Africa, Asia and Latin America—just as the previous generation of economists failed to cope realistically with economic fluctuations until after the depression had brought politically catastrophic results.

The life cycle of each period in the development of an economic doctrine is now familiar. Some great issue of public economic policy appears. At first, economists in high places refuse to admit that this is any concern of the profession.[2] Some of the more enlightened, it is true, find a place somewhere in the syllabus for the question (an additional chapter or an optional seminar), and discuss it in print, but the treatment is quite conventional and seems

1. I am grateful to Mr. Fei, Mr. Jolly, Mr. Kennedy, Mr. Reynolds and Mr. Worswick for comments on an early draft and to Mr. Streeten for an extensive critique, which has been of great help. I would like to take this opportunity to express my gratitude to the Economic Growth Center at Yale, which provided me with the respite from practical work and the professional stimulus to write this and other papers. The general argument was put forward in a discussion group of which co-organizers were Mr. Grunwald and Mr. Lamfalussy.

2. The story is told in Latin America of a Chilean graduate student who stated, in answer to a question by a very eminent London professor, that he wanted to specialize in the economics of development. "Oh!" said the professor. "What economics is that?" This was in the 1950s!

unrealistic. A few heretics make themselves unpopular by demanding much more emphasis and perhaps even a different theory, with different policy implications. One might call this the "Hobson phase".

Meanwhile political tensions mount; a growing proportion of younger members of the profession are attracted into this field; and the journals carry papers which cannot easily be fitted into the traditional doctrine, but which on the other hand cannot easily be ignored. This is the second, or "Kahn", phase.[1] Later, a sizeable number of the younger generation defects, led by a Keynes; they uncover what are now gaping holes in the current orthodoxy; demolish it enthusiastically, though not without arousing vehement protest; and erect a new system in its place. In university after university, as professors pass into retirement, the teaching syllabus is recast, and the fringe subject is given more importance, perhaps eventually central importance, so those in the profession who backed the right horse get their just rewards. It is then their turn, and their privilege, to block progress.[2] (Nobody burns his lecture notes until the next generation is already thundering at the door.)

If there was ever a time when one could see a major revolution in doctrine looming ahead, it is today. And the reasons are, as always, because the existing body of theory cannot explain what has to be explained, nor can it give the help that is politically essential. What has to be explained is why economies grow at different rates, and the help that governments need most desperately is advice on how to stimulate development.

It is clear where the force which will disrupt the subject is emerging. In the past five years, impatience with poverty has grown, but development has either slowed down in the poorer economies or been accompanied by increasingly severe tensions (e.g. payments deficits and inflation). In some of these, for example Argentina and Chile, the political position is now critical, and yet conventional economics does not have a great deal to offer by way of useful advice. Development is still considered as merely one branch, more an appendage than an essential element, of the syllabus. One hears the term "development economists" as if they were a race apart.[3]

1. Richard, not Herman, naturally.

2. This cycle is of course not confined to economics. Thus one could talk of the "Bruno phase", the "Copernicus phase" and the "Kepler-Galileo phase".

3. The question of why economists almost completely neglected overseas countries, and the central problems of growth, for so many decades, is an interesting one, but its answer lies in the field of sociology, not economics.

The political dangers are now so obvious that this state of affairs cannot continue. There are many pressing questions on which professional help has so far been very meagre. When is it justifiable to use labour-intensive but out-of-date techniques? How can one decide what to spend on education as opposed to capital investment? And on secondary education as against primary? Can capital-output ratios be used as a guide to savings needs, and if so which, and with what qualifications? To what extent, and when, does economic size limit growth? How does export diversification help to stimulate development? What sort of central bank should an exporter of primary products have? And so on and so on.

Attempts to deal with problems such as these will end, if the history of economic thought is any guide, by changing the attitude to development in industrial economies, and therefore the whole body of economic theory.

Naturally we cannot say what the changes will be. It is not for any member of this generation to anticipate the essential characteristics of the doctrine of the next. As has always been the case, we shall greet professional novelties with horror, fail to understand them, and fight against them vehemently. The date is too early to foresee what form the necessary (in fact inevitable) reconstruction of the subject will take. We are not even in a position to judge what has to be demolished of the old doctrine, or what can be saved and adapted for further use. This is still somewhere late in the "Hobson phase", or early in the "Kahn phase", of development economics.[1] The "Kahn article" may not yet have been published. A characteristic of this article is, of course, that nobody recognizes it as much at the time; only in the "Keynes phase" can its historical significance be appreciated. All one can safely say is that attempts to solve practical problems of development are going to teach us a great deal about processes of economic change, and the time is almost ripe for the appearance of a Keynes (though this task may be beyond the capacity of any single person.)[2]

One obstacle to the reconstruction of economics is that we have not really grasped, still less accepted, the point that the subject we

1. The transformation now is bigger and there are a number of candidates for being considered the "Hobson" of this generation—e.g. Myrdal, Prebisch, Singer and Nurkse. I would be inclined to nominate Prebisch, because it is a characteristic of a "Hobson" that he is effective partly because he does not quite realize what he is doing to the subject. Besides, Prebisch lives closer to the seismic fault from which the tremors are emanating.

2. We can hardly expect as much "explanation" (in a statistical sense) of growth as of cyclical fluctuations.

have inherited was built in and for countries with which the profession was familiar, namely developed industrial economies.[1] To paraphrase a dictum of E. H. Carr: Before you study economics, study the economist; before you study the economist, study his historical and social environment.

The whole business is made much more difficult by the widespread practice that authors and lecturers have, of not merely concentrating on the economics of some developed industrial country, but presenting it as universally valid. Textbooks or lecture courses with quite general titles, such as "Economic Principles", "Banking" or "Public Finance", turn out to be really treatises about economic principles, banking or public finance in the United States, the United Kingdom, or a typical developed economy.

In this respect economists are somewhat less than rigorous. A book is not called "Principles of Astronomy" if it refers only to the earth or the solar system or even the local galaxy. We justifiably expect a lecture course on geology to deal with other continents besides the one on which the author happens to live, unless the title is duly qualified. Even sociologists generally avoid this error.

The common failure to specify the frame of reference, which is so liable to mislead students and to hinder the subject's development, is at first sight puzzling, because the developed industrial economy is by no means typical. Viewed from the point of view of either history or geography, it is an extremely rare case, and obviously so. There have been only a few such economies for a few decades; even now they cover only quite a small fraction of mankind. It may be argued that economics is international in its scope, and provides an adequate basis for work anywhere. In fact, this *is* argued, and *must* be argued, since every aging doctrine must defend itself as best it can. (*A priori*, one can predict the moves of the defence just as in a taut chess game.) But here we can apply an empirical test. Are economists in fact successful when working in non-industrial countries? I would put in evidence (though you may have to take my word for it) a point on which there is widespread agreement, that economists are very little use working on the problems of under-developed countries, until they have done so for some years, and then only if they are unusually adaptable. Engineers are probably more useful than economists on economic problems in these parts of the world, at least until the

1. As Arthur Lewis says (*The Theory of Economic Growth*, Introduction), "There is a natural tendency to assume that the things which are associated in the society we know must necessarily also be associated in all other societies."

latter have had two or three years' experience. There is so much for economics graduates to unlearn—and unfortunately the abler the student has been in absorbing the current doctrine, the more difficult the process of adaptation.

In any case it is inherently implausible that a "general theory", or even propositions of any generality, can be derived from the experience of a few countries with highly unusual, not to say peculiar, characteristics. Teaching which concentrates on this type of economy is somewhat distorted, and the distortion is dangerous if those teaching fail to stress continually that they are dealing with what is a highly special case.[1]

The typical case is a largely unindustrialized economy, the foreign trade of which consists essentially in selling primary products for manufactures. There are about 100 identifiable economies of this sort, covering the great majority of the world's population. This is also fortunately the most interesting and important type of economy, for it is here that economic problems are really acute and the economist's help is most needed.

Economists were once more keenly aware of the limitations of what they taught. Thus John Neville Keynes quoted Bagchot as specifically limiting the subject to the study of a single kind of society, "a society of grown-up competitive commerce". While himself believing that there are some universally applicable abstract principles, the elder Keynes pointed out that, so far as concrete doctrines were concerned, "their relativity follows immediately from the realistic conception of this portion of the science adopted in an earlier chapter. It is as true of economic conditions, as of social conditions in general, that they are ever subject to modification. They vary with the legal form of society, and with national character and institutions. Even where the forces in operation are the same, the relative strength that should be assigned to each may vary indefinitely. Law, custom, competition, combination, are agents in determining the distribution and exchange of wealth, no one of which is probably at any time altogether inoperative. But the extent of their influence, and the manner in which it is exerted, are constantly varying; and such variations are always of importance as

1. Particularly dangerous if somebody who has learned Anglo-Saxon economics proceeds to reproduce it uncritically at a university in a non-industrial economy. Unfortunately, this happens only too often, so that many students find that the only way they can acquire the professional qualifications to work on their own country's problems is to take a course which may in fact make their job, at least temporarily, more difficult.

affecting the relevance of economic doctrines in relation to actual economic phenomena."[1]

As a rare modern example, Joan Robinson: "English economists, from Ricardo to Keynes, have been accustomed to assume as a tacitly accepted background the institutions and problems of the England each of his own day; when their works are studied in other climes and other periods by readers who import other assumptions, a great deal of confusion and argument at cross-purposes arises in consequence."[2]

Perhaps the strongest statement of the other side was by Robbins: "It is only failure to realize this [i.e. that certain basic assumptions are of universal applicability and that useful deductions can be drawn from them], and a too exclusive preoccupation with the subsidiary assumptions, which can lend any countenance to the view that the laws of Economics are limited to certain conditions of time and space, that they are purely historical in character and so on."[3] Also Bauer: "I am now convinced of the very wide applicability to underdeveloped countries of the basic methods of approach of economics and of the more elementary conclusions stemming from these."[4]

Characteristic features of the special case

What are the features of the private-enterprise industrial economy

1. *The Scope and Method of Political Economy*, pp. 294–6 (1897). It is interesting to speculate whether this Keynes would have entitled a book on the fluctuations of industrial economies a "general theory".
2. *Exercises in Economic Analysis* (p. xvii).
3. *An Essay on the Nature and Significance of Economic Science* (chap. III). In fact this very book has a number of propositions which are only true, if indeed they are true, under highly specific conditions. Thus it is held that redistribution of real income is virtually impossible, because changes in the structure of prices would thwart it. "This conclusion, which is obvious enough from the census of occupations, tends actually to be concealed by computation in money . . . if we compute the proportion of the population now producing real income for the rich who would be turned to producing real income for the poor it is easy to see that the increase available would be negligible." This seems rather a wild statement, even for an economy such as the United Kingdom in 1932. Was the subsequent redistribution of income entirely an illusion? Are resources so specific that they cannot move in response to moderate price changes? The proposition that income cannot be redistributed would hardly be of worldwide application.
4. *Economic Analysis and Policy in Underdeveloped Countries* (p. 15). Bauer goes on to state that he is thinking especially of the elements of supply and demand analysis, and his examples refer mainly to elasticity of factor supply. But examples in a narrow range and from a few countries would not necessarily substantiate a proposition of such generality. (The previous footnote suggests that Robbins would not agree that there is mobility of labour in the United Kingdom.)

that make it of limited professional relevance for work in other economies? I can only indicate these here in note form.

I. Factors of production

(*a*) *Labour:* Literate and mobile, mostly in employment; highly organized; racial, religious, and linguistic differences not sufficiently important to break up the labour supply; substantial quantities of skilled and professional workers.

(*b*) *Land:* Most available land cultivated, and by private owners (or farmers with secure leaseholds) in plots of economic size.

(*c*) *Capital:* All sectors heavily capitalized, with spare capacity; integrated and comprehensive systems of transport and power.

(*d*) *Enterprise:* A wide field from which entrepreneurs can be drawn, and a favourable climate for enterprise; firm legal basis for corporations.

II. Sectors of the Economy

(*a*) *Agriculture:* Wholly commercial, and flexible in response to price changes or technical advances; foreign ownership rare; extensive marketing network for foods.

(*b*) *Mining:* Of limited size and in the hands of local firms.

(*c*) *Manufacturing:* Diversified, with a large metal-using industry producing (*inter alia*) machinery and vehicles; some areas of competition.

(*d*) *Overall:* Manufacturing much larger than either agriculture or mining; natural resources adequately surveyed.

III. Public Finance

(*a*) *Revenue:* Strong reliance on direct taxes relative to import or export duties; tax laws enforceable.

(*b*) *Expenditure:* Includes big outlays on social security and agricultural subsidies, relatively little on public works.

IV. Foreign Trade

(*a*) *Exports:* Consist of several products for which there is a large internal market, and for which price and income elasticities are fairly high; export prices determined by local costs and stable; exports sold to many countries.

(*b*) *Imports:* Consist largely of primary products (some of which are also produced domestically) which come from many countries, and for which the income elasticity of demand is not high.

(*c*) *Capital:* Long-term capital flows and profit remittances of secondary importance.

V. Households

(*a*) *Income:* Distribution moderately equal (post-tax); very few living at subsistence level.

(*b*) *Expenditure:* Food not overwhelmingly important; standardization and mass production possible, because of equal distribution of income, national promotion and homogeneity of tastes; prestige of local manufactures high.

VI. Savings and Investment

(*a*) *Savings:* Mobilized by a capital market, comprising a stock exchange, a bond market and an extensive nationally owned banking system, with a central bank and a managed currency; personal savings significant.

(*b*) *Investment:* High (probably over 20 per cent of G.D.P.); but import content very low.

VII. Dynamic Influences

(*a*) *Trade:* No chronic tendency to deficit because of income elasticities (see above).

(*b*) *Population:* Growth of population slow (less than 2 per cent a year), and urbanization relatively moderate.

(*c*) *Aspirations:* Envy of foreign living standards not high or spreading as a cause of discontent.

II

In brief, what is assumed is an autonomous and flexible socio-economic structure, in which each human being responds individually to the material incentives offered, and which is subject to no formidable exogenous strains.

The extent to which various economic principles rely on the assumptions set out above is a matter of opinion. There are propositions of a very elementary sort which have some general validity (e.g. those showing the implication for prices if demand and supply curves have certain shapes and shift in one direction or another). But macro-economics is another matter. The burden is surely on those who claim that this is not highly specific to show how any macro-economic model fits various non-industrial economies, each with its own institutions and productive structure.[1]

It cannot even be taken for granted that the aggregative categories with which we now work (such as "labour", "full employment", "savings", etc.) are going to prove useful in non-industrial economies.

The major inadequacies of conventional economics for those dealing with the typical case are that analysis focuses on the wrong factors, and the models do not fit at all closely the way in which non-industrial economies operate.

One respect in which analytical emphasis is rather inappropriate is that although time can often be ignored when deriving propositions for developed economies, it certainly cannot in economies which are underdeveloped. In Asia, say, the need for social and economic development would be urgent even if there were neither population pressure nor rising aspirations. Consequently, purely static propositions are mostly irrelevant, if not actually misleading. Moreover, the fashionably uncommitted attitude to growth, intellectually cloaked in positivism, while perhaps justified by local circumstances in developed economies, has little place when onc is dealing with economic problems in a more general sense.

The second error in emphasis is that insufficient attention is paid to the social structure, feudal land systems, conventional work practices, the existence of foreign firms, disparities between regions, racial barriers, etc. It is arguable how much such factors hamper progress in industrial countries, but there is little doubt that they are more serious overseas as obstacles to growth. Conventional economics contains little discussion of the economic implications of policy tools such as land reform, nationalization, or capital levies, still less raising the educational level of the adult labour force. In brief, institutions are taken as given, whereas the question is precisely what institutions to change and how.

Thirdly, improvements in nutrition, housing, and health services are treated, if at all, as increases in consumption, rather than as influences on output. (This is still also partly true of education.) Here again, this is understandable in societies where economic progress is not conditional on raising the quality of labour.

It may be argued that false emphasis merely renders much of modern economics irrelevant. However, habituation, hour after

1. An E.C.L.A. study, *Inflation and Growth in Latin America*, assembles available Latin American material to show the extent to which these various assumptions are valid in the twenty republics of that region.

hour, year after year, to static models, assuming given institutions and neglecting the determinants of human capacity, makes a student gradually unfitted to understand, let alone solve, the problems of non-industrial societies.

Similarly, years of study and work with models devised to explain industrial economies make it hard for economists to grasp the operation of a very different type of economy. One main difference is that (except for a few large economies such as India) activity and employment in the non-industrial economy depend very much, in both the short- and the long-term, on the export sector. Moreover, the nature of the response to changes in exports depends on the organization of this sector, especially whether taxes, profits of foreign companies, or peasant incomes absorb the highest share of increments in income. It also depends on the type of product (particularly whether there is any significant domestic market). The role of the export sector is rarely stressed in conventional economies, and this for a very good reason—in an industrial economy hardly any major sector sells the greater part of its output overseas.

This leads to another point. Non-industrial economies cannot be understood unless studied in the context of the world economy. The sales of their particular primary products, and thus their development, are determined by (i) the rate of growth of the industrial economies that buy from them, (ii) the income-elasticities of demand for the commodities they export (which reflect, *inter alia*, the substitution of artificial materials for natural ones), (iii) protective measures that limit imports into industrial economies, (iv) influences on the distribution of the remaining markets between various suppliers (company policy, preferential tariff arrangements, etc.). One could argue that industrial economies would also be easier to understand, if the same approach were adopted. But they do not absolutely require this treatment—it may be reasonable to treat them, which is often done implicitly or explicitly, as if they were closed economies.

Of course, the development of non-industrial economies may become also partly independent of export performance. This implies, however, import substitution, which necessarily involves for these economies (in contrast to those which are already developed) the founding of completely new manufacturing industries. This in turn requires investments in transport and energy, and (defining "investment" slightly differently) in education, etc., and involves a shift in the composition of imports. But the substitution process eventually reaches a limit, which is set (in the main) by natural resources and the size of the local market. However, this process and these limitations are hardly discussed at all in conventional economics, which is so "global" that it misses essential characteristics of development.

Finally a word should be said about some of the peculiarities of fiscal and monetary sectors which affect the operation of industrial economies.

For example, because of the heavy weight of direct taxes and the scale of unemployment benefits, the public sector automatically compensates, in some measure, for fluctuations in the private economy. In non-industrial economies, on the other hand, a slump in trade can rarely be overcome by throwing the budget into deficit, because the only means of covering it will probably be to run down reserves. (This is obviously true of one particular type of non-industrial economy, an "open" economy; there a payments deficit appears immediately, if internal activity is maintained in a slump.) So the government may in time be compelled to raise taxes or reduce outlays, aggravating the initial downward impulse. Another feature of the fiscal system in industrial economies, but not in others, is that it operates to spread income more widely over the country's various regions and thus ensures that none get left far behind in an economic advance.

While all industrial economies have virtually complete monetary autonomy, this is by no means universally true. Even the larger non-industrial economies, which manage their own currencies, lack many of the means of influencing the supply of money, such as open-market operations; moreover, foreign companies and foreign banks, which draw finance from, or supply it to, their head offices, may be quantitatively important and their operation may affect the money supply more than any steps taken by the local central bank.

Because of their financial systems, industrial economies have boundaries corresponding to their political frontiers. But, when we look at the other types, we may wonder whether the nation is the correct unit of analysis at all. If fiscal and monetary systems are very tenuous, geographical or racial or religious barriers may seal off parts of the nation into virtually self-contained sub-economies. For this reason, national averages (e.g. income levels, wage levels, price levels, etc.) may have little meaning, whether used for comparison with other countries, or for measuring progress over time.

An example: the concept of the multiplier

The best way to demonstrate that concepts cannot readily be

generalized from industrial economies is to give an example. The usual treatment of income determination in modern economics rests heavily on the "multiplier" effects of investment. But the way in which income is created depends very much on whether the country makes steel and machinery itself or imports such goods. Every non-industrial country buys from abroad a large fraction of its equipment needs, and the great majority import all their steel too. Since the machinery content is very different for different types of investment, the effect on imports varies from project to project. Moreover, even as far as the local component is concerned, the implications for imports, employment, etc., depend on whether the investment is undertaken by contractors, public works department or private individuals, and also on whether it takes place inland or near ports (where the import propensities of consumers are higher).

Another point is that the effect of investment depends on whether local supply conditions are generally elastic, i.e. on whether there is unemployed labour of the right type, spare capital, and factor mobility.[1] For reasons indicated earlier, one would not expect these elasticities to be very high, particularly in agriculture. Consequently, the secondary waves of purchasing power will generate price rises, rather than higher domestic output and employment, even though there is considerable unemployment.[2]

What this means in practice is that the mechanism of income creation is highly complex, and the "multiplier" cannot be expected to have a stable value. Naturally, even in the United States the multiplier reaction is not the same for every single project, but one would hardly expect that the composition of total investment would change drastically from one year to the next in this respect. So the way in which the multiplier works can be considered stable for the purposes of teaching. In non-industrial countries, however, the commencement of investment in a particular large project may change the whole mechanism of income creation. And as capital

1. Formally, the lack of an equipment industry mentioned in the previous paragraph could be considered a special case, since it means that the price elasticity of domestic supply is zero.

2. This last point is stressed by V. K. R. V. Rao in "Investment, income and the multiplier in an underdeveloped economy" (*Indian Economic Review*, February, 1952); in an economy like India, the foreign trade aspect is much less important. Rao draws the conclusions that there is no such thing as a unique level of full employment in an underdeveloped economy. See also "Cual es la utilidad practica de la teoría del multiplicador?" by Osvaldo Sunkel (*El Trimestre Economico*, July–September, 1957), which puts more emphasis on the role of export fluctuations.

goods industries emerge, as import regimes alter, as internal communications improve and as agriculture is developed, the multiplier effects of all types of investment, and thus of total investment, will change significantly.

Furthermore, in non-industrial economies, foreign trade is a more important determinant of income than investment, except for a few special cases. Yet the mechanism of income creation attributable to changes in foreign trade may be quite different from what happens when domestic investment alters. One contrast with industrial economies is that we cannot usefully work with "net" foreign investment. A change in exports may be quantitatively the same as a change in imports, so that in each case net foreign investment alters to the same extent. Yet the repercussions may be entirely different, because the exporting and importing sectors are entirely different (perhaps hundreds of miles away from each other). In any case, import changes are (except in time of war or blockade) induced by income fluctuations, and usually follow export changes more or less closely. The appearance of an export surplus may reflect simply a delay in getting orders filled.

What is more important in practice, the magnitude and nature of the repercussions of export fluctuations depend on *which* exports have changed (because various export industries may be subject to high or low taxation, may or may not be in the hands of foreign companies, etc.), and secondly, on whether the change in the value of exports of a commodity was in the quantity exported or in its price. In mineral economies, for example, export fluctuations, especially when they are due to price changes, are to some extent offset by the variation in the profits of foreign companies.

Not merely is investment less important than trade in this context, it is very largely induced by trade, particularly in the more backward economies. Much investment is either in the export sector, in facilities for the movement and storage of exports and imports, or in the distribution of imports. The remainder largely depends on exports indirectly, through income.[1]

This does not mean that the idea of secondary waves of income creation is completely useless outside industrial areas. What it does imply is that, if the concept of the multiplier is to be generalized, attention has to be concentrated from the outset on the "leakage" due to imports (including profits made by foreign companies), instead of this being a qualification introduced later, as is usually the

1. This incidentally implies that "the accelerator" also cannot be treated as a global coefficient with a stable value.

case; secondly, exports have to be depicted as the motive force in income determination. The concept of a "multiplier", in the sense of a coefficient which can be expected to be the same whatever the economic stimulus and whatever the stage of development, is likely to mislead the student rather than to help him. It is a concept which was developed to meet a particular problem—namely how to understand the trade cycle in industrial countries, so as to devise policies for reducing the heavy unemployment of the inter-war years. Such a concept could hardly have been thought of if economics had evolved in countries exporting primary products and importing capital goods.

It may be argued that all these points can be accommodated within the traditional analytical frame; technically this is true, but in fact the subject is not taught in this way,[1] and the economist acquires a view of income determination which is a hindrance rather than an asset when it comes to working in non-industrial economies. He may, for example, easily adopt a naïvely optimistic view about the possibilities of compensatory fiscal policy.

Samuelson's "Economics" as a text

The textbook is what moulds the mind of the student more than anything else. This is something which he not only reads and rereads, but attempts to learn, as a source of truth. In order to see what sort of influence texts may exert on readers who will work on development problems (and who will themselves teach for decades in this field), let us look at one popular example, *Economics* by Paul Samuelson, a book very widely used in the universities of the underdeveloped and developed countries alike, and which is, of course, for many purposes, brilliant.

One reason for its success is the way in which contemporary material is used to illuminate problems. But this material is drawn almost exclusively from the United States. The reader gradually becomes accustomed to an economy with the abnormal features indicated above. Domestic investment is treated as the main determinant of income, for example, and the trade-cycle model presented is applicable only to a diversified economy.

Foreign trade is confined to a relatively small section late in the book, and there is no discussion of the different types of export sector, or their implications. Indeed the relation between trade and

1. A more radical line of criticism would be that concepts like "investment" (as a homogeneous category) do not help the student who will work on development problems.

the domestic economy is depicted in a way typical only of an industrial country; for example, it is alleged that devaluation tends to restore equilibrium by expanding exports and reducing imports.[1] Here again the case in the author's mind seems to be the United States. It is not obvious how devaluation of the cruzeiro could restore equilibrium in Brazil, say, in view of the fact that the price elasticity of demand for coffee is low; in fact there is now a quota on coffee exports. Could the volume of imports be reduced when they consist almost entirely of fuel, materials, and machinery? The evidence of Brazilian experience is really opposite; it implies that devaluation does *not* restore equilibrium. Of course, new exports might be stimulated on an adequate scale in a decade or so, but clearly the treatment is quite misleading for a Brazilian student, or someone who will work in Brazil or on problems of development or international economics.[2] It may be argued that Brazil is only one example, but a score of others could be given and a single exception is enough to overthrow an unqualified generalization.

Although reference is made to protective devices and the gold standard, there is no explanation of the critical difference between the functioning of "open" economies—i.e. those without exchange control, import licensing, or high tariffs—and of others. Nor is there sufficient material on the world economy to enable a student to see how any particular country would fit into it, or what are the main influences on a country's exports (and its rate of growth).

There is little mention of institutional change, which is perhaps only to be expected in a work dealing with an economy where such change has been limited in the past century. The question of whether existing institutions permit the resources of an economy to be mobilized, or prevent them from being, to feed, clothe, house and employ the public is not discussed (after all, one can argue that it is not a very pressing one in the United States).

1. Page 760 in the fifth edition, 1961, which is the edition under consideration here.

2. Discussing the applicability of the concept of an equilibrium exchange rate for pre-revolutionary Cuba, Henry Wallich points out: "But where the price mechanism has little influence, the equilibrium rate ceases to be clearly defined even if domestic and foreign incomes are given. In this the Cuban system differs radically from the industrial economies of Britain or the United States, where a few per cent in the price—or in the exchange rate—may decide whether their products can compete in the world market on even terms or not." This quotation is from *Monetary Problems of an Export Economy* (p. 216), which is one of the very few attempts to consider how appropriate conventional economic principles are for an underdeveloped economy which exports primary products. See also *Export Economies* by Levin.

Only at page 775 are problems of "economic growth and development" broached. Even here the role of industrialization in development is not brought out, nor for that matter is the reader told of the patterns of growth revealed by modern research.

One of the main weaknesses of this text, as of many, is that the argument is either at the "macro" level of the nation, or, more often, at the "micro" level of the firm or family.[1] Practically nowhere is there a discussion of the economics of either the world or the industry, which are precisely the interesting levels. Oddly enough, input-output analysis is mentioned only in an appendix on the history of economic doctrines, as a latter-day version of Quesnay's *tableau économique*

Finally, but above all, there is no description of the various types of economy (petroleum exporters, metal exporters, coffee exporters, etc.).

The title of Samuelson's text should not be "Economics", but "The Economics of the United States in the Twentieth Century". In fairness one should add that, at least in recent editions, the book shows relatively considerable awareness of the outside world (and of economic history); most other texts claim generality with even less justification.

The translator of the Spanish edition apparently felt vulnerable to the line of argument developed above. "Lo que deseo es justificar mi criterio sobre el problema planteado por les constantes referencias del texto a la realidad economica de los Estados Unidos."[2] He argues that to adapt the text to the needs of the reader's own country would be out of the question—quite different versions would be needed, say, for Chile and for Spain; anyway, the United States was a very important case, and worth study for its own sake. But, in his view the main consideration was: "Se encuentran las ideas generales con validex general para todos los situaciones estructurales."[3] In the fourth edition (1958) Samuelson himself made the

1. Samuelson justifies devoting most attention to micro-economics by saying (on page 412): "man has gained considerable mastery over his macro-economic problems". It is true that one can see the author is referring to the United States, but students may not all realize this. In any case this is no defence for a textbook with a title suggesting that it is, as it is often taken to be, a general text. The justifiable reaction of a student in Calcutta, say, would be that economics is not so much a dismal science, as a callous one. And is the statement true even for the United States?

2. Jose Luis Sampedro in the translator's introduction to the Spanish version of the third edition (Aguilar, Madrid, 1958). "I want to justify my judgment on the problem raised by the repeated references in the text to economic conditions in the United States."

3. "General ideas can be found with universal validity for all types of structure."

same point: "I like to think that the book's wide use abroad and translation into foreign languages . . . is a reflection of the relevance to societies of quite different institutional development." (This comment does not appear in the preface to the subsequent edition.)

These statements can best be judged if we see how they would look in another field. Suppose a textbook on zoology limited its descriptive material to horses and claimed that the big sales of an early edition showed its relevance to animals of quite different physiology?[1] Or could one defend issuing, without amendment, a special edition of the same book for keepers of domestic pets by stating that the horse was a very interesting animal, and that anyway if one tried to adapt the text for the needs of the home, one would have to write separate books on cats, dogs, etc.? Such arguments actually invite the student to fall into the trap of treating the special case as if it were the general one.

A Marxist text

I might add in passing that Marxist textbooks also seem to be of limited value for those who want to understand economically backward countries. A common example is *Political Economy*, prepared by the Academy of Sciences of the Soviet Union. This treatise can be found in students' rooms in many countries, and is a prescribed text for all departments in the three Cuban universities.[2]

Oddly enough many of the same criticisms apply. Here again a great deal of space is taken up by the workings of an industrial economy; foreign trade is not emphasized; the treatment is too global; and so on.

This text has, however, its own, though not unexpected, defects. Metaphysical questions such as "What is value?" are discussed at length, and the basic Marxist model for capitalism is elaborated, using categories such as "rates of surplus value" and the "organic composition of capital" which may have a political function, but do not seem very helpful to the economist. No attempt is made to compare values of these coefficients for different capitalist countries. Sections devoted to underdeveloped countries, including Latin America, treat them as if they were colonies, virtually without any heavy industries, and while emphasis is given to the role of foreign

1. In how many societies has man mastered macro-economic problems?
2. My comments are based on the Spanish-language edition (1959) now being used in Cuba, entitled *Manual de Economía Política*. Apparently a more up-to-date edition is now being prepared, but it will be surprising if it proves to be free of the faults mentioned here.

companies, there is no reference to their contribution to local economies (through taxes, etc.).

Naturally, one cannot complain that social issues are avoided—the description of the various social classes and of their political roles and ideologies would make more sense than Samuelson does to students who have first-hand knowledge of a partially industrialized society, for example Chile. Such countries are not wholly unlike what the economies of Western Europe were in the middle of the nineteenth century (which afforded Marx his material). The "industrial reserve army" of the unemployed is after all to be seen in the streets, and it does play the function of keeping wages down to subsistence levels. The attitude of the landowning classes to social change seems positively calculated to prove Marx right. Those from more backward economies, where there are large foreign-owned plantations, might find the account of imperialism fairly convincing.

But the standard Marxist scheme of stages of development—from a primitive economy through slavery and feudalism to capitalism and socialism—seems too rigid. Where would Ghana fit, for example, with different regions at different levels of development? And what would be its next stage, capitalism or socialism? The fundamental weakness seems to be that there is little attention to institutional development *within* societies at a given stage. This is no doubt a corollary of the simplistic view that revolutionary transformation of structure is the main form of social change.[1]

It seems that, apart from Lenin's "Imperialism", the material of which is also by now out of date, there has been little theoretical progress in a century. No use is made, or knowledge shown, of any advances in the social sciences. The treatment of Keynes is little short of scandalous. It is claimed (page 316) that he recommended raising profits by reducing real wages through inflation and that he advocated increasing the luxury expenditure of the rich and government expenditure in armaments.[2] The authors do not appear to be even aware of modern factual material that would be useful for propaganda (unemployment figures are quoted up to 1921).

Certainly there is no effort to adapt the doctrine to underdeveloped countries as they are today nor any scholarly discussion of their growth processes. The implication seems to be that if the shackles

1. I owe this point to Mr. Streeten.

2. The Quantity Theory still holds sway in these pages. Thus on page 176, inflation is described as a condition characterized by the presence of an excessive mass of paper money. In Marxist jargon, an argument of this kind, so comforting to the financial bourgeoisie, is objectively most reactionary.

of imperialism were removed, these economies would grow spontaneously.[1] There is not even an attempt to apply the lessons of Soviet experience to their problems.

It is sad to think that it is precisely the critical student in Asia or Africa or Latin America, aware of the limitations of Anglo-Saxon textbooks, who may turn to *this* as the main alternative. If Samuelson's text is to be retitled, the Soviet one should perhaps be called "A nineteenth-century Interpretation of Economic and Political Change, based on experience in Western Europe".

Other influences on the economist

The attitude of the student to development problems is formed both before and after he reads texts on economic principles. As a child and adolescent his experience is limited to the local economy, with which he gradually becomes very familiar. If he is brought up in a developed country, the newspapers, radios and television tell him mainly about its economy, and at school he acquires a heavily nationalistic approach to history. Economic relations with foreign countries are usually painted in a somewhat unreal way. It is not unusual for the university entrant to believe that the arrangements in his country, whichever that may be, represent the best to be found, and a model worth copying by the rest of the world. Side by side with this chauvinistic picture, he may be presented with a naïve internationalism, in a sense its counterpart, suggesting that foreigners are essentially similar to himself, sharing his own economic and political prejudices.[2] Such influences continue during undergraduate life, by which time the problem of finding a job comes to play an increasing part in the formation of attitude.

In the rest of the world, students may be even more chauvinistic than they are in industrial countries (some of which have a less insecure basis for their nationalism). While in certain fields this leads to attempts at an education suitable to the local society, in economics

1. The analysis of the developed capitalist economies is also highly unconvincing. The impression is conveyed that average real wages in the United States have declined since the end of the last century! Referring to one Bogart, the manual states that after prices started to rise in 1897, wages did not keep pace. It is also alleged that real wages fell in England and France in the first part of the twentieth century. One may be able to sell this to Russian students, but those elsewhere would know it to be nonsense, and is it really safe to bring up the future policy-makers so ignorant of the economic facts of life?

2. These errors are often aggravated by the gross distortions in the propaganda of the tourist industry. (Thus a picture is built up of inhabitants of the Caribbean islands as fortunate dwellers in a paradise of beaches and palm trees.)

(as in the natural sciences) the outcome is more often, especially in countries newly independent, an exaggerated respect for the mysteries of modern techniques.

The picture shown in the standard textbook is therefore accepted on all sides with little resistance. In the industrial economy, it more or less conforms to everyday experience, and the student is not experienced enough to realize its limitations. For students elsewhere,[1] an economics text shares the general glamour of all technical books from overseas.

Since undergraduate teaching does not do much, if anything, to break down parochialism and to bring home the realities of the modern economic world, the recruit to graduate school easily falls into the trap of admiring technique for its own sake. If the content is dull, the student turns to form, and this is indeed encouraged. Far from becoming more practical (as say, medical teaching does in its later stages), economics becomes still more abstract.

As H. R. Bowen has put it: "Graduate students of economics are confronted with a vast array of concepts, techniques, and detailed theoretical constructions. They perforce live in a strange world of indifference maps, kinked demand curves, cross elasticity, marginal propensity to consume, liquidity preference, net national product, sampling error, linear programming, and input-output matrices. They spend much of their time gaining familiarity with specialized concepts and techniques, and their success as graduate students is gauged largely by the degree to which they master them."[2]

A certain pattern of thinking becomes firmly implanted in the graduate student; intellectual agility is admired, irrespective of the purpose of the exercise. The highest praise for a paper is "elegant" rather than "useful"; conversely, work which is not narrowly economic may be described as "sloppy". Thus outlook becomes distorted in favour of the fashionable trivia. (Socrates was given hemlock for less!)

Seymour Harris, pointing out that mathematical treatment is particularly seductive, once said: 'the ablest young students take to this field and heavily concentrate on the relation of mathematics and economics. . . . Many of us are concerned lest by an overcon-

1. A special category is that of the student from overseas who wants to be accepted as a member of the profession in the United States or Western Europe. Like anyone bent on assimilation, he is unlikely to attempt a fundamentally critical reappraisal.

2. "Graduate Education in Economics" (*American Economic Review*, 1953 Supplement).

centration on mathematics the problems selected for study may be excessively those subject to manipulation by the use of symbols and also that many of the best minds in economics may be lost for the solution of the great public issues of the day."[1]

Highly abstract economics evidently has some aesthetic appeal, as well as the intellectual virtues of apparent precision and perfectability. (All logically possible exceptions can be discussed, so one cannot be taken by surprise.) As long as it remains abstract, the practitioner is preserved from the embarrassments of public controversy. An able young economist, searching for a topic for a thesis or first book, finds that mathematical manipulation has the particular and not inconsiderable advantage that it offers an unambiguous way of showing a certain type of ability.[2] (Genuine ability cannot, from its very nature, be demonstrated in such an easy way.)

Since I want to avoid the perennial and rather sterile argument about the role of mathematics in economics, I am not going to deny that mathematics may be very helpful, properly used, in economic argument. My point is that its charms are probably exercising an unhealthy influence, at this particular time in the subject's evolution. For one thing, progress in manipulation has contributed to the widespread, but really quite unfounded, belief that much progress has been made in economics. Secondly, since the processes of development, which are partly institutional, do not easily lend themselves to this type of treatment, the more able student may find the field unattractive. In the third place, those who do work on the problems of non-industrial economies usually try to force the material into some global model which they have been taught, passing over the question whether it was devised with a different type of economy in mind. They may also try to quantify the model, ignoring whether the statistics are good enough for the task.

It is not only the native of industrial economies who falls into this trap; precisely because of the reputation of technique as such, the

1. In *The Teaching of Elementary Economics* (edited by K. A. Knopf and J. H. Stauss), p. 241.

2. There are basically three types of economist: those who use numbers, those who use letters and those who use words. Very few are equally at home in all three means of communication, or even in any two. A preference for letters may conceal a lack of fluency in the use of language and a lack of interest in numerical information, and/or an approach to the problems of society which is highly schematic, because of a partially conscious desire to follow in the footsteps of the scientist proper. (For at least two centuries, however, natural scientists have not claimed that they could reach useful conclusions simply by sitting in studies and manipulating symbols). On the other hand, of course, aversion to letters may indicate lack of mathematical ability!

bright economist from overseas often does the same. Here authors of models are often largely to blame. Like the text writers, they rarely specify with sufficient clarity or emphasis the assumptions or state under what conditions they are likely to be valid. (This is all the more surprising in view of the fact that this branch of the profession prides itself on "rigour").[1] Models often rest on basic, but probably unstated, assumptions like a closed economy, perfect competition, constant tastes, constant income distribution and mobile factors of production, assumptions which are quite artificial even for industrial societies.

I do not deny that highly abstract models can be useful, at least for some types of problem. The question is whether there is room for them, in view of their limited application and inherent dangers. It seems odd to introduce students to symbolic economies before they are taught what they really do need to know, not merely for their professional work, but even to enable them to decide whether any model is useful—the structure of the world economy and how this structure is changing; the working of the main productive sectors, including the principal techniques in agriculture and industry, and their requirements of labour and other important inputs; the economics of population change; the organization and operation of commodity markets; the relations between economic size, structure and growth; the economic implications of various types of social institution; and so on. People are being turned out as economists who can draw diagrams illustrating the theory of duopoly, but who would not know how to start dealing with the question (say) of whether a steel industry should be established in Guatemala, or what it should make or how much. The majority do not know a great deal of the economic history even of their own country, let alone the problems and processes of development in the Soviet Union, Yugoslavia, China, Brazil, Egypt, India or Japan—to mention some of the more interesting cases. There is almost universal ignorance of current socio-economic theories such as Marxism, which any economist working overseas will come up against sooner or later.

It is true that there are usually seminars (as there are books) on "Development Economics". These are, however, often based on highly aggregative models of the Harrod–Domar type, together with some bits and pieces of information provided by the teacher (or

1. As Professor Ruggles once pointed out in the discussion group on development problems at Yale, merely to put an argument in mathematical symbols rather than words will not save it from any inherent imprecision.

author) on the basis of what he happened to notice in the countries he happened to visit. But a global approach may, for reasons already given, mislead the student. He may conclude, rather falsely, that he has learned what is known about processes of development.

Training in the use of statistical material could help to anchor a student's approach in reality. Unfortunately "statistical methods" as usually taught (as indeed I used to teach it myself) does not do this. It may even be positively damaging. Far from showing the student how to appraise and use material, the basic and central requirement, this subject is a museum of curious and ancient tools (mostly taken over from other fields, such as biology). The implicit assumption in examples and exercises is that the data used are absolutely firm and reliable. It is as if somebody learning carpentry was taught to ignore the properties of different types of wood. The student's attention is thus repeatedly diverted *away from* the essence of the problem; an uncritical attitude to data is gradually acquired, which it may take years to get rid of.[1] There is not even much attention to the theoretical propositions on errors and biases in various branches of the subject, though these would help the economist to take into account defects in the material, and decide under what conditions they affect one's conclusions.[2]

It could be argued that what an economist really needs is at least a year's work in a statistical office. Only by having to face, hundreds of times, the minor problems of tabulating trade returns, arranging departmental series for publication, and reporting surveys or censuses, does one acquire a genuine "feel" for the reliability of data, and therefore for what can and cannot be done in applied economics. Universities could, however, help shorten the probationary period by simulating practical experience. This means setting up research projects with actual material, such as successive censuses of agricultural or industrial production (or perhaps imaginary documents with constructed defects). The student would be forced to face the problems posed by changes in coverage, etc., when he attempts to compare productivity or price level from one census

1. It is interesting to speculate how this approach could ever have come about. Perhaps its root is the conventional division of labour between the menials who do practical work and the savants who know technique.

2. Questions of substance also come in here. The implication of the emphasis in economic theory suggested above is that inadequate time in statistical instruction is devoted to index numbers, including such points as "changing base years" (sometimes index number theory is almost entirely omitted, apart from a ritual mention of the twin deities, Paasche and Laspeyres.

year to the next. If the point is heavily emphasized that the quality of the material determines very largely what analysis can be carried out, there will be less temptation to use over-elaborate techniques.

The second defect in statistical teaching, which may show itself in the graduate's subsequent work, is analogous to one already mentioned in economics, namely that he is taught to manipulate, rather than to interpret. The emphasis is on how to fit regression lines (say), rather than on how one should read a regression diagram, how to decide whether there is any point in fitting a line at all, and how to choose (with an eye on the theoretical implications) between the different sorts of function. Analogous criticisms could be made of teaching in the interpretation of time series, and in drawing conclusions from samples.

The standard argument in defence of abstract techniques, in both economics and statistics, is that it teaches students "how to think". Since in the event they will mostly be involved in practical work, or at least in the discussion of current problems, I would argue that non-empirical instruction teaches them to think *in the wrong way*. (No doubt the same argument was put forward in the 1920s about the models then current.) It is rigid and narrow, and this leads students to pick up bad working habits, such as attempting to explain developments with linear functions chosen intuitively, and comprising a few selected variables (which are usually purely economic). But in any case, if the aim is to develop formal methods of thought, surely the subjects needed are mathematics and modern logical analysis. The drawbacks of the type of instruction which starts by giving algebraic symbols to "labour", "capital", etc., are twofold. First it encourages bogus theorizing by using concepts without specifying their context (or, often, their precise meaning). Secondly, since these concepts have real-life associations, it appears to be teaching the student something about economic relationships. Similarly, the danger of purely theoretical instruction in regression analysis is that it seems to be teaching the student how to do research.

There is really no need to search for material that teaches people "how to think". In many important fields of economics, patterns emerge which make rather complex analytical techniques appropriate, in fact essential. They include population movements (e.g. the use of a life table, the derivation of reproduction coefficients, etc.); inter-industry relations; demand trends; and the processes of producing and using energy. These provide adequate, and much more useful, opportunities for mental gymnastics.

The degree of generalization possible

Simple explanatory models can now be constructed for various individual economies, and these could be developed into models for the different types of economy. Steps in this direction, when they have been assimilated, will be particularly helpful to teachers working overseas who are anxious to try to relate material to their pupil's needs. At present they have to provide their own gloss on the available texts, such as Samuelson's, and this is of course a poor substitute for the texts that are needed. In any case there are very few teachers who have both the time and the capacity to do it at all adequately. Many of those teaching in underdeveloped countries have heavy schedules and/or full-time jobs outside the university. Some resistance is naturally felt to the idea that such a commentary is necessary.

But it would be worth while to attempt something more general. There are so many common characteristics that it would now be possible to write a text covering what is, and will be for several decades, the typical case in economics, the unindustrialized economy, even though such a text would at present be very rudimentary. For all such economies, a dynamic approach is needed, with heavy emphasis on trade, and therefore on the organization of the world economy and on the operation of commodity markets. There are certain similarities in their social and economic structures and in their problems, especially if they are grouped according to the stage of development.[1] Their growth processes show common features, and require analysis at a low level of aggregation. Recognizable patterns can be seen in the way they respond to short-period fluctuations, and again more so if we group them, this time, according to the organization of the leading export sector.

It is true that the material for writing such texts is as yet largely unorganized, the reason being that we have hardly started on the task of classifying the world's economies (always a very early step in a science), let alone making any comparative analysis, or exploring similarities. The developed economies have, like Narcissus, been interested almost exclusively in themselves. The great majority of research is still devoted to their local problems, and few economists even bother to read any periodicals other than American or British.

Instead of building up propositions from detailed observation of

1. Perhaps first dividing them according to the degree of central planning. It could be argued that this transcends the level of industrialization as a criterion of classification. Personally, however, I believe that for many analytical purposes, Cuba has more in common with (say) Venezuela than with East Germany.

scores of concrete cases, professional work goes mainly into the construction, largely *a priori*, of models which are provided, after their erection, with a very thin quantitative foundation (e.g. empirical verification for a single industrial country, covering at the most a decade or two), if indeed any numbers are used at all.[1] An increasing effort has, very recently, been devoted to the study of other economies—although the basic reason, one fears, is more often the Cold War than a desire to make economics a respectable subject. But since the institutions working in this field are doing little to co-ordinate their work, the task of drawing general conclusions will be far from easy.[2]

In all scientific subjects, progress has depended to a considerable extent on systematic and comparative research. The organized material on changes in economic structure is very thin. What does exist is due largely to three people—Clark,[3] Kuznets,[4] and Chenery[5]—and to the United Nations.[6] Apart from these, international research studies mostly cover particular industries or particular fields.[7] A basic framework exists, however, with material from a number of countries, in the writings of the Latin American school

1. "The understanding must not, however, be allowed to jump and fly from particulars to remote axioms and of almost the highest generality (such as the first principles, as they are called, of arts and things)" (Francis Bacon, *The First Book of Aphorisms*, C.I.V.). Bacon is interesting reading because he wrote at a correspondingly primitive stage in the development of the natural sciences.
2. A few Foundations provide much of the necessary finance and they could insist on a certain, even if limited, standardization. Foundation officials, however, have a misplaced (though comprehensible) fear of being considered dictatorial—and one must admit that there would be great dangers during the present early stage of the subject if its development were hindered by premature decisions on what factors are worth exploring.
3. *The Conditions of Economic Progress*. Most research workers now are somewhat cautious about using this material, but nobody can challenge Colin Clark's right to be considered the pioneer in comparative economics.
4. See his series of papers in *Economic Development and Cultural Change, seriatim.*
5. Especially, "Patterns of Economic Growth" (*American Economic Review*, September 1960), which is a candidate for being considered the Kahn article of this generation. It is perhaps worth noting that while British economists led the way in the previous major change in doctrine, the corresponding work today is being done almost entirely by Americans.
6. "World Economic Surveys", *seriatim*. For political reasons, it is hard for the Secretariat to use this material comparatively.
7. Mention should be made here of a new series on comparative economics, edited by Lloyd Reynolds. Two volumes have already appeared: *Foreign Trade and the National Economy* by Kindleberger and *The Economics of Labor* by Phelps Brown.

of structuralists, and this is sufficiently flexible, I believe, to be extended to other parts of the world.

The possibilities of generalization in fields such as money, banking, fiscal structure and the economics of the firm seem limited, because of the great institutional differences to be found. However, one should perhaps reserve judgment on this until a decade or two from now, by which time institutions in different countries will doubtless have been systematically compared.

It can, of course, be argued that in the universities of the developed countries, at least, texts *should* be based on the local model, as they are at present, because most economists will be working for local companies or governments. Because of the influence of such countries in the world economy, and their relatively successful functioning, there would also be something to be said for economists in non-industrial countries acquiring at least a general acquaintance with this model. This is all well and good provided it is recognized as a highly special case. Even then, it could be argued that much more provision should be made for the increasing numbers who will at some period or another be concerned in some way with the problem of non-industrial economies. However, in time, this objection will doubtless disappear. The growth of comparative economics should lead to the creation of a more general framework into which special cases (like industrial economies, say, or petroleum economies) can be fitted.

A useful guide in the reconstruction of economics which is now starting could be the following modest but revolutionary slogan: Economics is the study of Economies.

PART ONE

Papers submitted to the Conference

Part A. The State of Knowledge

EDITED BY JOHN KNAPP

Twenty Leading Questions on the Teaching of Economics

DUDLEY SEERS

A. *The task facing the profession in the 1960s*

1. Has the demand for economic development brought about a significant change in the work of economists?
2. How much does the question of development affect the work of specialized economists (for example, trade theorists)?
3. How much will students in the future be concerned, in one way or another, with the problems of world income distribution?
4. How much *should* the balance of professional research be changed in this direction?

B. *The record of economists in development work*

5. Do economists from industrial countries who work abroad contribute much to development policy?
6. Are they helping local universities align their teaching to local needs?
7. Are they using what they learn from each country's experience to adapt the general body of doctrine so as to make this more realistic?

C. *The adequacy of the present body of doctrine*

8. By what channels is the experience of Africa, Asia, Eastern Europe and Latin America being absorbed in the universities of the Northern Hemisphere?
9. How much has the body of economic doctrine responded to the acceleration in the last fifteen years in the growth of world population—and to the rising demand for civilized living standards?
10. Is Keynesian economics now an obstacle in the subject's development (because of its highly "global" approach, its emphasis on the demand side and the failure to specify the basic assumptions or to assess their relevance)?

11. Have we developed a coherent strategy for development comparable to classical liberalism or Marxism—or is this impossible in the second half of the twentieth century?
12. Do the significance and meaning of the concepts in use (e.g. "national income", "capital", "employment") need modification when one considers their *general* applicability in the world, i.e. in non-industrial economies?
13. What is the most productive way forward—to try to generalize economics, or to develop doctrines appropriate for different types of economy?
14. How much of "pure" theory will be left when the subject is generalized? (i.e., how much does "pure" theory in fact incorporate assumptions specific to the local circumstances of a few developed countries?)

D. *The relevance of the syllabus*

15. From what countries is drawn the material presented to students?
16. What attempts are made to show the geographical limitations of textbook presentations, and to assess their assumptions?
17. How much does the undergraduate learn today of the working of the world economy? Of the types of national economy? Of the main mechanisms of development? Of patterns of structural change? Of the role of social factors in development?
18. How much training is provided in handling statistical material (as distinct from "statistical methods")?
19. How much do the more advanced courses prepare students for work on the main economic problems of the world?
20. Can those who are receiving the bulk of their education in conventional economics understand a seminar in development? (And what difficulty does a member of a graduate school find with realistic courses in development economics after a conventional undergraduate course?)

Economic Theory and the Underdeveloped Countries

H. MYINT
Oxford University

How far is the economic theory of the industrially advanced countries applicable to the underdeveloped countries? This question has been raised, at one time or other by a variety of people. Some of the sociological writers have questioned the applicability of the concept of the "economic man" to the underdeveloped countries where traditional values and attitudes still prevail. The Historical and Institutional economists have argued that the generalizations of economic theory are based on the particular circumstances of the advanced countries and are therefore not "universally valid". Finally, there has been a long line of critics from the underdeveloped countries. In the nineteenth century, Hamilton, Carey and List questioned the applicability of the English classical free trade theory to the underdeveloped countries of that period, viz. the United States and Germany. They have been followed, amongst others, by Manoilesco from South-east Europe and Prebisch from Latin America. With the emergence of the underdeveloped countries of Asia and Africa, the questioning of the usefulness of the "Western" economic theory to these countries has become widespread. Now, many Western economists, not normally regarded as Historical or Institutional economists, have joined the ranks of the critics.

There are two main lines of criticism currently adopted against economic theory. The first is to elaborate the older line of criticism, stressing the differences in the social and institutional settings and stages of development between the advanced and the underdeveloped countries. This may be described as attacking the "realism" of economic theory. The second and newer line of attack is to question the "relevance" of economic theory to the underdeveloped countries. It is argued that "Western" economic theory is geared to the preoccupations of the advanced countries which, having already achieved sustained economic growth, are concerned with other problems, such as the optimum allocation of resources, the maintenance of full employment and perhaps the prevention of "secular stagnation". Thus the conventional economic theory is likely to be out of focus, if not largely irrelevant, for the central problem of the underdeveloped countries which is to initiate and accelerate the "take-off" into sustained growth.

Critics vary considerably in the emphasis they attach to these two different lines of attack.[1] But they share a common viewpoint on other issues. First, their attack on the applicability of economic theory to the underdeveloped countries is closely linked up with their attack on the applicability of free trade and laissez-faire policies to these countries. Thus, their sharpest attack on "Western" economic theory is reserved for the "orthodox" classical and neo-classical theory associated with the laissez-faire approach. The "modern" Keynesian and post-Keynesian economics is accepted less critically and is frequently used in support of deficit financing for economic development or as a basis for overall economic planning in terms of aggregate capital requirements to achieve a target rate of increase in national income, assuming a fixed capital output-ratio. Other modern developments of the neo-classical General Equilibrium theory, such as welfare economics, input-output analysis, linear programming, etc., are also acceptable provided they are used not as techniques for studying the performance of the market economy but as techniques of planning.

Further, all the critics share a common suspicion of the dispassionate "positivist" approach advocated by some of the orthodox economists.[2] The critics feel strongly that something should be done very urgently to relieve the poverty in the underdeveloped countries. They are also sceptical of the possibility of maintaining strict ethical neutrality in economics, and regard "positivism" merely as a cloak for inertia and an underdeveloped social conscience. Thus they feel that economists should give up the pretence of traditional academic detachment and become the champions and spokesmen for the underdeveloped countries. Some of them have come to look upon the economics of the underdeveloped countries not as a subject of impartial study but as an exercise in making out a persuasive case for increasing international economic aid to these countries.

1. D. Seers, "The Limitations of the Special Case", *The Bulletin of Oxford Institute of Economics and Statistics*, May 1963, stresses the "realism" aspect, while G. Myrdal, *Economic Theory and the Underdeveloped Regions*, London, 1957, stresses the "relevance" aspect.

2. E.g. G. Myrdal, *op. cit.*, ch. 12; Seers, *loc. cit.*, p. 83.

The aim of this paper is to clarify and appraise some of the issues which have arisen at the present stage of the discussion on the question of the applicability, particularly the "relevance" of economic theory to the underdeveloped countries. Since this is closely bound up with the further question of the applicability of the laissez-faire policy to these countries, we shall make use of the arguments directed against the market mechanism to illustrate the arguments directed against economic theory. To clear the air, the underlying standpoint adopted in this paper towards planning and private enterprise in the underdeveloped countries may be stated as follows. There is no reason to suppose that economic policies considered appropriate for the advanced countries will prove to be equally appropriate to the underdeveloped countries. But this "realistic" objection to generalizations should apply not only to the laissez-faire but also to the planning policies in the underdeveloped countries. Further, given the wide differences which exist among the underdeveloped countries themselves with respect, say, to the degree of population pressure, the overall size of the economy, the general level of administrative efficiency and the coherence of the institutional framework, etc., it is highly unlikely that any single standard model of development planning will be appropriate for all of them.[1]

The plan of the paper is as follows. In section I we shall examine the various arguments directed against the market mechanism in the underdeveloped countries and use them to illustrate and clarify the various arguments directed against the applicability of economic theory to these countries. In section II we shall argue that while the need for a greater "realism" is fully conceded, the arguments directed against the "relevance" of the "Western" economic theory to the underdeveloped countries are more debatable. In particular, we shall argue that the orthodox static theory of the optimum allocation of resources is as relevant as any other part of the existing economic theory. In section III we shall argue that a realistic approach to the underdeveloped countries has been hindered not only by the tendency to generalize from the "special case" of the advanced countries (as some critics have maintained), but also from the tendency to generalize from the "special case" of a particular underdeveloped country, such as India; and that this has been aggravated by the popularity of the "take-off" theory and by the tendency of some of the modern writers to treat the subject not as an academic discipline but as an adjunct to making out a persuasive

1. For a fuller development of this argument, see my book *The Economics of the Developing Countries*, Hutchinson, London, 1964.

general case for increasing international economic aid to the underdeveloped countries.

I

When the sociological writers questioned the applicability of economics to the underdeveloped countries on the ground that people there do not behave like the "economic man", they were questioning the "realism" of economic theory. It is not difficult to meet this type of criticism by showing that, with suitable adaptations to take into account local circumstances, the demand and supply analysis can be made to explain the behaviour of individuals in the market and the prices and quantities bought and sold, etc., in the underdeveloped countries as well as in the advanced countries. For instance, the much cited case of the "backward-bending" supply curve of labour in the underdeveloped countries (even if it really exists) can be explained in terms of the demand and supply apparatus, not to speak of refinements such as the "Income Effect" and the "Substitution Effect". Similarly, even the reaction of the "subsistence sector" to the impact of the exchange economy can be dealt with by extending the concept of "retained" demand and supply and the factor-proportions analysis of the international trade theory.[1] But this type of defence does not impress some of the modern critics who are questioning the "relevance" of economic theory to underdeveloped countries. They are not really concerned with the question of whether the basic tools of economic theory, such as the demand and supply analysis, can explain economic behaviour in a wide range of underdeveloped countries. What they are concerned with is whether it is *important* for the underdeveloped countries to give a central place to the study of the market mechanism and how far the theory of the optimum allocation of resources which goes with this approach is relevant for countries seeking rapid economic development.

Now, the discussion would have been much simpler if the critics had simply concentrated on this suggestive line of attack. We could then go on to discuss the usefulness or otherwise of the concept of the static optimum for economic development. But what they usually tend to do is: first to identify the existing "orthodox" theory with the laissez-faire approach; next to argue that the free play of market forces in the underdeveloped countries will not lead to an optimum allocation of resources because the conditions of Perfect Competition, such as perfect mobility and divisibility of

1. Cf. H. Myint, "The 'Classical Theory' of International Trade and the Underdeveloped Countries," *Economic Journal*, 1958.

resources and perfect knowledge, are lacking; and finally to emerge with the twin conclusion that both the existing economic theory and the laissez-faire policy are inapplicable to the underdeveloped countries. This type of argument tends to obscure a number of issues.

First, take Perfect Competition. It may be taken for granted that the ideal conditions required by it will not be fulfilled in any real life situation, whether in the advanced or the underdeveloped countries. What is more interesting is to find out how far these two types of country suffer from the same types of market imperfections and how far the existing theories of imperfect competition arising out of the problems of the mature industrial economies are relevant to the underdeveloped countries at a much earlier stage of development in market institutions. Further, given the important differences in population pressure, the overall size of the economy, and the general stage of development, etc., among the underdeveloped countries, it would be interesting to find out how far the different types of underdeveloped country suffer from different types of market imperfections. But many critics have been distracted by the easy target offered by the Perfect Competition model from making a "realistic" exploration of how the market mechanism actually works or fails to work in the different types of underdeveloped economic framework.

This has an interesting consequence on current writings on "planning" in the underdeveloped countries. On the one hand, we have the rejection of the Perfect Competition model. On the other hand, it is quite fashionable to formulate "pure" planning models, with given target figures of outputs, given production functions with constant sectoral capital-output ratios, and given supplies of resources, and make a great show of testing the formal consistency of the plan. Such a plan is supposed to cover the economy as a whole, but the fact that most governments of underdeveloped countries control a relatively small part of their G.N.P. (10 to 20 per cent) through taxation is used as evidence that there is a larger scope for the expansion of the state sector rather than as the evidence of a need for a more systematic analysis of how the private (including the subsistence) sector will react to government policy. Although some lip service is paid to the role of the fiscal, monetary and commercial policies of the government, the attention is focused mainly on the "quantifiable" aspects of the plan. Thus much in the same way as the Perfect Competition model fails to tell us how the market mechanism will actually overcome the existing immobility of factors and particularly existing imperfect knowledge, the "pure" planning model fails to tell us how the state mechanism will actually perform these tasks in the given administrative and institutional framework of an underdeveloped country. The substitution of the word "planning agency" for the "market mechanism" merely glosses over the actual problems of the mobilization and allocation of resources according to the plan and above all the problems of co-ordination and flexible readjustments. Thus the failure to study systematically how the economic forces work in the private sector of the underdeveloped countries, which produces the bulk of their G.N.P., has contributed to the failure to develop a satisfactory analysis of the "mixed economy" in the underdeveloped countries.

Next, take the Optimum. Much confusion has been caused by the habit of identifying the laissez-faire approach with the theory of the optimum allocation of resources. Although there is a historical association, there is no necessary logical link between the two. Thus it is possible to accept and work on the basis of an optimum allocation of resources without accepting the laissez-faire policy: for instance, welfare economics is mainly concerned with correcting the market forces to get closer to the optimum. Conversely, it is equally possible to reject the concept of the optimum as being too "static" and yet advocate a laissez-faire policy. The case for laissez-faire can then be made on other economic grounds, such as that it is likely to impart a "dynamism" to the economy by stimulating enterprise, innovation and investment. Thus in criticizing the working of the market mechanism in the underdeveloped countries, it is necessary to distinguish clearly whether we are concerned with its defects as the means of attaining the (accepted) norm of the optimum allocation of resources or whether we are concerned with the inadequacy of the concept of the optimum itself for the purposes of promoting the economic development of these countries.

Few critics have done this. Instead, they tend to bring out further objections against the market mechanism in the underdeveloped countries which are also used as the arguments against the applicability of the existing conventional economic theory to these countries. These various arguments may be grouped under four main lines of attack on the market mechanism.

(1) The first type of criticism runs in purely relative terms.[1] It is argued that the market mechanism works *more* imperfectly in the

1. Most critics have put forward this argument at one time or another. For a clear exposition of this view, see T. Balogh, "Economic Policy and the Price System", *United Nations Economic Bulletin for Latin America*, March 1961.

underdeveloped than in the advanced countries for various reasons, such as, a greater degree of immobility and indivisibility of resources and imperfect knowledge. Thus free market forces will lead to larger deviations from the optimum, requiring a correspondingly greater degree of state interference in the underdeveloped countries compared with the advanced countries. This type of criticism implies that the market imperfections in the advanced and the underdeveloped countries differ in degree rather than in kind and that the existing theory of the optimum and the deviations from the optimum may be usefully extended and adapted to deal with the problems of the economic development in the latter countries.

(2) The second type of criticism is based on the view that the most important problem facing the overpopulated underdeveloped countries is that they suffer from a surplus of labour and a shortage of other factors, viz. capital and natural resources. It is argued that this fundamental disequilibrium in factor proportions cannot be corrected merely by improving the allocative efficiency of the market mechanism on the basis of *given* resources, techniques and pattern of consumers' demand.[1] So long as these structural determinants of the economy remain unchanged perfect competition, even if it were attainable, would merely bring out this problem sharply; according to the logic of the optimum theory, since labour is redundant relatively to given wants and technology, it should have zero wages. This type of criticism implies a rejection of the concept of the static optimum. But, unfortunately, in the absence of a thoroughgoing dynamic theory, many exponents of this view revert to the conventional methods of correcting the deviations from the static optimum. This can be best illustrated by the argument that the manufacturing sector of an underdeveloped country should be subsidized or protected because it is having to pay positive wages to labour whose social opportunity cost in agriculture is zero.[2]

In this connection, it may be noted that current writings tend to restrict the market mechanism too narrowly to its role of allocating given resources, neglecting its possible longer-term effect on the supply of factors, particularly capital.[3] Private savings may increase

1. Cf. e.g. R. S. Eckaus, "The Factor-Proportions Problem in the Underdeveloped Countries", *American Economic Review*, September 1955.
2. Cf. e.g. W. A. Lewis, "Economic Development with Unlimited Supplies of Labour", *The Manchester School*, May 1954, p. 185.
3. In international trade theory, there has been some discussion of how far the expansion of primary exports of the underdeveloped countries tends to aggravate the initial "skewness" of their factor endowments. Cf. C. P. Kindleberger, *Foreign Trade and the National Economy*, chapter 3.

through improvements in the market for finance or through a rise of a capitalist class ploughing back profits. Even if it is decided that savings should increase only through public channels, such as taxation, marketing boards and the issue of government securities, the success of such a policy will still depend considerably on the market factors including the stage of development of the exchange economy and the development of a capital market.

(3) The third type of criticism is based on the view that the underdeveloped countries are trapped in a very stable low-income equilibrium and that they can be jerked out of this only through a "balanced growth" development programme big enough to overcome the smallness of the domestic markets and to take advantage of the economies of scale and complementarities. It is argued that at its best the market mechanism can only make one-at-a-time "marginal" adjustments, whereas an effective development programme requires large "structural" changes introduced by a simultaneous expansion of a wide range of complementary industries.

Without going into all the different versions of the "balanced growth" theory, it is sufficient to point out that we can adopt at least two different attitudes towards the role of the optimum allocation of resources in economic development, depending on the version of the theory we favour.

(*a*) One version emphasizes the overall size of the investment programme which must be large enough to overcome technical indivisibilities and the smallness in the size of domestic markets caused by the low levels of purchasing power in the underdeveloped countries.[1] Those who adopt this version tend to attach a greater importance to the problem of the aggregate level of investment and effective demand than to the problem of better allocation of resources at a given level of economic activity. Professor Hirschman has justifiably described this as "a variant of the Keynesian analysis of the slump".[2] Many of the "balanced growth" economists of this school would, for instance, be willing to put up with the possible distortion in the allocation of resources through inflationary methods of financing development rather than cut down the overall size of the investment programme. (*b*) This may be contrasted with

1. The most notable exponent of this version is P. N. Rosenstein-Rodan. Contrast, however, his early paper, "Problems of Industrialisation of Eastern and South-Eastern Europe", *Economic Journal*, 1943, with his *Notes on the Theory of the* "Big Push", 1951.
2. A. O. Hirschman, *The Strategy of Economic Development*, p. 54.

the other version of the "balanced growth" theory which stresses the interrelationships between investment in different sectors of the economy and the need for a government "planning agency" to co-ordinate the investment plans so as to achieve an optimum allocation of resources.[1] Those who adopt this version believe that the market mechanism is ineffective in the underdeveloped countries, not because the people there do not behave like the "economic man" in responding to its signals, but because the market signals themselves are defective and cannot accurately forecast what the future economic situation would be, after a complex of large-scale interrelated projects has been carried out. Thus, far from belittling the importance of the optimum, this second group of "balanced growth" theorists have made important contributions to the theory of the optimum involving complex interrelations between investment in different sectors of the economy over a period of time.

(4) Finally, there is the criticism which is based on the view that the free play of market forces tends to fossilize or exaggerate the existing market imperfections and the inequalities in income and bargaining power which are to be found in many underdeveloped countries.[2] The idea of the cumulative disequalizing forces has been applied both to the international economic relations between the advanced and the underdeveloped countries and to the internal economic relations between the "advanced" and the "backward" sectors or groups of people within each underdeveloped country. This type of criticism attempts to break sharply away from the conventional ideas of a stable equilibrium and the optimum and focus attention on the concept of the "dualism" in the economic structure of the underdeveloped countries which underlies most other types of criticism of the working of the market mechanism in these countries.

Although the ideas contained in this line of attack are suggestive, they have not been satisfactorily formulated so far. The concept of "dualism" needs more systematic study and the theoretical mechanism of how the cumulative disequalizing factors work has been sketched out in a rather impressionist manner. For instance, while the fragmentation of an economy into an "advanced" and a "back-

1. Cf. e.g. T. Scitovsky, *Two Concepts of External Economies, J.P.E.*, April 1954, and H. B. Chenery, "The Interdependence of Investment Decisions", in Abramovitz *et al.*, *The Allocation of Economic Resources*, Stanford 1959.
2. Cf. e.g. T. Balogh, *Static Models and Current Problems in International Economics*, O.E.P. June 1949; also H. Myint, *An Interpretation of Economic Backwardness*, O.E.P. June 1954; and G. Myrdal, *op. cit.*, chapter 3.

ward" sector will lead to a deviation from the optimum in a static sense, might not "dualism" have certain dynamic advantages enabling the "leading" sector to drag the "lagging" sector in its wake? Following the trend of thought suggested by Professor Hirschman's "unbalanced growth" approach, might not an attempt to impose a dead-pan uniformity and equality between the different sectors of the economy lead to the elimination of "growth points" and dynamic tensions for further economic development? These questions bring us to the difficult problem of choice between economic equality and rapid economic development. Here the critics are not always clear whether they object to the free play of market forces because they want to prevent economic inequality for its own sake or whether because they think that this inequality will in its turn inhibit the growth of the economy as a whole.

II

The relations between the four main types of criticism of the market mechanism in the underdeveloped countries and the theoretical approaches they suggest for development economics may be summed up schematically as follows:

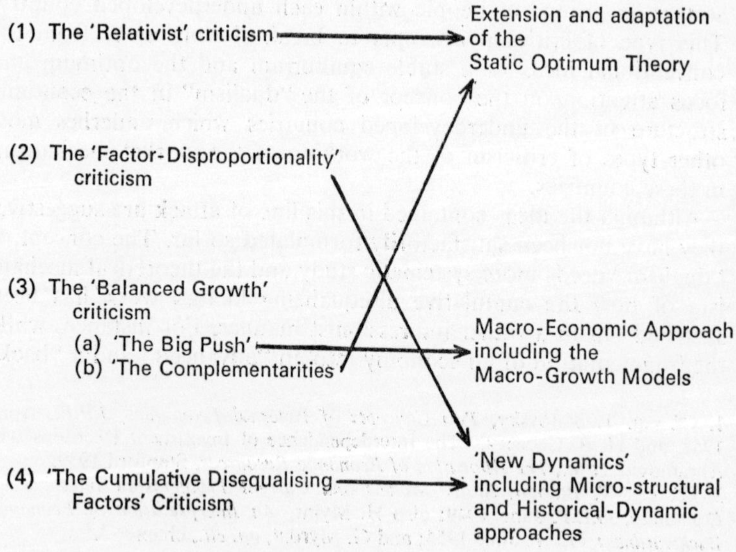

We are now in a position to appraise the criticisms directed against economic theory (as distinct from those directed against the market mechanism) in the context of the underdeveloped countries. There can be no serious quarrel with those critics who stress the need to increase the "realism" of economic theory by taking into account the various social, historical and institutional differences between the advanced and underdeveloped countries. If anything, our analysis has suggested the need also to take into account the differences between the underdeveloped countries themselves with respect to the degree of population pressure, the overall size of the economy, the general level of economic development and institutional framework and various other factors which may be expected to introduce significant differences in the structure and texture of their economic life. In particular, we have suggested that a failure to study systematically how the market forces actually work or fail to work in the different types of underdeveloped framework has contributed to the failure to develop a satisfactory analysis of the "mixed economy" in the underdeveloped countries. A study of the different patterns of market imperfections in different types of underdeveloped country is largely an unexplored subject.[1]

The argument of those critics who question the "relevance" of "Western" economic theory, in particular the relevance of the "orthodox" static theory of the optimum allocation of resources to the underdeveloped countries, is more debatable. In the light of the criticisms (2) and (4) above, few will question the need for a thorough-going "new" dynamic approach to economic development involving changes in the supplies of factors, techniques of production and the "transformation" of the whole organizational structure of the economy. It may be that such a new approach means widening the scope of conventional economics to take into account the broader sociological factors which made up "Political Economy" in the classical sense. But there is no need to argue about this since orthodox opinion has never imposed a methodological interdict on such a process. As Marshall wrote: "each economist may reasonably decide for himself how far he will extend his labour over that ground".[2]

What is really at stake is how far we should discard the existing static optimum theory before we have time or are clever enough to

1. For a pioneer effort in this field, see Morton R. Solomon, "The Structure of the Market in Underdeveloped Economies", *Q.J.E.*, August 1948.

2. *Principles*, p. 780; see also Robbins, *Nature and Significance of Economics*, 2nd ed., p. 150.

build up a satisfactory "dynamic" approach to the underdeveloped countries. That is to say how far are we to follow Professor Myrdal's advice to the "young economists in the underdeveloped countries" to "throw away large structures of meaningless, irrelevant and sometimes blatantly inadequate doctrine and theoretical approaches".[1] There are a number of considerations against following this advice, if this means throwing away the static optimum theory.

The first and most powerful is that the underdeveloped countries are too poor to put up with the burden of preventable waste which arises even within the static framework of given wants, techniques and resources. As Professor Galbraith has suggested in his *Affluent Society*, only the richer advanced countries can afford to take an indulgent view towards the misallocation of resources. There is a real danger that in searching for newer approaches and more advanced techniques of analysis, the economist (particularly if he is a visitor) in the underdeveloped countries may easily overlook quite glaring sources of wastage through misallocation, whether due to spontaneous market imperfections or inept state interference.

To give an example of the latter: after her Independence, Burma followed a policy of cutting out all private middlemen from her rice marketing board operations and opening numerous state buying stations all over the country to purchase rice directly from the peasant producers. Until very recently, the government insisted on paying the same fixed price all the year round, to cut out "the speculators". It also insisted on paying the same fixed price to all inland rice cultivators, irrespective of their distance from the main seaports (on grounds of regional justice). The consequences of conducting a marketing board on the basis of zero rate of interest and storing cost and zero transport cost are apparent from elementary optimum theory. As it happened, the rice crop, which normally took about four to six months to be cleared under free market conditions, now had to be cleared almost at once, since no one had any incentive to hold the rice stocks. This would have wrecked a very much more efficient marketing machinery than the government had been able to provide: the wastage and deterioration of the rice through bad storage, e.g. fire, rain, theft, mixing of different grades, etc., was enormous. Further, the remoter regions which used to grow rice for local consumption now sold their crop to the state buying centre, which sent it down to seaports for export, so that consignments of milled rice from the seaports had to be sent back to these

1. G. Myrdal, *op. cit.*, p. 101.

remoter regions to prevent food shortages, entailing two useless journeys on the country's limited transport system. Yet many economists visiting Burma during this period characteristically overlooked this "simple" but extremely wasteful misallocation of resources in their preoccupation with the more elaborate development plans, including the expansion of investment in "infrastructure". It is hard to believe that this is an isolated instance.[1]

If the underdeveloped countries are too poor to put up with the waste from preventable misallocation of resources, they are presumably also too poor to forgo immediate sources of relief from poverty for the sake of larger benefits promised in the future. Here, the time-preference which the critics have adopted on behalf of the underdeveloped countries shows a curious kink. In arguing for more international aid, they stress the urgent need to do something to give immediate relief to the underdeveloped countries; but in other contexts they tend to adopt a much lower valuation of the present in favour of the future. Thus they generally stress the longer-run social benefits from various forms of development expenditure to justify their immediate cost to the developing countries. Again, as against the orthodox presumption that the underdeveloped countries should choose less capital intensive methods of production with quicker returns, some of the critics would defend capital intensive methods on the ground that these are necessary for a higher rate of economic growth in the future. Thus the critics may be regarded as exercising the same pattern of time-preference in the choice of theoretical techniques when they urge that the existing static theory should be discarded in favour of a new dynamic theory which is rather sketchy at present and which promises to yield results in the somewhat indeterminate future. There are strong reasons to be worried about the future of the underdeveloped countries, but there are equally strong reasons to be worried about their present poverty, and the former should not be stressed almost to the exclusion of the

1. See however A. C. Harberger, "Using the Resources at Hand more Effectively", *American Economic Review*, May 1959. Harberger argues that for economies like Chile, Brazil and Argentina, reallocating resources, with existing production functions, "would raise national welfare by no more than 15 per cent". He considers that although substantial, this is relatively small compared with the large potential dynamic gains to be obtained from technical improvements raising labour productivity. One may reply that any source of gain is likely to appear small compared with the gains from technical improvements. But from the point of view of this paper Harberger's article remains an interesting attempt to apply the optimum analysis in a quantitative manner to the underdeveloped countries.

latter. If it is urgent to give immediate relief to the underdeveloped countries by stepping up international aid, it is equally urgent to find out how far they can help themselves by stopping obvious sources of waste through misallocation of resources. The significance of the conventional static theory of the allocation of scarce resources to the underdeveloped countries can be properly appreciated only in this perspective.

So far we have been concerned with criticisms (2) and (4). Let us now turn to criticism (3*a*) which may be regarded as the Keynesian criticism of the orthodox economics. This tendency to neglect the problem of allocating scarce resources in the writings on the underdeveloped countries has been aggravated by the "backwash" effect of the Keynesian Revolution. In the early post-war years at least, the Keynesian reaction against orthodox economics was automatically extended from its original context in the advanced countries to the underdeveloped countries. The Keynesian approach was enthusiastically adopted both as a basis of economic planning at macro-economic level and also as an argument for the deficit financing of development plans. Since then there has been an increasing realization of the need to probe below the macro-economic approach into the "structural" and "frictional" factors in the underdeveloped countries. Nevertheless, the point raised by criticism (3*a*), viz. how far we should put up with the possible distorting effect of inflation on the allocation of resources before cutting back the overall size of the investment programme, still remains a live issue dividing the expansionist and the orthodox economists. But even here an important change is noticeable. In the earlier days, the case for deficit financing of economic development was made mainly at the macro-economic level. Thus it was argued that the investment expenditure financed by pure credit creation would expand the money incomes but keep them stabilized at a certain level according to the Multiplier theory. Thus the increase in physical output from the newly created capital goods would have a chance to catch up with the increase in money incomes until at last prices were restored to the initial level and inflation destroyed itself.[1] More recently, however, the structural and allocative factors have been brought into the forefront. It is now argued that a mere negative elimination or ending of the

1. W. A. Lewis, "Economic Development with Unlimited Supplies of Labour", *Manchester School*, May 1954, p. 165. Lewis himself points out "the usual objections against applying multiplier analysis to inflationary conditions, namely the instability of the propensity to consume, the effect of secondary investment and the dangers of cost inflation".

inflationary pressure will not lead automatically to an optimum allocation of resources and that what is really needed is "carefully discriminatory policies" designed to correct the structural imbalance and market imperfections in the underdeveloped countries.[1] One can follow up this point by asking how far the government of an underdeveloped country will in fact be in a position to pursue such discriminatory policies effectively and consistently after the inflationary pressure and balance of payments difficulties have got beyond a certain point.[2] But for our present purpose it is sufficient to point out the shift of emphasis from the Keynesian approach to the optimum approach.

We can now pull together the threads of our argument so far. As shown by our chart, the various criticisms of the working of the market mechanism in the underdeveloped countries have suggested three types of theoretical approach to these countries: viz. (i) the extension and adaptation of the existing static theory of the optimum allocation of scarce resources; (ii) the extension of the Keynesian macro-economic approach, including the macro-growth models of the Harrod-Domar type; and (iii) the introduction of a new thoroughgoing dynamic approach which is capable of dealing with the changes in the long-run supplies of factors of production and changes in the techniques of production involving the "transformation" of the whole organizational structure of the underdeveloped economies. In the post-war writings on the underdeveloped countries there has been some progress made in the application of the optimum theory to development economics, particularly on the problems of complementary investment and of optimization over a given plan period.[3] But, nevertheless, the optimum approach to the underdeveloped countries has been unduly neglected by the critics of the "orthodox" economics, partly because they identify this with the laissez-faire type of liberal economics, partly because they feel that

1. T. Balogh, "Economic Policy and the Price System", *U.N. Economic Bulletin for Latin America*, March 1961, p. 53.

2. For instance, the differential advantages offered by tariff protection to "infant industries" are likely to be swamped under random short-term speculative rises in prices of the non-protected imports when successive rounds of quantitative import restrictions have to be imposed because of a balance of payments crisis. For a fuller treatment see my paper, chapter 7 in *International Trade Theory in a Developing World*, eds. R. Harrod and D. C. Hague, Macmillan, London, 1963.

3. E.g. H. B. Chenery, *loc. cit.*, in Abramovitz *et al.*, "The Allocation of Resources", and also "Comparative Advantage and Development Policy", *A.E.R. Proceedings*, March 1961, also A. K. Sen, *The Choice of Techniques*, 1961, and O. Eckstein, "Investment Criteria for Economic Development and Intertemporal Welfare Economics", *Q.J.E.*, February 1957.

anything short of a thoroughgoing dynamic approach should be discarded, and partly because of the "backwash" effect of the Keynesian Revolution. While fully admitting the need to develop a new dynamic approach to the underdeveloped countries, we have tried to show: (1) that the orthodox static theory of allocation of scarce resources remains as "relevant" to these countries as any other part of economic theory so long as they suffer from serious misallocations of resources which they can ill afford, and (2) that the optimum approach can be made more fruitful by a "realistic" study of how the market forces actually work or fail to work in the different settings of the different types of underdeveloped country.

III

Some critics have attributed the lack of "realism" in the current writings on the underdeveloped countries to the tendency of the Western economists to generalize from the "special case" of the advanced countries.[1] But this is only half the trouble; the other half of the trouble must be traced to the tendency to generalize about all underdeveloped countries from the "special case" of a particular type of underdeveloped country; and this has been aggravated by the tendency to treat the whole subject as an adjunct to making out a persuasive case for increasing international aid. Thus it is no accident that the theory of economic development of the underdeveloped countries should come to be dominated by a "conventional" model of the underdeveloped country which most closely resembles India. For the case for increasing international aid to the underdeveloped countries is strongest when we have a country like India. Given India's acute population pressure on natural resources and material poverty, the case for increasing aid to her on purely humanitarian grounds is obvious. Given her low ratio of foreign trade to national income, she cannot hope to earn enough foreign exchange through the expansion of her exports even if the market prospects for them were brighter, and when she has reached the limits of borrowing on commercial terms, there is little alternative but to rely on aid. One further consequence of a low ratio of foreign trade to national income is that foreign exchange shortage cannot be overcome by increasing domestic saving. Again, given the very large overall size of her economy, it is reasonable to suppose that she will be able to reap the economies of scale from setting up a

1. E.g. Seers, *loc. cit.*, pp. 79–83, and *passim.*

large and interrelated industrial complex, including a capital goods sector orientated towards the domestic market. Finally, whatever our views about India's chances of ultimate success in achieving economic development through integrated economic planning, it is generally admitted that her general institutional framework and her administrative and planning machinery are well in advance of other developing countries. Thus in India's case both the need to receive material aid and the ability to absorb aid for successful economic development are stronger than in most other underdeveloped countries. Only Mexico and Brazil, at about the same stage of general development as India, but without her population pressure, seem to have a comparable capacity to absorb material aid.

Now there is nothing wrong with concentrating on such a type of underdeveloped country, provided it is clearly recognized as a very "special case". The danger arises from trying to generalize from the Indian case and, in particular, trying to apply the standard Indian model of development planning to other underdeveloped countries. Here are some of the more obvious limitations of this "special case". (i) Although population is growing very rapidly all over the underdeveloped world, there are still many sparsely populated countries, covering most of Latin America, considerable parts of Africa and most of South-east Asia, where the Indian type of extreme pressure of population on natural resources does not apply. The concept of "disguised unemployment" has limited application for these countries and their problem is how to make the best use of the available elbow room of natural resources before plunging into the more heroic measures of development required by the Indian situation. (ii) Even among the overpopulated countries, the overall size of the population and area of India has no peer except for China. Many of the overpopulated countries are much smaller countries which, unlike India, have a high ratio of foreign trade to national income and which because of their smallness cannot hope to imitate the Indian model of industrialization based on a substantial capital goods industry and orientated mainly towards the domestic market. Short of organizing themselves into larger common market units for which they are not politically ready, exports, particularly export of primary products, must continue to play an important role in their economic development. In this respect the position of the smaller overpopulated countries, some of them overcrowded islands, is harder than that of a big overpopulated country like India with a domestic market potentially large enough to yield the economies of scale. While a few small countries like Hong Kong and Puerto Rico may have found an escape route in the export of "simple manufactures" and/or emigration, this is not likely to be open to the others because of various obstacles, partly of their own creation, and partly created by the advanced countries. (iii) Above all, it should be stressed that the underdeveloped countries are at widely varying stages of general social, political and economic development. At one end of the scale are a few countries, like India, Mexico and Brazil, which have reached a stage of development where they may be considered to be within a reasonable striking distance of the "take-off". The rest of the underdeveloped countries are at different sub-stages of the "pre-take-off" phase, tailing off into a considerable number of countries which are hard put to maintain even the minimum of law and order, political stability and public services and which clearly do not yet possess the necessary institutional framework to carry out elaborate economic development planning.

Given the popularity of the conventional Indian model of economic development, however, most underdeveloped countries have tried to fulfil the first and the second of Professor Rostow's conditions for the take-off: viz. "(*a*) a rise in the rate of productive investment from (say) 5 per cent or less to 10 per cent of national income (or net national product); (*b*) the development of one or more substantial manufacturing sectors, with a high rate of growth." But in their preoccupation with quantitative planning and target figures, they have neglected his third elusive condition: "(*c*) the existence or quick emergence of a political, social and institutional framework which exploits the impulses to expansion in the modern sector and the potential external economy effects of the take-off and gives to growth an ongoing character".[1] It turns out that condition (*c*) is the most important of the three in the sense that unless it can be fulfilled it is not possible to keep the other two conditions fulfilled for long. It is also the most important factor determining an underdeveloped country's capacity to absorb aid productively.

Yet in spite of the fact that the majority of the underdeveloped countries are either just emerging from the "traditional society" or are somewhere in the "pre-take-off" stage, the discussion of this earlier phase is perhaps even more unsatisfactory than the rest of the take-off theory.[2] The central problem of these countries is not how

1. W. W. Rostow, "The Take-Off into Self-Sustained Growth", *E.J.*, March 1956, p. 32, and "The Stages of Economic Growth", p. 39.
2. Cf. S. Kuznets, "Notes on the Take-Off", in the *Economics of Take-Off into Sustained Growth*, Rostow *et al.*, Macmillan, 1963.

to plan for an immediate take-off but how to compress the pre-take-off phase into a few decades instead of "a long period up to a century or conceivably more" which the Western countries are said to have taken. Here, one may agree that if these countries are not yet ready for the final "big-push" into take-off, they need not rely solely on the unaided working of the market forces to shorten the preliminary period. In the past, even the so-called laissez-faire colonial governments encouraged the growth of the exchange economy, particularly through the provision of better transport and communications. But beyond this, analysis has not proceeded very far.

For instance, the success of a policy of concentrating on "infra-structure" investment will depend on the various economic factors determining the structure and behaviour of the "subsistence sector" and on the question how far its persistence is due to the limitations on the demand side, i.e. lack of marketing facilities and outlets, and how far it is due to limitations on the supply side, i.e. lack of a marketable surplus. Yet there is little systematic study of the mutual interactions between the "subsistence sector" and the "money economy" (including the government sector) in the different types of underdeveloped country, taking into account the differences in the degree of population pressure, the nature and extent of the export production and the urban manufacturing sector. In this context, we may also ask how far the more sophisticated monetary policy of deficit financing is really suitable for the earlier stages of the development in the money economy, when we should be concerned with encouraging the people from the subsistence economy to use money not only as a medium of exchange, but also as a unit of account for a rational economic calculus and as a store of value. Recently there has been a shift of interest from investment in material "infra-structure" to "investment in human capital", particularly in education. Yet so far this line of approach has been limited by too much emphasis on what the government should do in the way of a "crash programme" in education combined with too little analysis of the demand and supply factors affecting the market for skilled labour at various stages of economic development.[1]

All this is merely another way of stating our argument at the end of the last section that we need to have a more systematic study of

1. For further discussion, see my papers, "The Universities of South-east Asia and Economic Development", *Pacific Affairs*, Summer 1962, and "Social Flexibility, Social Discipline and Economic Growth", *International Journal of Social Science*, Paris, 1964.

how the market forces actually work or fail to work in the different types of underdeveloped country. Applied to the majority of the underdeveloped countries at the earlier "pre-take-off" stages of economic development, this now assumes a special significance. The degree of effective control which the government of such a country can exercise over the rest of the economy depends more clearly than elsewhere on the growth of suitable monetary, fiscal and market institutions through which it can extend its control. Thus we may reasonably suggest a more systematic study of the market forces in such an underdeveloped country even to the most planning-minded economist.

To sum up: current writings on the underdeveloped countries have been vitiated not merely by the tendency to generalize from the "special case" of the advanced countries, but also by the tendency to generalize from the "special case" of a particular type of underdeveloped country, notably India. This in its turn has been aggravated by the popularity of the idea of development planning based on the "take-off" theory and by the tendency to treat the subject not as an academic discipline but as an adjunct to making out a persuasive general case for increasing international aid to the underdeveloped countries. The new crusading spirit has rendered a valuable service in getting the idea of giving aid to these countries firmly established in the advanced countries. But now that the general good will towards these countries seems to have outstripped an accurate knowledge of how the economic systems of these countries really function, one may venture to urge the revival of the traditional academic approach to the subject.

What we do not know about the Economics of Development in Low Income Societies

E. E. HAGEN

Massachusetts Institute of Technology;
Tavistock Institute of Human Relations

THIS is a précis of a long argument, intended as a basis for discussion.

An implicit assumption that is common in economic theorizing in economically advanced societies concerning economic growth in low income societies (hereafter, underdeveloped countries, or udc's) is as follows: We in the technically advanced societies have higher productivity. The people of every society prefer more goods to less goods. People in udc's can obtain more goods by adopting our methods. Hence economic development in udc's is "natural". If they do not develop, it must be because some economic barriers peculiar to the udc's are present in them.

Until the last few years, economic theorizing concerning the problem has taken technical advance (movement southwestward of the iso-product curves on a production function) for granted, and has considered that the barriers must be blocks to capital formation. This emphasis results in part from the history of the development of economic theory. From Mill to say Marshall, theorists progressively ruled technical progress out of their analytical models, and since Marshall it has been absent, whereupon the only path to increased income per unit of labour input, in economic theory, has been increase in capital per unit of labour input. The habit of centring attention on capital formation has continued even when the problem was economic progress in udc's, a process in which technical advance is the central characteristic.

Hence without empirical evidence we have assumed that the "peculiar barriers" must be barriers to capital formation. From this assumption have derived several hypotheses which are probably (almost certainly) false. The paragraphs which follow state such hypotheses and the relevant probable facts.

1. Hypothesis: The level of *per capita* income in udc's is too low to permit net saving.

Facts: The distribution of income after taxes in most udc's is probably more unequal than in the advanced economies. That the people of udc's in general live above the subsistence level is evidenced by the fact that population is increasing. Hence the upper income classes—say the upper 10 to 15 per cent—could live well by the standards of their societies and simultaneously save a fraction of the national income easily adequate to finance economic development. Moreover, such societies, as Arthur Lewis has noted, seem always to have the resources necessary to finance wars.

Further fact: In almost all udc's, even though the top income families lived well by Western standards, they could do much saving.

2. Hypothesis: Even if the facts asserted in (1) are correct, the high income families in udc's are psychologically barred from saving by the "demonstration effect".

Fact: The demonstration effect operates in face-to-face contacts. It does not seem to operate between low-income and high-income communities, even within the United States, with the intimate communication between them via press, television, cinemas, etc. (See Dorothy S. Brady, "Research on the Size Distribution of Income", Part I, *Studies in Income and Wealth*, Vol. XIII (New York: National Bureau of Economic Research, Inc., *c.* 1951).) Hence, that it has an important influence across the boundaries of societies is doubtful. Note: Under certain conditions of intense psychological pressure of conquering intruders on the élites of udc's, the phenomenon known to psychoanalysts as "identification with the aggressor" probably occurs, and the demonstration effect becomes important. That such cases are frequent enough to provide the basis for an economic hypothesis is doubtful. Hence the demonstration effect of contact by high income families with Western societies may have influence on *how* they consume, rather on the level of their consumption.

3. Hypothesis: The markets of udc's are so small that they do not provide an outlet for the output of minimum size modern plants. Hence there is no incentive for investment.

Fact: Many udc's provide too small markets for the output of a steel mill, an aluminium refinery, an electric light bulb factory, etc.; but virtually every udc provides a market more than adequate to take the output of an efficient size plant in sugar, sugar products, rice or wheat milling, textiles, textile products, shoes or sandals, and various other mass consumed consumer goods.

4. Hypothesis: Economic progress in udc's requires as a basis certain "social overhead capital" or "infrastructure" projects feasible

only in units so large that the economy cannot accumulate the lump of capital required.

Counter-hypothesis: The technological paths available are not inflexible, as this hypothesis suggests. There are many paths of technical advance in udc's where methods are still traditional which do not require large s.o.c. projects as a base. Indeed, many large s.o.c. projects are uneconomic at low income levels and with non-modern technology the prevalent type. Their capacity would be so little utilized until considerable change in methods had occurred that the cost per unit of their services would be exceedingly high. At this stage, dynamically as well as statically many other types of investment are more economic. The appropriate time for most large s.o.c. projects is later, and at a later time financial capacity is greater.

Relevant fact: Governments now typically have or can borrow the resources to finance large s.o.c. projects. However, the counter-hypothesis above, which I believe to be realistic, suggests that the absence of these s.o.c. projects was not an important barrier to development even before governments had that capacity.

Added fact: Improvement in transportation in small doses is feasible. This is true even of railroad transportation, and much more so of road or water transportation.

5. Hypothesis: Because the economies of udc's are on dead centre, government planning for simultaneous advance in various sectors is necessary to get development going.

Theoretical considerations: This hypothesis rests on hypotheses 3–4 above. If these are incorrect, this one is less persuasive. This hypothesis also assumes that only investment to increase output is in point. Technical change to reduce costs needs no expansion of the total market. On the other hand, it causes expansion of productive capacity, and with appropriate fiscal-monetary policy, expansion of the market will occur. The usual process of growth is through one investment project after another, induced by the possibility of cost reduction or the judgment that this process of expansion will continue, or both. Thus expansion of the economy gradually gains speed. The metaphor of "dead centre" is inappropriate.

(It does not follow that government planning is not in point. Planning to provide "public goods" and other services most economically provided by government, needed to complement and facilitate private expansion, to regulate the level of aggregate demand, to manage foreign exchange problems, and to serve non-economic goals, is of course essential.)

6. Other hypotheses, e.g. by Balogh, Eckaus, and Lewis (also

many others), present descriptions of economic conditions in udc's that seem plausible.

However, except tautologically they neither indicate the "natural history" of the changes that will cause growth nor convincingly suggest policy measures that will bring growth. (Nor do they all claim to do so.) As economists, we do not know why growth varies among societies.

7. Hypothesis (usually implicit): The udc's can develop largely by a process of imitation, since more productive techniques are available for borrowing from the West.

Fact: These techniques work well in the West in part because of the technical, economic, social, and cultural complex in which they function, and because of the nature of personality in Western societies. To adapt almost any technique (even the spade, to replace the digging hoe) so that it will work well in a society with a quite different social and cultural complex and different personalities requires a very high degree of creativity. (Note: this is asserted not as an hypothesis, but as empirical fact.)

Counter-hypothesis: The factor centrally responsible for the absence or sluggishness of economic growth in udc's is the absence of a sufficient and sufficiently widespread degree of creativity directed toward technical and economic problems. The problem is not economic; its analysis lies in the area of sociological-anthropological and, especially, personality theory.[1]

8. Addendum, after reading Hla Myint's paper: Nothing above is intended to suggest that conventional economic theory, macro- or micro-, is inapplicable in udc's. The writer believes both branches of theory applicable, but only with large adaptations required because of absence of market mechanisms, uncollectibility of progressive income taxes, etc.

1. Paragraphs 1–6 above are largely a précis of chapter 3 of E. E. Hagen, *On The Theory of Social Change: How Economic Growth Begins* (Tavistock Publications, 1964). Chapters 4–12 suggest why inadequate technical and economic creativity is manifested in "traditional societies" and the "natural history" of the process by which creativity increases and is directed increasingly toward technical, economic, and related problems.

The Use and Abuse of Models in Development Planning[1]

PAUL STREETEN

Oxford University

THE following criticism is not intended as a rejection of all models in the analysis of underdevelopment and in planning for development. All thought presupposes implicit or explicit model building and model using. Rigorous abstraction, simplification and quantification are necessary conditions of analysis and policy. But models must be realistic, relevant and useful. The trouble with many current models is that they are shapely and elegant, but lack the vital organs.

SYSTEMATIC BIASES

Model thinking shows four systematic biases, which are related to each other and overlap, and which can be called:

1. Adapted ceteris paribus or automatic mutatis mutandis;
2. One-factor analysis;
3. Misplaced aggregation;
4. Illegitimate isolation.

1. *Adapted ceteris paribus or automatic mutatis mutandis*

It is interesting to note that the conclusions of orthodox liberal and of Marxian economics, though derived from very different premises, converge in this respect. The separation of parameters from variables in Western orthodox models is partly determined by what is appropriate for advanced industrial nations, partly by ideology and vested interests, and partly by convenience of analysis. Thus psychological attitudes and valuations and social institutions are normally assumed to be given and adapted. We assume that

1. I am indebted to Miss P. Ady, R. Portes, Mr. M. F. G. Scott and D. Whitehead for helpful comments. The paper owes much to collaboration with Professor Gunnar Myrdal and Mr. M. Lipton.

there is a legal framework, that contracts are enforced, that an efficient civil service carries out government orders and an honest judiciary adjudicates; that people are able and willing to work if opportunities arise, that they are literate, skilled and able to co-operate with discipline, appearing on time and carrying out orders, that money spent is efficiently spent and not diverted into the pockets of corrupt officials, that alternatives are considered largely on their pecuniary merits, etc. It follows that none of these matters is considered a suitable area for planning.

In the Marxian scheme (though not always in Marx's own writings), what are parameters become dependent variables. Cultural, political and social institutions are the superstructure, which is determined by the methods of production. It reflects these conditions and gives rise to tensions and contradictions in due course. These tensions between the degree of development of the forces of production and the prevailing relations of production (the institutions and attitudes) in turn give rise to revolution. After the revolution the attitudes and institutions reflect the new conditions of production. Hence social, cultural and political attitudes and institutions, the so-called "relations of production", though dependent variables, are, after a time-lag, adjusted to the extent required by the dynamic productive forces. Once again, though for fundamentally different reasons, planning the superstructure is not in question. It would be futile before the revolution and unnecessary after it. It was indeed for their attempts to speculate on how social attitudes and institutions could and should be reformed that Marx and Engels ridiculed the "Utopian" thinkers. Yet, in many ways the early Utopian socialists were more akin to modern planners, including the planners in Soviet Russia, than many of the cruder versions of Marxian thought.

Thus the conservative judgment that a reform of attitudes and institutions is undesirable, and the Marxian judgment that it is either impossible or inevitable, lead to the same conclusion, distracting attention from conscious policy directed at a radical reform of the so-called "non-economic" factors in economic development. It is, of course, true that textbooks, articles and plans pay lip service to the need to reform the social framework before economic planning can begin. But these declarations are usually forgotten later when the discussion turns to the conventional concepts of income, employment, savings, investment, etc. At that stage either the assumption of *ceteris paribus* is tacitly reintroduced, so that the conventional economic variables can be considered in isolation, or the assumption of automatic *mutatis mutandis* is made, implying that where other things cannot be assumed constant, they will without special policies be adapted to the required extent as a result of economic transformation.

The intellectual framework, which reflects this bias, is supported by value judgments and by vested interests. As we shall see, reforms of institutions and human attitudes violate entrenched interests and are therefore more painful to implement than financial expenditure programmes.

In a bias-free model, the distinction between parameters and variables would be determined, not by ideological preconceptions, but by the situation to which the model is intended to apply and by the questions asked about this situation. To be useful, models will have to be, at least initially, much more specific to individual cases and much less general and "theoretical". In particular, the distinction between parameters and variables should not run along the line drawn between "economic" and "non-economic" factors operating in a situation. Thus social and political reform should neither "precede" nor "follow" economic development: social reform must accompany development, reinforce it, create the conditions necessary for it, but is itself promoted and determined by development. The process is one of continual mutual causation.

2. *One-factor analysis*

Although economists ought to be particularly trained to discern interdependence and particularly immune to uni-causal explanations, it is a fact that frequently one factor is selected as the strategic factor in development, although the choice of this factor is subject to fashion and ideology. If the Physiocrats stressed *Land* as the source of all wealth and the classical economists *Labour*, *Capital* has recently played the strategic role. Keynes's emphasis on the income-creating aspect of capital was combined with Marx's emphasis on its output-creating aspect in the Harrod-Domar model which has strongly influenced planners. The relationship which equates the rate of growth of income to the savings ratio divided by the capital/output ratio has been one of the chief vehicles by which Western economic thought has been carried into the plans and discussions of the plans of underdeveloped countries. Capital is sometimes regarded as a necessary and sufficient condition of growth, sometimes as the strategic variable. It became soon obvious, however, that numerous other conditions both account for past growth in advanced countries and are required for development in underdeveloped countries. But instead of embarking on a careful analysis of the necessary co-ordination of policies in particular cases, a new one-factor analysis has tended to replace the old one. *Education* is now the craze and one cannot open a journal or read a speech concerned with development without being told of the high returns that "investment in human beings" yields. There is often little thought as to education of whom, for what, how long, in conjunction with what other measures. It is interesting to speculate what other factors will be singled out as discussion progresses. "Research and Development" are already popular, and perhaps we shall soon study the returns from appropriate child-training, which produces experimental innovating personalities, or from expenditure on child prevention.

3. *Misplaced aggregation*

Almost all concepts formed by aggregation suitable for analysing Western economies must be carefully reconsidered before they can be applied to underdeveloped economies. "Capital", "income", "employment", "unemployment", "price level", "savings", "investment", presuppose conditions which are absent in many underdeveloped countries. "Employment" presupposes a fairly homogeneous, mobile labour force, willing and able to work and responsive to incentives. In a society of isolated communities, some of them apathetic or with religious prejudices against certain kinds of work, illiterate and unused to co-operation, the notion "Labour Force" does not make sense. Similarly "underemployment" or "disguised unemployment" presupposes that if only demand and machines were available, men and women would be able and willing to work. In fact, much more would be required: a breakdown of caste prejudices, of apathy, of lack of interest in money rewards, of resistance to co-operation, discipline and punctuality, etc. Any attempt to calculate "disguised unemployment" also presupposes a value judgment as to the length of the appropriate working day and working week.[1]

If economies are divided into sectors between which there is little or no substitution, either in consumption in response to changes in relative prices, or in production in response to changes in relative factor rewards, aggregation of incomes or prices is inappropriate. Even though the indigenous sector may sell its surplus in the market, and even though some of its members may occasionally participate in the transactions of the money sector, if the

1. For a more detailed discussion see the last section on the Reform of Concepts.

indigenous sector neither depends upon nor interacts with the capitalist sector, aggregation can be meaningless. The income of an industrial enclave may grow, while real income per head of the indigenous population stagnates or declines. In what sense is "average income" rising? The problem is not merely how to get at the facts in the indigenous sector and how to appraise them properly. More fundamental is the problem what weights to attach to a small decline of essentials and to a large increase of non-essentials. Paasche and Laspeyres indices may give contradictory results. Habits of thought induce us to use concepts which are applicable to one set of conditions, because substitution is possible, responses exist, and value judgments are appropriate, in an entirely different context, where these presuppositions of legitimate aggregation are absent. The statistical manifestation of this would be contradictory results according to which of several equally plausible sets of weights were applied to the same change. Using base period weights, we should register a rise in income per head, and therefore conclude that development is proceeding, while we have begged the political question "development for whom?"[1]

The distinction between consumption and investment can have various justifications. In the context of development, it is based upon the assumption that investment enables us to produce more later than we would otherwise have done, while consumption is current enjoyment. But if more food and better health now reduce apathy and raise ability to work, they share in the characteristics of investment: consumption, too, is productive of more output.[2] If different investment projects require different sums to bribe corrupt officials, what guide is their cost to the resources used up? To abstract from the differences in such cases is to pour out the baby with the bath water.

It is correct to say that a man is male, a woman female, but it does not make sense to ask: "Is your family male or female?" One can discuss the differences between the British and the French Constitutions, and also the connections between the Cabinet, Parliament and the Church of England, but it does not make sense

1. I am aware that I shut my eyes to these problems in the "Sketch of a Model of Development".

2. "It has been estimated that the combined effect of malnutrition and ill-health in Ecuador, for example, reduces the average worker's production to 48 per cent of his potential capacity, as opposed to 93 per cent in the United States (see Hector Correa, *The Economics of Human Resources* (Den Haag: Drukkerij Pasmans, 1962), p. 44)."—Anthony Bottomley, *Economic Journal*, March 1964, fn. 2, p. 233.

to ask "What transactions go on between the House of Commons and the British Constitution?"[1] Similarly, it is what philosophers call a "category mistake" to ask what is the capital, income, employment, price level, etc., of a society sharply divided into non-communicating sectors. Just as words can be spelt, but letters of the alphabet cannot be spelt, not because it is very difficult but because it is an improper request,[2] so asking questions about certain aggregates commonly used in advanced industrial countries in the context of underdeveloped countries, is improper. The solution of a jigsaw puzzle consists in putting each piece where it belongs, not in lumping them together arbitrarily.

Two separate problems arise here. First, category mistakes are made where a category is applied to a field of experience to which it is inappropriate. It is quite possible for this category to be appropriate for advanced countries, but not for underdeveloped ones, just as it is legitimate to ask in some cities "Where is the University?" but not in Oxford.

Secondly, there are instances in which the category *might* be appropriate if we knew what it meant when applied to a situation of underdevelopment. Thus the distinction between consumption and investment can be misplaced aggregation in either sense, depending upon the definition. If investment is defined as "abstaining for the sake of higher consumption later" the first problem may arise. But if investment is defined as any input which yields higher output later, irrespective of whether it involves "abstaining" or not, the second problem arises and the error is not a conceptual one but simply of failing to group certain activities under "investment" which, in advanced countries, are classified as "consumption".

4. *Illegitimate isolation*

The converse of misplaced aggregation, but related to one-factor analysis, which is a particular manifestation of it, is the bias of illegitimate isolation. It consists in assigning the role of sufficient condition to what may or may not be one of several necessary conditions of development. If a component is illegitimately isolated from its necessary complements, and then aggregated with others similarly isolated, we get a combination of misplaced aggregation and illegitimate isolation. The case can be illustrated by successive missions going to a country. The first says entrepreneurial *incentives*

1. Gilbert Ryle, *The Concept of Mind*, pp. 17 and 168.
2. *Op. cit.*, p. 206.

are inadequate, and if we nurse these by *low taxes*, resources will soon become available. The next goes and says *resources* are the bottleneck and decisions will soon come forth if we set free resources by *high taxation* to generate a high budget surplus. But the correct policy would be high taxation of certain incomes and property, perhaps land, combined with generous investment allowances and incentives where these yield results. The division should not be resources *versus* incentives, but certain incentives combined with certain resources.

Education, which is now often advocated as a panacea, may simply result in a group of educated unemployed and unemployables, as in India. Equipment may lie unused and unmaintained. Irrigation water flows unused and reservoirs are silting, because "investment" has not been co-ordinated with the right kind of education, land reform and civil service reform. The price we pay for misplaced aggregation and illegitimate isolation is wasted resources and possibly hardened resistance to and growing cynicism about the process of development.

The problem is illustrated in the first table. The horizontal groupings indicate the conventional Western categories of thought and, if applied to underdeveloped countries, misplaced aggregation; the vertical groupings indicate "packages" relevant to development and, if torn from their vertical links, illegitimate isolation. Expenditure on birth control, like expenditure on health and teachers' salaries, is normally classified as consumption. But in conjunction with the construction of clinics and schools and the reform of the administrative system, it is in many societies the most important single *per caput* income-raising force. Much of the potential benefit of irrigation schemes is wasted because schistosomiasis is spread and reduces human efficiency, or because land ownership systems deprive peasants of both incentives and opportunities to make use of the water even if they wanted to raise yield. The vertical groupings represent blocks of sufficient conditions for accelerated development, whilst the horizontal groupings apply the false Western categories according to which institutions and attitudes are given (Liberalism) or adjusted to the required extent (Marxism), consumption is current enjoyment which does not contribute to higher production later, and investment is the strategic instrument to raise output and income.

The second table illustrates the misplaced aggregation of all forms of education and the illegitimate isolation of certain forms (agronomy, engineering) from the necessary equipment which is required to embody the knowledge and apply the training.

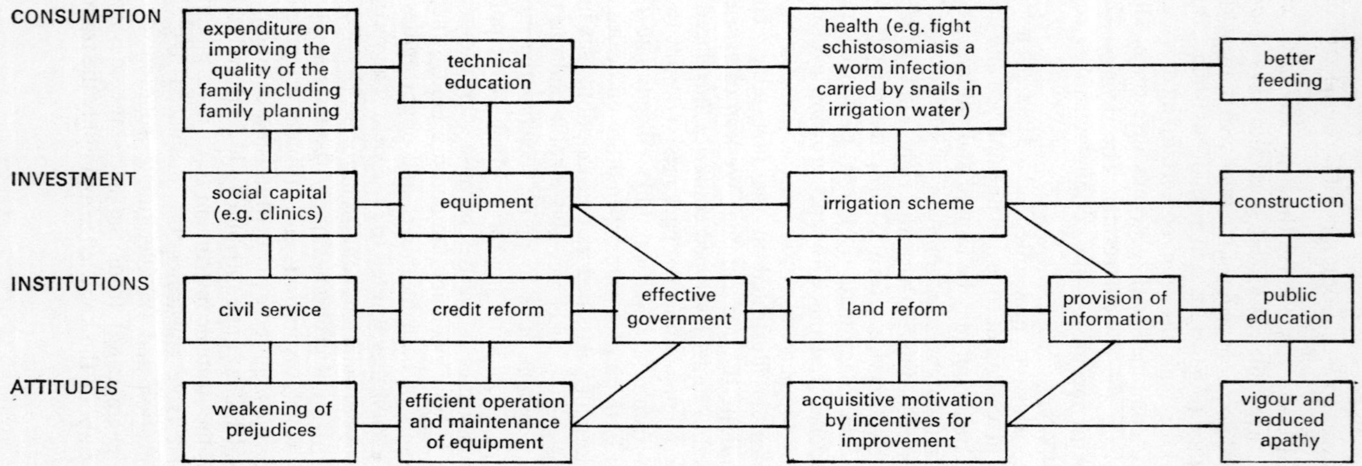

CONSUMPTION
INVESTMENT
INSTITUTIONS
ATTITUDES
expenditure on improving the quality of the family including family planning
technical education
health (e.g. fight schistosomiasis a worm infection carried by snails in irrigation water)
better feeding
social capital (e.g. clinics)
equipment
irrigation scheme
construction
civil service
credit reform
effective government
land reform
provision of information
public education
weakening of prejudices
efficient operation and maintenance of equipment
acquisitive motivation by incentives for improvement
vigour and reduced apathy

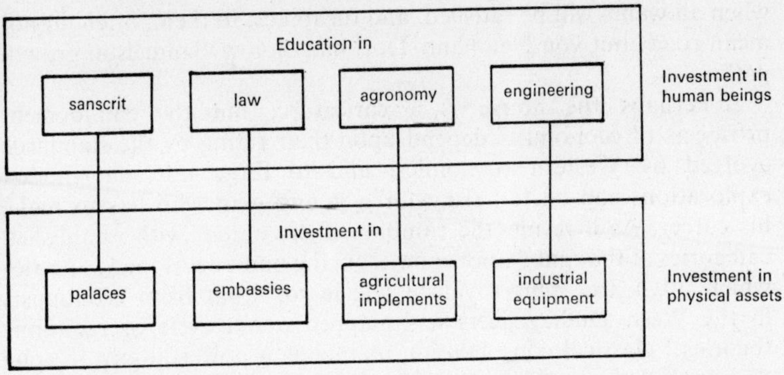

An illustration of a shift from a horizontal to a vertical alignment can be found in the recently popular notion of technical knowledge embodied in new equipment. In the old framework, "the state of the arts" or technical and managerial knowledge were separated from physical equipment. In the new models, knowledge is infused through equipment and the productivity of the total stock of equipment is a function of its age composition.

Sociology of Knowledge

It is not enough to point to biases, particularly if they are so plain. The interesting question is, how is it that they have such a strong grip on thought, in spite of their obvious faults? This is a question in the sociology of knowledge, or rather the sociology of ignorance or of false belief. It is a strange fact that social scientists, whose special interest is social reality, are exceedingly naïve when it comes to examining the social origins of their own theories and models. We investigate workers, priests, prostitutes, entrepreneurs, soldiers, politicians, and analyse the social roots of their behaviour. But rarely do we examine the social determination of our own thought. It is as if a physician were able and ready to cure others but unwilling or incapable of healing himself.

There are perhaps six reasons, not of equal importance, why these models have such a strong hold on our thought and are even more deep-rooted in the discussion in underdeveloped countries.

1. Western economics has a high prestige value. With its "Effects", "Processes" and "Mechanisms", it is admired in underdeveloped countries, and the highest honours in the profession go to those who work on the most esoteric mathematical problems. Economists from underdeveloped countries write about the problems that arise

when all wants will be satisfied, and turnpikes, to them, often do not mean roads but von Neumann–Dorfman–Solow–Samuelson growth paths.

2. Perhaps the above is a caricature, but the employment prospects of economists depend upon their rating by the standards evolved by Western economics, and to forge into unorthodox explorations can be too risky for a young man who has to make his career. As a result, the rumbles of discontent with established categories of thought do not come from the underdeveloped countries which often are "plus royaliste que le roi", but from economists in the West. Dudley Seers has mapped out a cycle of economic theories:[1] classical consolidation maintains a powerful grip in spite of accumulating evidence against it. Thus economists refused to permit under-employment equilibrium into their analysis in spite of the plain facts around them. An underworld of Hobson, Gesell, Major Douglas, pointed out the obvious, but were dismissed as cranks. Although their instincts were right, they did not formulate them in an alternative rigorous model. Then Keynes replaced the old orthodoxy by a new one, articulating clearly the feelings of the underworld, which now became respectable, because the inadequacies of one model were shown up by a different model. It may be that underdeveloped economics is now, as Dudley Seers suggests, in its Hobson–Gesell phase, the underworld worthily represented by Myrdal, Prebisch, Singer and Co. Will there, or can there, be a Keynes to articulate the instincts which, as yet, have not found coherent expression?

3. A third reason is that attitudes and institutions can, as we have seen, legitimately be separated in advanced Western countries. These habits are transferred to underdeveloped countries. Developed markets, the dissemination of information, an educated labour force, transport and power facilities, flexibility of resources, an honest and efficient civil service, effective tax legislation and tax collection, all make it legitimate to assume a hinterland adapted to the conduct of economic activities and suited for conceptual aggregation.

4. Fourthly, "economic facts" are *rightly* considered more accessible to investigation and quantification than "non-economic facts". It is easier to calculate how much different irrigation works will cost than to calculate how many peasants will use and maintain them. It is easier to specify the costs of a pump or a steel mill than to predict how effectively it will be used, how long it will take to

1. "The Limitations of the Special Case", *Bulletin of the Oxford University Institute of Statistics*, May 1963.

build, and what people will learn from using it. It is easier to say how much contraceptives cost than to say how human beings can be changed to wish to use them.

5. Fifthly, "economic quantities" are *wrongly* thought to be more objective than non-economic considerations. The economic calculus is often contrasted with moral and political choices. It is now well known that this view is false and that all economic choices presuppose moral and political valuations. The weighting system by which a heterogeneous collection of goods and services is made homogeneous and comparable with other collections, and on which "economic" choices are based, expresses social valuations of the relative social significance of different goods and services. If these comparisons pretend to be "objective", the underlying valuations are tacit (such as the acceptance of a given income distribution implied in freely determined market prices as guides to income distribution) and therefore *less* objective than choices based on explicit valuations.

The difficulty is acknowledged but not overcome by the employment of concepts such as "accounting prices" or "shadow prices". Jan Tinbergen defines these as the "intrinsic values that would prevail if (i) the investment pattern under discussion were actually carried out, and (ii) equilibrium existed on the markets . . . ."[1] Although the concept is useful in bringing out the arbitrary nature of actual market prices as a basis for planning, it is misleading because it begs a number of questions and recreates a spurious impression of objectivity. In particular, it begs the question of equilibrium in other markets and the question of the length of the time period over which equilibrium is assumed: is it before the investment projects are carried out, while they are under construction or after they have been finished? It also fails to distinguish sufficiently clearly between the use of prices as the basis for taking decisions as to the allocation of scarce resources and their use as incentives and deterrents. And finally it fails to bring out the need to postulate an income distribution and social objectives *before* the appropriate equilibrium prices can be determined.

Though logically fallacious, this type of reasoning, which attempts to substitute "objective" criteria for political choices, provides an intellectual escape mechanism from difficult or unpleasant political decisions.

6. The intellectual escape mechanism is powerfully supported by a moral and political escape mechanism. Strong obstacles amongst

1. Jan Tinbergen, *The Design of Development*, p. 39.

those whose activities are planned, and serious inhibitions in the minds and hearts of the planners, who are themselves part and parcel of the society which they intend to reform, stand in the way of economic development. Land reform may be opposed and may hurt one's cousins and friends. To sack corrupt officials may be disloyal and may incur wrath. To change one's own mind and heart may involve a more radical conversion than is humanly possible. In view of these difficulties, an easy escape is offered. Concentrate on financial expenditure, select variables that hurt least and side-step the crucial decisions! Soft handling, reluctance to use force, can then be rationalized as the democratic process, reinforced by disparaging allusions to colonial oppression and Soviet labour camps. Thus economic models support the forces of resistance to change. Much easier to say money spent on investment or on education yields high returns than to carry out a land reform, impose an effective tax system, or clean up public administration.

We have already seen how Marxism, with its diametrically opposed premises, leads to very similar conclusions. Although attitudes and institutions here are not parameters but dependent variables, they adjust to the required extent. Planning and social engineering are futile or unnecessary. Marxists have often been very naïve about the problem of planning. Marxist theory has, ironically, a strong laissez-faire streak. But Soviet practice diverges substantially from this theory. Soviet Plans did not just stress the accumulation of capital. The savings *squeeze* (inferred from a model of capital accumulation) was reinforced by a consumption *twist*. It was clearly seen in practice, though not in theory, that the promotion of certain forms of consumption, in particular better feeding of workers, improving their health and literacy, but keeping down house building, can accelerate development.

Again, Japanese and German development in the nineteenth century started with a thorough reform of attitudes and institutions. One wonders what would have happened if Japan and Germany had then had the benefit of the advice of modern economists. But perhaps we are too presumptuous in our claims for the influence of economics. Economics is possibly just a modern theology. Perhaps only a small part of the iceberg – the planning ideology – is visible above the water, while the larger part of the actual practice of planning is carried on sensibly, paying attention to the right combination, co-ordination and timing of policies, without heeding distinctions between "economic" and "non-economic" variables. This conclusion, though pessimistic from the point of view of the significance of economics, would be optimistic from the point of view of development. But one cannot help expressing a faith, perhaps irrationally, in the value of rationality and the contribution that an economic theory which is realistic, relevant and applicable could and should make to effective planning for development.

A Sketch of a Model of Development

The following sketch outlines a possibly fruitful approach to the analysis of underdevelopment and to the policy of planning for development. The model is essentially that used by Mr. Kaldor to analyse the trade cycle[1] and by Professor Trevor Swan to illustrate mutual causation between White prejudices against Negroes and Negro standards of living. This note follows closely Professor Swan's article.[2] Cumulative processes have been analysed by Wicksell and have been emphasized in various contexts by Myrdal.

In Figure 1 we trace on the horizontal axis an index of the level of economic development and on the vertical axis an index of the forces that raise the level of development. A good index of economic development has not yet been designed and we have therefore recourse to income per head as a rough-and-ready index. There are, as we have indicated, numerous difficulties both in giving precise meaning to *per caput* income and in using this as an index of development. The average may conceal wide dispersions; a rise in income per head may be due to improved terms of trade, the benefit of which accrues to a small enclave, etc. But it will do for the moment, if we bear in mind its limitations.

The index of the income-raising forces is even more difficult to devise. Investment, education, market size, economies of scale, human attitudes to growth and change and, above all, family limitation, may all contribute to development if applied in conjunction with the appropriate measures. We shall specify some of these forces later. We require an independent measure for each of these forces separately and we can then combine them, weighting each by their respective contributions to output and income. The situation would be exactly like that of different inputs and their contribution to increases in output. Ideally, one would want not a combined index but separate relations, connecting each of the forces both to its effects on income and to other forces. In order to simplify such n-dimensional functions and illustrate them on a

1. *Economic Journal*, 1940.
2. *Economic Record*, 1962. See also H. Leibenstein, *Economic Backwardness and Economic Growth*, chapters 3 and 8.

two-dimensional diagram, we assume the possibility of such an index. The problem is further complicated by the fact that there are income-*depressing* forces, above all a high rate of population growth, but also various resistances to development: inertia, prejudice, etc. Ideally, the index should be an index of the excess of raising over depressing forces, i.e. it should be *net*. There would then be a zero point, below which the income-depressing forces would prevail. But this raises a further difficulty. The index of the forces should be related not to the level of income, but to the (positive or negative) *rate of growth* of income, while it is the *level* of income which determines the forces. The model would be exactly parallel to the accelerator-multiplier model.[1] But for our purposes we regard the income level determined by the income-raising forces as an average over the planning period.

It may well be that these difficulties are fatal and that no such index can be constructed. But let us assume that it is possible to devise an index of the net forces raising income per head which does not use shares of income generation as weights.

We next note that the Income-Raising Forces and Income per Head interact: there is a feedback. The higher is Income per Head (Y), the stronger will tend to be the Income-per-Head-Raising

1. The path taken by income if the Forces $F = f(Y)$ and $\frac{dY}{dt} = ø(F)$ can be illustrated on the following diagram. Income at time t_0 is at A_0; this income determines the level of Forces at B_0 which in turn determine the increase in income in the next period at C_0. OD_0 is added to A_0 after a period at t_1 (so that $A_1 E = D_0O$) and the same process is repeated from A_1.

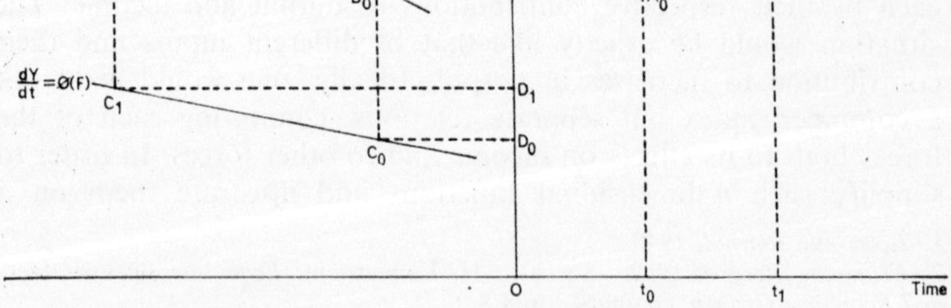

Forces (F), and the higher the Forces, the higher will tend to be Income per Head. The former relation may be due to the ability to extract a larger savings and investment ratio, the existence of a larger market with economies of scale, a weakening of tradition, improved education, etc. Obviously, the higher the level of F the higher will be Y.

The fact that there is interaction (mutual causation, feedback) between F and Y is not sufficient to produce instability, although, in certain conditions, it can have snowball effects (cumulative processes). If the coefficients are as illustrated in Figure 1, this will be the case. At any point to the left of the line F→ Y (showing the level of Income as a function of the Forces) Income will be less than that generated by the Forces, and the Forces will tend to raise Income. At any point to the right, Income will be larger than that which is generated by the Forces and they will tend to lower Income.

At any point above the line Y→ F (showing the Forces as a function of Income) the Forces are greater than is warranted by the Income level and will therefore contract. At any point below, the Forces will expand. These causal relations are clearly subject to time-lags. The lines show the long-run static relationships towards which the values will tend to move. The point of intersection U in Figure 1 is a point of unstable equilibrium. The smallest deviation sparks off a vicious or a virtuous circle.

In Figure 2 we have reduced the response coefficients of both functions so as to produce a stable equilibrium at S, in spite of mutual causation. The Forces are less responsive to Income and Income is less responsive to the Forces and a disturbance will not cause a permanent alteration. In order to make interaction yield cumulation, the response coefficients must be above certain critical values. This explains why, in spite of the ubiquity of interdependence in social life, development (or decay) is a rare phenomenon. While this is a pessimistic conclusion for those who hope for cumulative processes wherever there is interdependence, it opens a wider range of policies to planners.

There are important differences between a situation as depicted in Figure 1 and Figure 2 according to whether we apply a once-for-all push (say a single injection of foreign aid) or a sustained development effort (say an annually recurrent sum of aid). In unstable equilibrium (Fig. 1) there is no difference between these two policies. Either will induce development. But in stable equilibrium (Fig. 2) a once-for-all push will not alter the final position of the system, whereas a sustained effort of a given size will be exactly like the multiplier process: the process will converge towards a higher new equilibrium position which will be a multiple of the size of the sustained effort.

We know from the most casual observations that neither the stability of Figure 2 nor the instability of Figure 1 corresponds to reality and, like the archetypal model of Kaldor and Swan, we must postulate non-linearity and multiple equilibria as in Figure 3. S_1 and S_2 are points of stable, U of unstable equilibrium. It is not difficult to think of reasons why the sensitivity of both functions should be low for both low and high values, and high for intermediate values. At low levels Y will not have much effect on F because tradition has a strong hold, the forces of resistance are strong, it will be difficult to squeeze out even a moderate investment ratio, the market will be small, ignorance and imperfections will prevail, etc. F in turn will have small effects on Y because population growth will wipe out a large part of any increase in income per head. Similarly, one may speculate that, at high values, people get tired of the effort required by growth, the third generation has less vigour, opposition and destructive criticisms grow. One could build a philosophy of history upon the values of these functions. For intermediate values responsiveness will be high, both because the obstacles to development will have been overcome successfully, particularly population pressure, and because the higher income level makes it much easier to do all kinds of things conducive to faster development.

Planners now have a choice between three types of policy.

(*a*) They may go for the "Big Push", or the "Critical Minimum Effort", or to rev up to "Take-Off Speed". This means accepting the response coefficients and raising the system from S_1 to just above U. Beyond that they can rely on automatic development.

(*b*) They may attempt to shift the curves to tangency. They can either lower the $F \rightarrow Y$ curve (so that for any given level of the Forces the resulting income will be higher) or raise the $Y \rightarrow F$ curve (so that for any given level of Income the resulting Forces will be higher).

(*c*) Finally they may attempt to change the relative slopes of the curves, thus turning S_1 into an unstable equilibrium, though they must also take care to avoid a downward slide.

An illustration of (*a*) would be a large and long industrialization programme, combined with improvements in health and education, as Russia experienced under Stalin. An illustration of (*b*) would be fairly simple measures such as an effective land reform or the establishment of an effective tax system, which, in Argentina or Chile, might be quite sufficient to induce growth. Illustrations of (*c*) are more difficult to think of, although the Argentine case might do, where Peron may have changed the slopes of the curve so as to produce decay.

As for historical explanation, the length of the distance between S_1 and U explains why the same events have different consequences in different historical contexts. At certain times, in certain places, quite small events spark off revolutionary sequences. At other times and places, the same events are swallowed up by the big waves of history. It explains why, sometimes, small causes have large effects, while at other times large causes are required to produce these same effects: why history sometimes seems like a thick syrup and at others like a plaything of accidents. A Polish inventor invented machinery for weaving cloth in the twelfth century and was hanged for threatening the established order. The same invention in the eighteenth century triggered off the Industrial Revolution. Hero of Alexandria, and before him Ctesibius, had invented the piston and the steam engine and other sophisticated mechanical devices. But these were used to enable the priesthood of Alexandria to impose on the simple-minded. Hydraulic bellows operated by the doors of the temple sounded a fanfare of trumpets whenever a worshipper entered. Another device, fixed below the altar, operated levers which led to the holy shrine. The altar stone was heated during sacrificial burning, the air below expanded, pressed on the lever and opened the door, revealing the image of God. This could be carefully timed according to the amount of heat generated on the altar. The knowledge of electricity and steam power was used, not to move the wheels of industry, but the minds of men, in a direction inimical to development.[1] S_1 and U in those constellations were far apart. In eighteenth-century England they were close together.

The task begins when we attempt to specify and to construct an independent index for the income-raising and income-depressing forces and to analyse their interaction. The following list contains a possible way of classifying these forces, although no attempt is made to indicate the numerous possible links between them. The formulation is in terms of obstacles, inhibitions and limitations, but can easily be translated into their opposites.

1. The story of a premature innovator in ancient Rome, confronted with an Emperor reluctant to apply these innovations and aware of some of the obstacles, is told by William Golding in his story "Envoy Extraordinary".

1. Output/worker
   Income/population

"*Economic*" *forces operating on 1.*

2. Conditions of production
   - small industrial sector
   - absence of economies of scale
   - primitive techniques
   - absence of specialization
   - low capital intensity
   - scarcity of products requiring much capital
   - low savings
   - little enterprise
   - inadequate social overhead
   - low labour utilization
     - low participation
     - short duration
     - low efficiency

3. Levels of living
   - under-nutrition
   - malnutrition
   - bad housing
   - bad hygiene
   - inadequate medical attention
   - absence of training facilities
   - inadequate education and cultural facilities
   - illiteracy

"*Non-economic*" *forces operating on 1.*

4. Attitudes to production and living
   - no discipline
   - no punctuality
   - caste prejudice
   - superstition
   - lack of foresight
   - lack of ambition
   - weak acquisitive motivation
   - apathy
   - lack of adaptability
   - unwillingness to bear risks, venture, innovate
   - inability to co-operate

contempt for manual work
submissiveness
low standards of hygiene
work-spreading attitudes
absence of birth control

5. Institutions
   land tenure hostile to improvements
   imperfect markets for labour, credit, capital
   poor information
   weak government (national and local)
   political uncertainty
   corrupt, inefficient and inadequate administration
   rigid class, caste system
   inequality
   absence of opportunities
   arbitrary legal administration
   non-enforcement of contracts

6. Policies
   soft state: unwillingness to enforce law and to legislate for development
   concentration on "economic" action
   ineffective taxation

The possible links are numerous, but a few can be indicated by way of illustration.

Positive feedback

1. Higher income—higher savings/income ratio—higher investment/income ratio—higher income.
2. Higher income—better health—greater vigour and ability to sustain work—higher income.
3. Higher income—greater economies of scale—higher production—higher productivity—higher income.
4. Higher income—stable government—increased political and business confidence—greater national solidarity—higher income.
5. Higher income—reduced caste prejudice—less corruption—better administration—higher income.

Negative feedback

1. Higher income—faster population growth through reduced death rates—reduced *per caput* income.
2. Higher income—more change—stronger resistance to change—reduced income.
3. Higher income—faster population growth—employment of more labour intensive techniques with low learning content—reduced rate of growth of *per caput* income.
4. Higher income—faster population growth—work-spreading habits and attitudes both among employers and employees: premium on preserving low productivity ways lest someone loses his job: obstacles to innovation—reduced growth rate.
5. Higher income—higher unemployment—introduction of capital-intensive production methods—greater social prestige attached to better off not doing manual work but leaving it to the poor—reinforcement of attitudes that despise manual work and attach low social prestige to it—reduced growth.

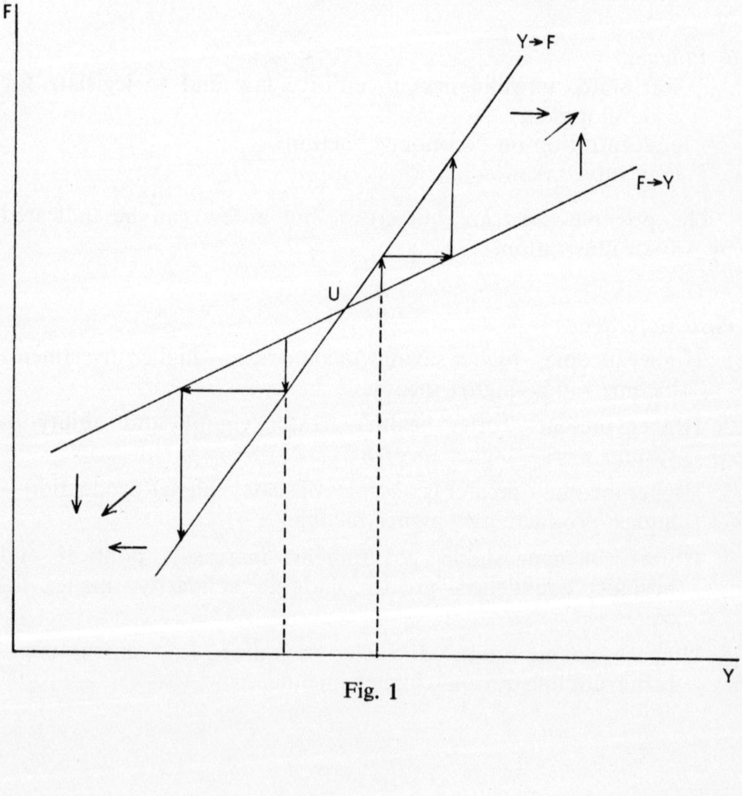

Fig. 1

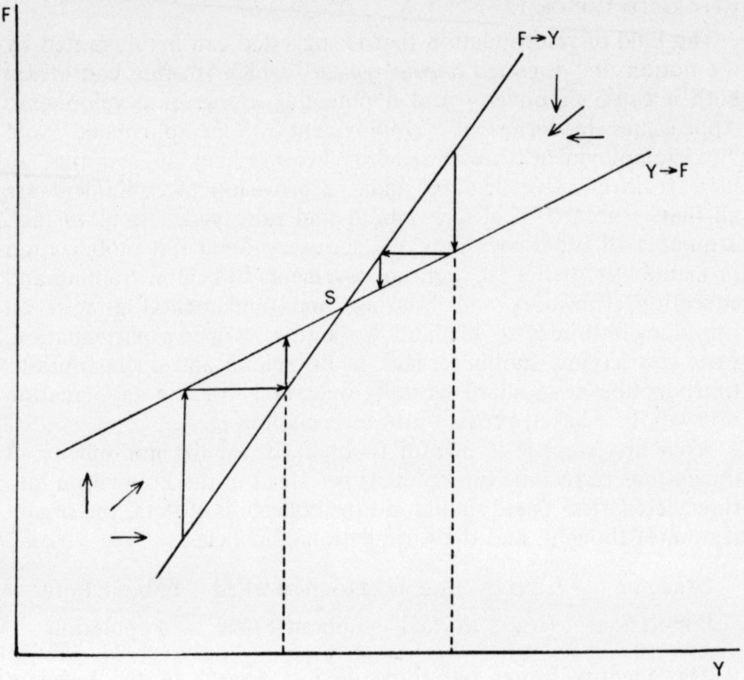

Fig. 2

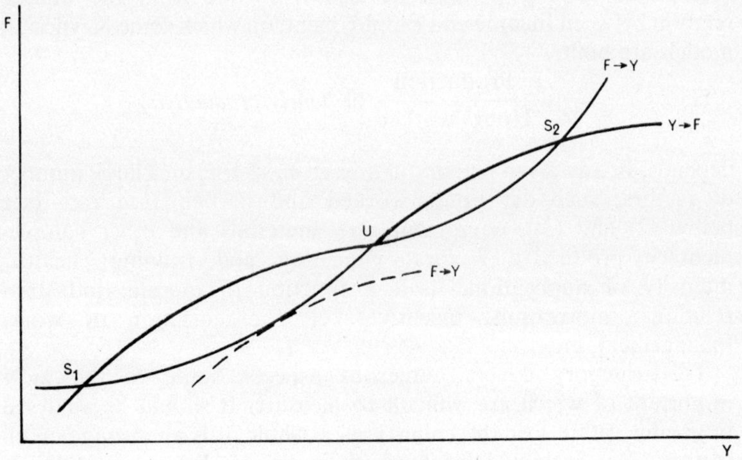

Fig. 3

REFORM OF CONCEPTS

The kind of reformulation that is suggested can be illustrated by the notion of "*disguised unemployment*" which is often considered both a cause of poverty and a potential source of development. Approaches in terms of "employment", "unemployment" and "underemployment" are misleading because they suggest that an increase in effective demand and the provision of equipment are all that is needed to absorb labour and raise production. In fact, a number of other measures are necessary for a full mobilization of manpower: better feeding, improvements in health, training and education, transport and housing, and fundamental attacks on prevailing attitudes to life and work (e.g. women's participation, caste restrictions, snobbery, lack of discipline) and on institutions (introduction of standard working week and working day, creation of a labour market, provision of information, etc.).

As a first step, it is helpful to break down the multiplicity of dimensions of Income (or Product) per Head of the Population into three categories. These should aid the collection of data, the organization of thought, and the formulation of policies.

$$\frac{\text{Income}}{\text{Population}} = \frac{\text{Production}}{\text{Hours worked}} \cdot \frac{\text{Hours worked}}{\text{Labour Force}} \cdot \frac{\text{Labour Force}}{\text{Population}}.$$

This identity brings out three distinct aspects of the Level of Living (= Income per Head) on which more information would be useful for framing policies. It also frees one from the unique relation between Income and Employment, on which some Keynesian models are built.

(1) $\frac{\text{Production}}{\text{Hours worked}}$ or *hourly productivity*

depends, in any given activity in any given sector$_2$ on a large number of factors, such as: hours worked and participation rate (see below (2) and (3)), equipment, raw materials and other complementary productive factors; education and training; health; intensity of application, itself a function of morale; industrial relations; motivation; incentives, etc.; organization of work, management, etc.

This category covers numerous aspects, some of the most important of which are difficult to measure. It should be analysed in greater detail. For the country as a whole, it is an average of all sectors, each weighted by its share in the total number of hours worked. If we denote the sectors as 1, 2, 3, etc., and their shares in total working hours as h_1, h_2, etc.,

$$\frac{\text{Output}}{\text{Hours}} = h_1 \frac{Y_1}{H_1} + h_2 \frac{Y_1}{H_2} + \ldots$$

Hourly productivity can be raised if all other things remain constant, either by transferring workers from low-productivity to high-productivity sectors, or by raising productivity within sectors.

(2) $\frac{\text{Hours}}{\text{Labour Force}}$ or *working time*

depends on organizational and institutional factors: whether there is a standard working day and working week; whether overtime is worked; whether multiple shifts exist; whether time is wasted in idleness waiting for materials and components, or spent on holidays and feasts. It also depends on natural factors such as the weather. The ratio will depend both upon the level of demand and on the availability of essential supplies. A shift of rural labour to urban industry raises output not only by changing the weights attached to low- and high-productivity sectors, but also by raising hours/labour force. Unemployment of people both willing and able to work will show up as low hours/labour force. But the distinction between ability to work and willingness to work may not always be easy to draw or even logically legitimate. (E.g. Moslem women?)

(3) $\frac{\text{Labour Force}}{\text{Population}}$ or *participation rate*

depends on attitudes to work and to gainful activities (their dignity or ignominy), housing and transport facilities, legislation about minimum working age, compulsory full-time education, etc. Removal of caste barriers and of objections to certain kinds of work, increased incentives to earn money, emancipation of women, improved mobility, etc., will raise participation rates.

Since each category is an average of sectoral ratios, the identity can be rewritten as

$$\frac{Y}{P} = \left[h_1\frac{Y_1}{H_1} + h_2\frac{Y_2}{H_2} + \ldots\right]\left[l_1\frac{H_1}{L_1} + l_2\frac{H_2}{L_2} + \ldots)\right]$$
$$\left[p_1\frac{L_1}{P_1} + p_2\frac{L_2}{P_2} + \ldots\right]$$

where Y is total income (output)
H is total hours worked
L is labour force
P is population
h is share in total hours worked
l is share in labour force
p is share in population

and the suffixes indicate the different sectors.

The conventional presentation suffers from the fact that intensity of work, skill, organization, education, health, etc., are assumed given. Thus the only variables are demand and equipment. Furthermore, the assumption is usually made that unemployment and underemployment are "involuntary". This implies that willingness and ability to work are present. Unemployment and underemployment must also be defined with reference to some standard of working hours per day and working days per week. But such standards do not exist in large parts of underdeveloped economies and are therefore introduced, usually implicitly, from outside. The whole set of questions relating to participation and organized work is thereby begged and a number of important relationships are concealed.

Policies can then be classified according to whether they use compulsion, permission or persuasion. The following table provides illustrations.

	Compulsion	*Permission*	*Persuasion (incentives)*
Output/Hour	Make pay depend on minimum output	Forbid trade union restrictions	Piece rates
Hours/Lab. Force	Fix 8-hour day	Improve diet	Overtime rates
Lab. Force/Population	Lock up workless, conscript, poll tax	Raise demand, provide equipment	Raise wages, supply incentive goods

The relations can be illustrated in the following figure.

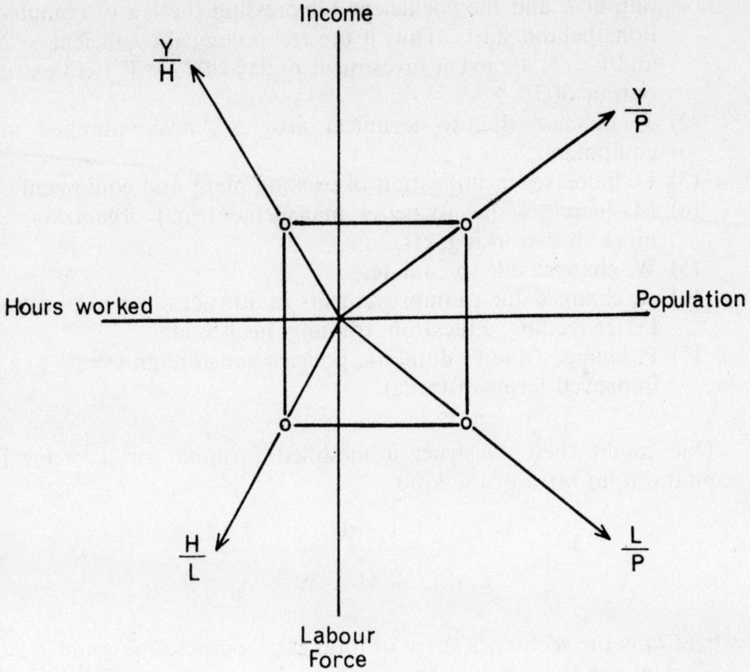

Another concept which might gain from a more detailed breakdown is the *capital/output ratio*. One might try to allow for a number of special influences:[1]

A. On the side of investment, we may distinguish in each sector between the following:
   (1) I, the cost of the investment project under consideration, all other things assumed constant, and labour in abundant supply.
   (2) D, expenditure to save labour and other inputs without increasing output.

B. On the side of output:
   (1) $\frac{I}{fk}$, the increase in output resulting from I, all other things assumed constant and abundant labour supply, given the technological ratio between finished machines and extra

1. See W. B. Reddaway, *The Development of the Indian Economy*, Appendix C.

output k and the coefficient f expressing the lag of completions behind starts. Thus if the technological coefficient $= 2$ and $f = 6$, a current investment outlay of 12 will yield extra output of 1.

(2) T, increase due to technical progress, not embodied in equipment.

(3) U, increases in utilization of existing plant and equipment.

(4) M, increases due to better management and organization, more shift-working, etc.

(5) W, changes due to climate.

(6) A, changes due to improvements in attitudes and responses, better feeding, education, training, health, etc.

(7) P, changes due to domestic policies and foreign events (e.g. improved terms of trade).

One might then construct a modified formula for a sectoral capital/output ratio of the kind

$$\lambda_1 \frac{I + D}{\frac{I}{fk} + T + U + M + W + A + P}$$

where λ_1 is the sector 1's share in total extra output.One could get a coefficient for the whole economy by adding up the coefficients of each sector weighted by its share in extra output. Those who believe in the usefulness for planning of a technological capital/output ratio implicitly assume that $f = 1$ and that all terms except I are negligible. Once the other influences are recognized, it would be possible to maintain a modified capital/output ratio (no longer equal to the technological ratio k), if the other terms were (*a*) fairly stable and (*b*) independent of each other. But the terms cannot be assumed to be stable, for the purpose of the development effort is precisely to change some of them drastically (e.g. to raise f, T and M). Hardly any of them is a wholly independent variable. Many depend upon the composition of I and on history. All are asymmetrical for upward and downward moves. The valuation of output and its flow through time involve political judgments.

But even if all these difficulties could be overcome and all the relevant facts were known, the global coefficient would provide no useful information. If the sectoral ratios are known for any specific project at a specific time, the global ratio is unnecessary. If they are unknown, the global ratio is impossible.

Finally, it might be useful to specify in what respects we should particularly beware of possible traps in established doctrines and in what ways these can be either improved or replaced. In addition to the already discussed problems of misplaced aggregation and illegitimate isolation, one might consider the following points.

(1) Be on guard against assuming continuous and smooth functions. Discontinuities and kinks may occur in relationships such as capital coefficients, supply of effort, production functions, foreign trade, etc. Consider Indivisibilities and Complementarities.
(2) Be not content with less than at least two sectors where inter-sectoral relations are crucial to a problem. Clearly, the marginal returns from disaggregation decline and may become negative, but Keynesian aggregation too is often misleading.
(3) Consider the implications of unstable equilibria, whether static or dynamic. Cumulative processes and polarization are not as exceptional as the concentration on stable equilibrium suggests.
(4) Include, where necessary, variables which are exogenous in advanced countries, as dependent variables. Examples are administration, political stability, acquisitive motivation, population growth, technical progress.
(5) Keep in mind the specific limitations of the free market system as a guide to certain important decisions. Distinguish clearly between the free market system and price policies. The latter are an instrument of planning.
(6) Beware of abstracting from time: the phasing of projects, the time-flow of consumption, the effects on learning are crucial.
(7) Be content to provide (at least initially) *sufficient* conditions for certain sequences rather than full *explanations*. Discard these sufficient conditions only if they are contradicted by observations.

The Economics of Educational Planning: Sense and Nonsense

THOMAS BALOGH

Fellow of Balliol College, Oxford

A NUMBER of interrelated misconceptions have become fashionable of late in the field of educational planning and policy. While these are perhaps of little importance in fully developed areas where resources are abundant and some waste does not matter, they may have extremely pernicious results in underdeveloped areas which struggle with insufficient resources, including foreign aid, in situations of great difficulty, to achieve self-sustaining growth.

I shall try to discuss the more absurd ones in this paper.[1]

I

(1) The first of these fashionable misconceptions is the implied assumption that the contribution of "investment in the human factor" can somehow or other be isolated in the process of historical growth, and that numerical magnitudes can be assigned to it which can then be used for extrapolation for policy purposes.

These calculations of the impact of education on economic progress turn out, on closer view, to suffer from practically all the possible fallacies of which anyone can be guilty in an enquiry of this kind.

(2) First of all, they derive from a model of the economic system which is completely static in character. But, worse than that, they assume a production function—the Cobb-Douglas formula—which even among all the inapplicable static models is the least plausible. In this the national income is expressed as the product of capital, labour and a "residual", which stands for the "human factor", including improved "knowledge", improved health and skills; for better organization and management; for economies of scale; for external economies and changes in the composition of output, and

1. I have made use of some earlier papers, and I wish to acknowledge my debt to Mr. Streeten, who clarified and developed my views.

whatever is not explained by the increase in capital and labour. In this way, what is not caught among the assumed effects of capital and labour is attributed to a "residual". The formula which they use thus *assumes* and does not empirically ascertain or *measure* the impact of the increase in the capital or labour (if one could measure the latter).

(3) Some authors, Mr. E. F. Dennison for instance, simultaneously assume a linear homogeneous production function and perfect competition, i.e. universally increasing costs, in order to be able to use average return per unit of factor as a measure of its marginal value product, *and* also attribute a substantial proportion of the residual growth to economies of scale, i.e. decreasing costs. There is complete inconsistency in this treatment which is based on an implied theoretical description of the past arising from the assumption that additional increasing quantities of productive factors, such as labour and capital, will yield diminishing returns in a particularly unconvincing equiproportionate fashion. The possibility that the relationship is different (and, of course, those authors who try afterwards to correct their results by assuming the impact of increasing returns to scale implicitly acknowledge this fact), or that it might mathematically be less easy to work with because of changes through time, is disposed of by dismissing or disregarding it.

(4) The systematic relationship implicit in the figures is then calculated and from the assumptions it follows that, if a decrease in returns is not experienced as the quantity of the respective factors of production is increased, this failure of the returns to decrease in fact, according to the theoretical assumption, is then declared to be accountable for only by the "residual factor". This extraneous factor is once more analysed into a systematic trend-like movement which is called technical progress, or increased knowledge, or what have you, and the residual of the residuals has lately been attributed to education.

(5) The pitfalls and fallacies of this type of reasoning are too obvious to need consideration, except that in fact a whole school has grown up doing this exercise all over the world, and policy recommendations have been based on it.

(6) In the first place, as we have already said, the basic relationship between capital, labour and output has not been *demonstrated* on the basis of technological enquiries: it has been *postulated*. Therefore, the conclusion that a divergence from it must be due to an improvement in knowledge or education amounts to no more than begging the question. Yet it should have been clear that the answer

to the question of what was the contribution of Factor X can only be found by answering the different question of what would have happened if the Factor X had not been present in the past, or if it had been present in a different quantity, or *horribile dictu*, a different quality. This last and most disturbing of these criticisms is dismissed by assuming that *education is a homogeneous input*, and dismissing the further objection that improved knowledge might have only become effective as a result of investment and exploited in specific ways within the framework of a certain ethical or motivational system which is dependent on historical, i.e. cultural, religious, institutional and political factors.

(7) The very assumption that education can be a homogeneous input is absurd. The teaching of a certain classical type might have not merely no positive results on output, it might impede it. Teaching itself can have no influence in the abstract, but only if those taught are given jobs and not despised for their knowledge as tradesmen or experts. The isolation of education from other measures completely ignores the ineradicable complementarity of measures, and the aggregation of all types of education obscures the type of education needed for, or conducive to, development. The procedure, as Mr. Streeten has pointed out, therefore suffers from both illegitimate isolation and misplaced aggregation.

(8) In truth, we do not know exactly how education is related to technical progress, nor do we know how technical progress and investment are related. Nor do we know why the relationship between volume of capital and its yield varies so much from one country to another, and is so different at different times in the same country. What we do know is that the relationship has hardly ever been constant, and only the least plausible explanations have as yet been offered.

(9) It must be said in all fairness that most authors are rather coy when dealing with this problem, though not when putting forward vast schemes for research which *a priori* do not seem to have much sense. They will not, in their opening chapters or conclusions at any rate, say outright that educational or technical progress *was* the cause of the increase in production. They merely say that it was associated with it, or contributed to it, or is observable. When it comes to policy recommendations or demands for further research projects, however, this scientific modesty is rather discarded and the qualifications disappear.

(10) But even the more detailed and less assertive efforts seem to be obnoxious. It is quite illegitimate to claim that an educational

system which in the general cultural and political framework of the United States, and given the American endowment with natural resources, has led to or was accompanied by a certain growth rate, economic activity and wealth, will be accompanied by a *similar growth rate* elsewhere under totally different conditions.

(11) It is equally illegitimate to assume that, on the basis of these data alone, a *different growth rate* can be calculated for other countries by assuming constant parameters and substituting different variables for the educational effect. Such an education in the feudal aristocratic countries of South America, the colonial aristocratic areas of British Africa, or the literateur colonial area of French Africa, might not produce any growth at all, but discontent and the possible refusal to work on farms, accompanied by an increase in urban unemployment, subversion and collapse.

(12) Thus, approaches which try to estimate the contribution of education to national prosperity in the past, or projected on the basis of certain claims for the future based on the past, have no value at all. They have no value because:

(*a*) They derive a *residual growth rate* which they attribute to education by wholly illegitimate methods, on the basis that it cannot be explained by the increase of the other factors of production. Thus they beg the question by their own procedure. They estimate the answer, and their conclusion is unproven and unprovable.

(*b*) They assume, equally unwarrantably, that investment in education is not merely a cause but the sole sufficient and necessary cause responsible for the whole, or certain artificially selected portions, of the residual growth rate which has been experienced in certain historical examples.

(*c*) Finally, they assume that this causal connection which has been assumed and not proven would not merely hold in a completely different context and historical setting, but would remain valid in an operational sense, i.e. in the reverse direction.

(13) An additional and interesting fact is that, throughout, the models assume complete mobility, perfect competition and full employment. In actual fact, in all the historical examples which have been analysed, there was no free mobility, no perfect competition, and the economic systems analysed suffered from violent cyclical fluctuations. Thus, even if the procedure did not suffer from

fatal logical flaws, the quantitative relationship obviously would change completely in a different context with different doses of imperfections in the resources and product markets.

II

(14) Even worse is the second group of fallacious attempts to calculate the rate of return on capital investment in education for the individual. These have been evolved, I suspect, for political motives, in order to substantiate a plea for a laissez-faire finance of education, to make it "pay for itself", to abolish free education and institute a system of giving loans to prospective students, to be paid back from the increase in their earnings as a result of their being educated.

(15) Thus there is a specious plea of equity—specious because the sons of the rich would not be burdened with such obligations. These proposals are usually accompanied by suggestions to cut personal taxation in order to increase incentive. Besides fallaciously mixing up necessary and sufficient conditions, and confusing causes and effects, these calculations seem also to assume that the *social and political framework* is a strictly *neutral* influence. Yet surely it must at least *a priori* be suspected that it might contribute to, if it is not wholly responsible for, the differential between professional and skilled remuneration.

(16) Accordingly the differential remuneration is attributed purely to the difference in the cost of education, on the one hand, and the loss of experience due to not being in a job while receiving education, on the other. A sort of perfectly competitive education opportunity system is imagined in which relative prices express relative social costs, and scarcity and marginal private product seem to be supposed to be strictly proportional to what is "desired". The authors forget that what might be correlated with increase in income need not be caused by differential education. They also forget the tremendous force of monopolistic factors.

(17) This view of the world is fantastically untrue even in the United States, though there individual effort, if backed by exceptional ability, might get people up the educational ladder. Even there it is absurd to maintain that equal opportunity is accorded to equal talent. In fact, from this viewpoint, the concentration of economic power has in recent times made mobility less, not more. The view that the investment in education proceeds in an optimum serial framework is surely completely out of focus even there. In the first

instance, it can be shown that there are groups in America which are increasingly falling back in the educational and social ladder, and that their falling back can be attributed to the initial inequality in their incomes and in the income of the community in which they live. It has also been shown that equal education by no means provides equality of opportunity in getting jobs. In fact, even in the United States, the initial class situation of an individual decisively determines his career opportunity, and who would dare to assert that the income differentials in the management ladder are in any way established by pure and perfect competition.

(18) Far worse, the calculations ignore both the indirect returns accruing to others than the educated individual, and the direct non-financial returns of the cost of investment. On the other hand, they pay a good deal of attention to income foregone during study which constitutes a large proportion of investment, presumably because it is calculable. But neither the income foregone by other groups in society (such as housewives, voluntary workers, people in some favoured occupations, like universities, accepting a lower income than they could get in other occupations), nor the non-financial benefits enjoyed during education, are estimated.

(19) Finally, as the returns have to be calculated over a lifetime, the present income differentials between educated and less educated, if they can be attributed to the difference in education, refer to the educational situation in the 1920s. It is, to say the least, doubtful, and ought to be doubtful even to the economists of the Chicago school, that educational developments since then might have some results on the expected returns available to education at present, especially in underdeveloped countries to which they are now being applied. There the difference surely would have to be attributed (if it can be attributed to education) to a feudal status of the educated incompatible with economic development: literates there refuse to undertake manual labour.

(20) But even if these objections could be overlooked it would be rash, even in the United States, to attribute the differential rate of remuneration and thus establish a rate of return to cost for education. In countries other than the United States, and especially the countries on the road to development, all these problems are exaggerated by the defective sociological framework, and are the result of monopolistic influences due to feudal aristocratic or cultural and tribal restrictions on class mobility. Expenditure on education by family is highly correlated to the income and wealth of the parents, to ability and motivation, to educational opportunity

vouchsafed by urban residence and proximity to educational centres. On the other hand, the access to well-paid jobs is reserved for family connections. Even in England, professional differentials are dictated not by free competition of the individuals but by monopolistic restraints deeply embedded in the social organism. Far worse is the situation in ex-colonial territories, including Latin America. There, and in Africa, in most countries of Asia, and even in a number of Mediterranean countries, these factors are so strong as to be able to account, either by themselves or in conjunction with some of the others, for the whole of such income differentials. An almost impenetrable barrier exists between rural misery and the life of capital cities containing the administration and the professional classes.

(21) The income differential between urban and rural incomes might be as 1 to 4, or 1 to 5. All that this shows, however, is not that there is a high return to education but a successful acquisition by the upper class of an incomes scale which evolved in the colonial period with no close relationship to the national average. In the civil services and universities, income levels will be governed by the traditional standards of feudal or expatriate colonial oligarchy, and could provide no clue as to the relative rates of investment in the "people". It would be dictated not by the relative actual productivity or usefulness of the experience or knowledge of the individual enjoying it but by the injustice of the system.

(22) In the colonial regime, moreover, the service administrators had to obtain recruits from the metropolitan country. They were therefore forced to pay salaries commensurate with (but much higher than) the income levels of the metropolis. This was tolerable so long as the function of the administration was merely to preserve law and order. In a "night-watchman state" the numbers required would be low. This would not matter. The burden of the high salaries could be borne. It would, however, be impossible to sustain an administration needed by a modern state on this basis. Thus all calculations made about "profitability of education" are not merely devoid of meaning, or fallacious, they have a deeply immoral political implication.

(23) If this conclusion seems self-evident, why has it not had any deterrent effect on these arithmetical manipulations? This failure can be explained partly by their appeal to snobbery and to the self-esteem of the educated. Moreover, it appears to provide an economic justification for existing income differentials and tends to buttress vested interests and deter reform.

(24) The creation of agricultural extension services and of an educated agricultural credit system, the real organization of civil service, the establishment of state corporations, all these are complex and difficult matters and involve a change of attitudes, a reform of institutions. They reduce privilege. How reassuring and simple it is to be served up by econometricians with an elegant mathematical model out of which a residual can be lifted representing the complex conditions of progress, in this case "the vast heavy investment which all countries undertake at all times in the development of their human resources" and a mathematical "demonstration" attributing to it a definite causal force.

(25) This is contrasted with any reactionary design of fobbing off the newly independent areas with a second-rate or worse system: " . . . Poor nations should not waste their resources on education; they should have only as much education as they could afford. At best, quantitatively they should not have more primary, secondary or higher education than was needed to run their public services. Qualitatively that system should be so devised, so cut, reduced, economized on and made into a multi-purpose hodge-podge seeming to serve all kinds of mutually contradictory purposes at the same time, that it cost the country and its resources the minimum possible, preferably nothing at all."

(26) Instead of having to specify which type of education combined with what other specific measures (such as investment in improved methods of cultivation, provision of the right equipment, creative skills, and ability and willingness to work efficiently), and complemented by what general reforms would produce progress, one item is singled out, either as the necessary and sufficient condition, or as a principal strategic variable of development.

(27) *But the wrong kind of education, unaccompanied by the required complementary actions, can check or reverse the process of development*. An unemployable "educated class" can be the cause of uncertainty and risk prejudicial to economic activity, and young people brought up to despise manual work can reinforce the resistances to development. Growth rates derived from the experience of the United States cannot be used to calculate the returns on education in the entirely different setting of underdeveloped countries. The same "input" could result in refusal to work on farms, an increase in urban unemployment, subversion and collapse. The wrong type of education can also produce a ruling élite which gives the wrong kind of advice, as well as setting up ideals that stand in the way of development. It can encourage ignorance of, and contempt

for, the professional and technical qualifications which are a condition of economic development.

III

(28) The third fashionable fallacy in treating the economic aspects of education is to assume a fixed relationship between global expenditures and the global effects, that is, to assume that education is homogeneous. This characterizes both mathematical approaches to educational planning. It is especially pernicious in the context of the development of poor, primitive, agricultural territories to which it has recently been applied.

(29) Education is not a homogeneous input. This has been recognized in a rough-and-ready manner by dividing it into consumption educational and investment educational expenditure. Unfortunately the division between these two is exceedingly difficult to draw and has in most cases been drawn in a manner which, to my mind, is entirely inconsistent with the true situation. In particular it has been assumed that certain types of education, the introduction or generalization of which has coincided with a tremendous acceleration of economic development in Western Europe and North America, would do the same in other, differently situated countries having different economic, social and political frameworks and institutions.

(30) This feature of the educational debate is the more pernicious as there has been in all continents a tendency to imitate the educational institutions which have won a high reputation in Europe.[1] Even those countries which shook off colonial dependence before the industrial revolution in their home countries, such as the independent states of Latin America, have nevertheless been influenced by the culture of the mother country which they faithfully copy. Thus it comes about that the Latin American universities are in the same way Law and Literature oriented as would be a university in Old Castile or Leon, or for that matter Portugal. There is the

1. We in Oxford are subject to this stupidity in a most peculiar way. Oxford grew out of Padua and adopted a timetable which is dominated by the climate of Padua. This, being extremely hot in summer, demands a long vacation beginning at the end of June. In Oxford, on the contrary, we usually have a heat-wave, if at all, in late May and early June. July and August seem to be the worst of the rainy period. Nevertheless, we have our examinations in the former and take our holidays in the latter, in slavish imitation of the famous North Italian institution.

same disdain for technical education, the same neglect of agriculture, the same exaltation of what was called liberal education.

(31) Great Britain and France, though they should have learnt better, have given an identical ethos to the countries under their dominion in Asia and Africa, and from there it spread to those areas which were semi-independent under a mandate. The heavy weight of Oxbridge classicism, combined with a muscular Christian masculinity, characterizes the ex-British territories from St. Steven's College in Delhi to Legon in Ghana. The even less appropriate Sorbonne disdain of the littérateur for technical culture has a heavy responsibility for the almost complete absence of any type of technical education in the ex-French area.

(32) The insistence on "quality" has meant such bankruptcy in quantity that the closely restricted circles of "culture" have no relevance at all to the problems of the masses in these territories. Worse than that, in the process of naturalizing the civil service and the higher echelons of the foreign private enterprises, which, under a colonial regime, were strictly reserved for the nationals of the metropolitan country, the colonial nationalist movements, eager to strive for equality, have poisoned the social structure of the new countries. The independence that was achieved under feudal leadership in Latin America has led to a strengthening of the feudal hold over land and the worsening of the situation of Indians and landless Europeans. The grant of European salaries has stabilized inequality in Africa, the Caribbean and Asia.

(33) This development is obviously quite incompatible with the legitimate striving of these countries for accelerated and balanced development. On the one hand, this is made unlikely, if not impossible, by the crushing burdens which such a development would entail in the framework which has been created, and which has its roots in a completely different situation. In the second place, the whole tendency and direction of development planning points the wrong way and is extremely likely to stifle such development programming as there will be.

(34) These two factors, combined, have resulted in plans being put forward to create educational systems in Asia and Africa akin to those of Western Europe or North America. Oddly enough perhaps the North American model would be less dangerous than the Western European for reasons which will be made clear below. Education is to be concentrated on literacy and a full complement of secondary and higher education, and research facilities are to be provided within an exceedingly short period of less than a score of

years. This is to be accomplished in ways which are familiar to us in Europe. (In fact, plans such as have been put forward for these countries have been implemented by the French under the Constantine plan in Algiers, including lovely prefabricated school buildings, institutions for nuclear research, etc.)

(35) The building programme alone would imply the absorption of a large part of the present investment capacity even if we assume that foreign aid would rise very sharply. Salaries as they are contemplated are obviously more akin to professional salaries in high income countries than anything which could be accommodated in Africa or elsewhere on the basis of primitive agriculture. If, for instance, we in England were to pay our school teachers relatively to average income as some proposals suggest in Africa, their salaries would be between £5,000 and £6,000 a year. On the same basis the capital cost of a place in a university would be £50,000 in contrast with the actual English figure of, say, £2,500–£3,000. The nonsense of this approach is obvious as soon as the comparison is made. The crucial point in this type of approach is that it does not pay the slightest attention to the need for balanced development. It will prove impossible to increase educational expenditure in this way (even if it were desirable, and its desirability is not at all proven), and still have sufficient resources to devote to directly productive investment for the acceleration of economic growth.

(36) Yet without such growth educational progress will produce a discontented, unemployable class of young desperadoes just waiting to be led into violence. Welfare and administrative services must not pre-empt the whole of the resources potentially available for development, because if they do they will be self-defeating and the failure of the economic development will push everybody towards complete totalitarian mobilization.

(37) A second characteristic of a large portion of development programmes and development planning looks for an improvement in these territories towards accelerated industrialization. Inasmuch as the rural squalor is unspeakable, inasmuch as the incomes attainable in the cities are immensely higher, and consumption tenfold higher than rural incomes, it is obvious that there is a flight from the countryside, and that the government, faced with the problem of urbanization and urban misery, tries to escape by planning industrialization at any cost.

(38) Two things need to be said in this respect. The first is that if industrialization programmes were as successful as in England and America in the nineteenth, or Russia and China in the twentieth

century (which is not at all probable, because of the great handicaps and the poverty in natural resources per square mile of land) it would be impossible to absorb even the increase in the population into industry. The absolute numbers of rural population must be expected to increase indefinitely. Premature industrialization based on single small units such as have been created would permanently cripple all efforts to lift the standard of life towards European levels.

(39) Any relief from misery for the population of Africa must depend on rural renascence, especially on the evolutionary improvement of food production and nutritional habits. The old Africa of the jungle and of wild life so prized by some well-meaning do-gooders cannot possibly provide a decent life for men and women. The exciting and hopeful thing is that the physical possibilities for such a transformation are stupendous.

IV

(40) What are the needs of a new educational drive? Education must be made part of a general campaign for the renascence of the countryside integrated with a purposeful mobilization of this one great asset these countries possess, the available manpower in slack seasons. If the people themselves, with expert guidance, build their own educational system and "pay for it" in a very different sense from the traditional manner, the esteem of the new facilities will be enhanced and a large step will have been taken forward in the general social and economic development of the country.

(41) The problem of the psychological attitude of educators to techniques and vocational training does not end here. The connection which grew up between the universities and research institutions of the African territories with the metropolitan institutions, and the understandable ambition of the research workers and teachers eventually to obtain employment in their own countries, further strengthen this anti-technological, anti-vocational bias in the social structure and educational system. Practical work concentrated on solving particular problems of the territories concerned might not easily entitle the performer to accelerate his progress in his own profession. In order to obtain recognition, he had to strive in practice to show his excellence as a pure scientist.

(42) This meant, however, that African *academic* research work, such as it was, as also much of the research of the metropolitan areas, in stark contrast to the example of nineteenth-century America and present-day Australia, became to a large extent irrelevant from the

point of view of the African territories. The numerous research institutes (especially in the British zone) mainly concentrated their research activity on cash crops according to their importance for the Metropolis, while the neglect of food crops of primary importance to the people of the dependencies was startling. Even so, the results obtained in these institutions were not, in many cases, made immediately and emphatically available to the population, but regarded rather as the result of scientific endeavour *per se*. Consequently, a great deal of knowledge has been stored up which awaits us, while a reorientation of research activity might accelerate its gathering in harmony with the relative needs of the African states.

(43) A balanced programme must give the highest priority to general education and training for rural advance. The provision of technical knowledge, both in the rural area and for the urban industrialization programme, must be oriented from this basic viewpoint.

(44) In the second place, the cost of such a widespread and effective education and training programme must not be so crushing as to prevent its harmonious integration into a general development programme. The distance and dispersion of the population will demand a disproportionately heavy sub-structure investment which will contribute little to national income. If, then, a balanced advance is to be accomplished, extreme conservatism will be needed in limiting expenditure.

(45) In the third place, the programme should be so conceived that both the creation of a new administrative, technical, and teaching cadre and the general education system should concentrate on producing the framework in which co-operative, communal work can flourish so as to increase productivity. This demands a basic reorientation of educational policy because until recently, training and education were undertaken on a selective basis not always favouring the most efficient solution for a mass advance in welfare. There has been, in particular, integration of general agricultural extension work and education with political administration and with the institutional organization needed to increase the effectiveness of work. The consequence is that a number of very ambitious schemes have been started which, though extremely costly, have little, if any, impact on the life of the population as a whole. This is not merely so in the case of the existing organs for higher education, but also in rural settlement schemes, the cost of which is so heavy as to exclude any generalization. They are thus irrelevant for the solution of this socio-economic problem of the countries of Africa.

(46) A change can only come by linking educational advance closely with rural change and with the modernization of agricultural production, including marketing and credit. In addition, the administrative hierarchy has to be made to fit into the reorganization so as to promote and assist rather than to deter modernization and the acquisition of technical knowledge and its application.

(47) (*a*) *Elementary education.* Elementary education must strive to impart directly available technical knowledge to the rural youth, enabling them to increase production. The possibilities in this respect are immense. Better seed, the treatment of seed, the use of better implements and techniques, of fertilizers, the right choice of the planting period, could easily double output in vast areas in five years. Education also must embrace alimentation, one of the most awkward problems of Africa. Improved feeding must be demonstrated, not discussed in the abstract. No better use could be found for food surpluses than such a campaign. It could palpably demonstrate the superiority of the new ways of life and give incentive to changes in production.

(48) Above all, elementary education must cease to alienate pupils from their environment and render them unfit for the purpose to which education ought to be dedicated, namely, the rise in rural welfare. The reorganization of elementary education ought to be so conceived as to create prestige and status for agricultural work. It must, therefore, go hand in hand with a change in the rural framework and rural life towards increased productivity. At the same time, its expansion must not absorb too large a proportion of available scarce resources relative to the other needs of the country. All these requirements could be met by using the only economic reserves of the African countries, the large-scale underemployment of their population.

(49) The rural elementary school must be made the centre of rural renascence. This means that in its curriculum, rural science, such as elementary biology, elementary soil chemistry, and elementary technical knowledge and use of implements and of crop management, must be given an increasingly important place. Teaching must be followed up by doing. It is not only essential that schools should have land attached on which the children can be trained in more effective methods of production without being for one minute divorced from their original milieu, but, in view of the overall economic problems facing most African countries, that the school should become more or less self-supporting and thus diminish the draft on the general resources of the country.

(50) At present, elementary education follows closely on the European pattern. It starts at the age of 6 or 7 and, theoretically, gives four to five years' education. There is no reason whatever why this pattern, which was evolved in Europe in the early nineteenth century because children of 11 or 12 were then not exempt from factory employment, should be perpetuated. Education should begin when the adolescent is at his most absorptive from the viewpoint of learning, and can also contribute positively to the work of the model school farms. At the same time, special facilities should be provided for talented children to continue their education through scholarships.

(51) The school building and the teacher's residence should be constructed by the villagers with some help, in terms of modern building material, given by the Central Government. It should be emphasized, however, that these buildings must be in keeping with the new *national* character of the teaching service in contrast to the metropolitan standards of the pre-independence educational system. And if the salary of the teacher is to be in tolerable relation to the average national income, and, nevertheless, a very large number of able and ambitious young people, capable of giving effective, indeed revolutionary, leadership to the rural communities, is to be recruited, other, non-material incentives must be provided. I shall return to this problem.

(52) (*b*) *Extension work and co-operatives.* The accent on self-sustaining education for higher productivity must be paralleled by training to fit adults, especially young workers beyond school age, for co-operation, the success of which in the end will determine whether Africa can rise towards a standard of life comparable to that of highly developed areas. Without co-operatives capable of applying modern techniques and servicing individual members, both with implements and with economic facilities, African productivity and income will necessarily remain at an unsatisfactory level. If co-operative endeavour is to succeed within the old framework of the extended family ownership yet, at the same time, infused with a new modern content, it will be necessary to inculcate a new spirit. This calls for self-discipline and capacity for sacrifice. Fortunately, this restraint can be shown to benefit all and within a measurable time. This, and the upsurge of new consciousness of national endeavour as a result of independence, should make such a call for co-operative work possible.

(53) The rural school would thus become the centre of improved productive activity. There is a grave shortage of manpower to lead

this advance. Its full utilization demands also that adult education and especially extension work should be concentrated into it. If the extended family or village holding will have to be made the basic operational unit of the new improved agricultural activity, in order to utilize a valuable traditional authority and influence, as well as the old legal framework for a new purpose, it would be essential to bring the extension service gradually right into every village.

(54) It is a question of organizational convenience whether the village-level monitors or extension officers should be trained as teachers or the other way round. There is no problem of principle involved, merely one of convenience. At present (and for some time to come), even the application of very primitive improvements in production techniques would give very considerable results. There is no need to teach complicated things. Thus it is unnecessary to have elaborate training schemes for extension workers or to demand very high technical qualifications. That is a matter for the further future. What matters now is enthusiasm and leadership.

(55) Adult education should also be organized round the practical task of improving the general welfare in the village, preferably in conjunction with community development schemes, which it ought to strengthen. These might take the form of rural public works partly paid for, partly performed in discharging a tax obligation for rural improvement, either in terms of a money payment or in terms of labour service. Personal interest should be engaged by giving people good opportunities to prove their capacity in the execution of public works and in adult education, and acknowledge their merit by enabling them to rise to better (possibly paid) positions, provided they are willing to undertake training.

(56) The closest consultation with the population ought to be attempted in deciding on the plans for improvement schemes for each rural community which will be executed by these public works programmes. They should comprise quick yielding schemes if possible, e.g. access roads, small dams, etc., and not merely amenities. Once the decision has been taken on the local development plan, however, the power of taxation of the State and/or the local authority (whether newly organized on an electoral basis or based on the traditional rural authority of chiefs) would have to be used to ensure its execution.

(57) Everyone should have to contribute either in terms of money or of labour. The money value of labour should be set very high to encourage general contributions in labour, so as to create some

feelings of equality and reduce prejudice against manual labour Twenty or thirty day's annual contribution to there building of Africa is a small price to pay (provided the plans are well conceived) when the work-year is less than 200 (and often less than 150) days. It would make all the difference between stagnation and cumulative growth, and the relief of poverty and sickness. Unfortunately, past experiences in this field represent a terrible psychological hindrance. All such schemes based on direct contributions have a fatal (if superficial) resemblance to the forced labour of the colonial past (especially in the Belgian and Portuguese, and in some British territories).

(58) The more foreign help is available, the more the Government could rely on incentives. But the problem has to be faced of the dead hand of the compulsion of traditional living which has hitherto blocked progress. It must be weakened, if not altogether eliminated, if reconstruction is to be successfully accomplished. It would be unforgivable if all available social forces could not be used to promote progress because of an unjustifiable reluctance to use compulsion when necessary. It is necessary to offset the malign influence of the compulsion of traditional but inappropriate social institutions. This problem cannot be evaded by some unctuous platitude about democracy.

(59) Failure would retard rural renascence and there is no time available: the increase in population, the exhaustion of natural resources, and the growth of expectations in combination render delay dangerous. Special care must be taken, however, to provide safeguards, to enable the population at large to have recourse to some process of accountability on the part of those who exercise traditional or newly-created authority in rural life. It is the irresponsibility of authority, and therefore the likelihood and facility with which authority can be abused, that is so objectionable in the present systems of social compulsion in Africa, quite apart from their self-perpetuating, indeed, self-aggravating character which prevents the basis for freedom of choice from being established for the majority of the population.

(60) (*c*) *Creating the technical cadres*. The new concept of the role of education inevitably implies a vast increase in the need for teachers cum agricultural monitors. The target should be at least one monitor teacher for each one to two thousand families in each village. A crash programme for training might be planned. Every district should have a large camp-institute for the purpose, also on a largely self-supporting basis. Subsequently, as specialized teaching becomes

available, extension work and elementary teaching might be separated on the higher echelons, yet without cutting its closest relationship in the field.

(61) Centres for higher education and specialized research should be regional, based on the fact that the political boundaries in Africa cut across the natural climate, soil, and water resource regions with common problems. The establishment of such common teaching and research institutions should promote the feeling of unity in Africa which is so indispensable for its future progress. It is essential that a certain unity should be maintained in these services.

(62) The need must be stressed for a practical and technical bias in higher education, and attention called to the ineffectualness to date of the reports which have emphasized this need in the past. Adequate attention is not paid to the vital middle echelons, who are, after all, the indispensable agents to popularize and carry into effect innovations in rural and indeed in urban life.

V

(63) This brings me to the problem of educational planning.

(64) Does my criticism of the ramstam methods hitherto adopted by over-eager or just simple econometricians and mathematical economists add up to a complete repudiation of all quantitative analysis? Nothing could be further from my thoughts. Qualitative meditation without the discipline of quantification would certainly not produce an acceptable alternative to the approach I criticize. It was in fact this sort of humanistic-littérateur approach which resulted in the present dearth of technical talent in many European countries, but even more in the colonies of which they had charge. Because of the long gestation period in education, we must try to plan ahead in some detail, over extended stretches of time. It is impossible to escape the need for detailed quantitative planning.

(65) Educational long term perspective planning, however, must —in my opinion—start with a rather detailed plan of socio-economic development. It cannot start just from some arbitrary global hypothesis on the interrelation between educational input which is assumed to be homogeneous within each stage of the educational structure, these stages differing from one another only in their quantitative relationship to global "progress".

(66) (*a*) In particular, such a perspective plan must embrace a serious politico-sociological study of the problem of how, and how far, traditional educational patterns had contributed to the failure

of social and economic progress in the past. Such a study is the essential basis of all educational planning. It must discover whether the attitudes which are hostile to economic progress have been the result of a specific structure of education, and what modifications of that structure are needed to obtain a new approach to the technical requirements, in terms of knowledge and training, of accelerated economic expansion. In both the formerly English, and in the formerly French territories, a disdain of technical education has grown up, for instance, which has been exacerbated by the relatively lowly status of technical schools and the restricted career possibilities open to their pupils. So long as the Civil Service and those appointments which are controlled or influenced by it—and they are the majority, if not the totality, of all worthwhile posts in the newly free areas—are the preserve of the non-technically educated, the best ability will obviously be diverted into non-technical education. This will both justify and increase the initial disdain, and render economic and social progress more difficult, as first-class technicians needed for it just will not be available; first-class talent will ensconce itself in the capital in nice administrative jobs.

(67) On the basis of this study a new educational structure can be planned which will give adequate status to those qualities in the educated élite which harmonize with technical requirements of accelerated progress, while at the same time such a reform of the choice of the élite is initiated as would attract the best ability to the new type of education, by giving it sufficient scope.

(68) (*b*) The second aspect of the job of a long term perspective educational planning demands an idea of the shape of economic development that is hoped for. A perspective twenty- or twenty-five-year plan will have to be produced because (and in this I fully agree with Professor Tinbergen) the gestation period for educational preparation is very long indeed.

(69) I do not think that technical shortcuts such as, for example, the methods advocated by Professor Chenery[1] will be much good in this respect, but they are certainly far better than Professor Tinbergen's approach of simply writing down an arbitrary equation. Professor Chenery wants to base planning on the assumption that the distribution of manpower between different occupations at each stage of economic development in different countries is identical or closely similar. This methodology neglects the fact that past experience can only be drawn from cases which evolved as a result

1. "Patterns of Economic Growth", *American Economic Review*, September 1960.

of *spontaneous* growth (or its failure). It would be wrong, or at least illegitimate, to assume that this experience is applicable to *deliberate* efforts to *accelerate* growth. And can such efforts be successful if plans are not adapted to overcoming the *specific difficulties* which were responsible for the failure of growth in different countries? These hindrances are likely to *differ* widely from country to country, while the states which have shown some progress in the past have shown success in a few categories for broadly *similar* reasons. I feel very sceptical under these circumstances about the legitimacy of Professor Chenery's method.

(70) Far more promising is the approach adopted by Mr. Pitambar Pant of the Indian Planning Commission, and by Mr. Dhusis of the Greek Ministry of Co-ordination, of drawing up a long term perspective plan for industrial development and then to see (on the basis of current experience) what detailed categories of education and training, and in what quantities, are needed to meet the requirements of the expansion of industry and agriculture if the direct development goals are in fact to be achieved. Even present trends might be misleading because of the rapid changes in technique.

(71) (*c*) This list will have to be detailed as education is by no means homogeneous and the sociological difficulties in the way of changing attitudes are very strong indeed and take a long time to overcome. At the same time it is obvious that the educational effort will be extremely expensive in the sense that, at each stage of economic development, an educational system needed for the *next* or even *subsequent* stage of economic progress will have to be supported. These are commensurately expensive. Thus, educational planning (unless technical assistance can be expanded far faster than now seems likely) will have to be extremely conservative and expense-conscious. Such conservative advice is politically difficult because very unpopular, and in great tracts of the world also suspect of racial discrimination. Commensurate efforts must, therefore, be made to dispel prejudice against a balanced educational plan as a part of a balanced overall plan, preferably on a multi-country regional basis (e.g. West Africa). *The larger the area for which collective planning can be initiated, the greater the scope for, and the less the danger of, those specialized institutions* (e.g. *nuclear physics*) *which are so expensive, so unrelated to immediate economic and social progress, so conspicuous, so status-symbolizing between countries, and therefore so coveted.*

(72) I do not underestimate the difficulties of a new approach. The whole historical framework, the social and political trend,

militates against a reconsideration of present policies which secure privilege.

(73) The way to a solution is being pointed by the Economic Commission for Africa. Sub-regional balanced planning of all phases of economic development, coordination of all aid-giving agencies, here are the rudiments of a better era. Let us hope that UNESCO and FAO will give a new lead.

Part B. Teaching Economic Development

EDITED BY KURT MARTIN

Teaching Economic Development in the U.K.: Some Analytical Aspects

PETER ADY

Fellow of St. Anne's College, Oxford

TEACHING economic development in the U.K. involves a problem in communication at two levels. There is firstly that of communicating an understanding of the difficulties of individual underdeveloped countries to those who are familiar with the discipline of economics and understand its application (and its limitations as a system of thought) in modern industrial societies. Secondly there is the task of teaching would-be developers from the poorer countries in just what way, if any, economics as a discipline can be useful to them in acquiring a clearer appreciation of the forces that are holding back their growth and thus in helping them to design economic policies to foster change along chosen lines.

Both these tasks imply, however, that the system of postulates developed for the economic analysis of industrial societies can be used in those of a different economic structure.

Given that our economic models are useful at all (a point contested with respect to some of them), are they equally applicable in underdeveloped countries? Model building is only an attempted approximation of the real world, models based on static general equilibrium criteria being easiest to fault even in developed countries on the score of inapplicable assumptions. Much the most successful models have been those based on Keynesian accounting concepts, whether designed for the study of cycle or of growth, yet even these have come under attack in recent years as conceptually unsuited to the analysis of growth in countries at an early stage of development. While some critics have discussed them as conceptually unsound,[1] others, like Seers, consider that they are ill designed to show the nature of the processes at work.

1. See, for example, Paul Streeten's paper in this series. Also W. Barber, *Bulletin of the Oxford University Institute of Economics and Statistics*, 1963.

In what follows one should try to keep separate the criticisms of economic theory as such from comment on its relevance in non-industrial societies. This presupposes that those studying development are already sophisticated about the limitations of the tools of economics. For if not the foundations of any course in economic development may be very shaky. There are two sources of danger. The elegance of formal models, if such are used, may be apt to obscure the limitations imposed by their assumptions. What begin as postulates become "laws". Or on the other hand, "teaching" may become a series of recipes for social change, with the student given no criteria for choice between the receipts.

Assuming for the moment that the student will already be aware of the limitations of the tools at our disposal as economists, do these tools apply at all in the context of underdeveloped regions? We may ask this question under a number of heads.

1. Are there basic differences in the behaviour of individuals as consumers or producers which render the usual price-quantity relationship in reverse or even inoperative?
2. What is the character of the market economy? Does it escape the imperfections which make the price = marginal cost assumption unrealistic in developed countries?
3. Is the economic community non-homogeneous? The usual assertion is that a dualism exists, with a traditional, backward subsistence sector living side by side with an advanced and vigorous market economy. There are other reasons for non-homogeneity: the dominance in many countries of a sector producing only for export, the high preponderance of foreign capital and of foreigners in the cadres of skilled and managerial labour.
4. What are the implications, if any, for our macro-economic accounting concepts and models if the answer to some of the above questions is affirmative? Thus if dualism of the first kind exists, do the concepts of "Income", "saving" and "consumption" have the same meaning in underdeveloped countries? If the dualism is only of the second variety,[1] what are the implications for our accounting concepts and more particularly for the parameters of our macro-economic models?

1. Arising from the foreign trade sector.

These different questions are not all on the same level of discourse. If the producer in underdeveloped countries responds "non-rationally" to economic incentives, economics must yield place to sociology or psychology in the study of social change. For similar reasons if the subsistence sector is the large and unresponsive segment usually pictured, the implications are far-reaching both for market models and for our aggregates. By contrast a recognition of the other features indicated by our questions leads to no more than a change of emphasis. Questions of the kind we have before us are capable of empirical treatment and I have tried where possible to give orders of magnitude to the elements with which the argument is concerned.

Economic man and the market economy

The famous case of the backward rising supply curve need not detain us, although it has had a long history and has even had its day of influence upon colonial policy.[1] In one sense this question is an empirical one. Is the general response to prices in underdeveloped countries positive (equated to rational) zero or negative? The empirical evidence as to the typical response either way is slender. Negative responses to price changes have never been demonstrated to empirical enquiry to be typical of underdeveloped countries or even to occur on any scale. Yet, like the Indian rope trick, cases of them abound in travellers' tales. On the other hand, well-designed investigations on this subject are also rare,[2] only a few peasant crops having been studied. In all cases the indications were that the long run supply function was positively inclined.

Some of the assertions about negative responses have, of course, been due to ignorance about supply conditions in certain crops. An increase in output at a time of falling prices has often been due to cobweb effects where there is a long time lag between planting and production. Similarly the short-run elasticity popularly attributed to peasant inertia has more likely been due to the technical condition of production.

Negative responses in isolated cases are in any case not "irrational"

1. The government of one British colony reduced the price it paid for wild rubber in 1943 in the hope of getting increased output, but raised it again in 1944 after finding that supplies had actually fallen.

2. See P. Ady, *Bulletin of the Oxford University Institute of Statistics*, December 1949, and P. Bauer, *The Rubber Industry*, Appendix, p. 359, respectively. Also R. M. Stern, *American Economic Review 1962*, for some other cases.

in all circumstances. Where the seller comes to the market with unsatisfied residual demand for his own produce it is rational to keep more for his own consumption when prices rise. The individual's unresponsiveness to team incentive payments is well known in industrial management: it would, therefore, be no surprise to find family labour in peasant societies individually unwilling to undertake more arduous work, when the increased output from the land is to be shared by all in relation to need rather than to work done.

In the towns the common practice of work sharing has its own rationale, for the employed are the sole source of support for the unemployed. Refusal to undertake work single-handed when it is traditionally sufficient to employ two persons is not due to laziness so much as labour loyalty.

All these "rational" explanations for the oft-cited cases of individual labourers who refused to undertake heavier work or longer hours cast doubt on the value of individual instances as evidence in support of the contention that peasants in the tropics have a high leisure preference. This is surely belied by the ceaseless flow of migrations of men in search of wage paid work. Indian coolie labour is to be found all over the tropics. African labour from Nyasaland migrates as far south as Johannesburg, to which also comes the migrant labour of Northern and Southern Rhodesia and of Mozambique. This is *not* just a drift to the towns: it occurs whenever wage-paid employment is available. Ghana cocoa farmers' efforts are supplemented by labour from the Saharan savannas; the Gezira cotton scheme by migrant labour from Northern Nigeria; and Malayan rubber and Mauritian sugar plantations, in common with many other tropical agricultural enterprises, employ Indian labour on a large scale.

Market or dual economy

These misunderstandings are symptomatic of failure to reinterpret the reaction of individual producers in the context of economic conditions obtaining in underdeveloped countries, a feature of which is the prevailing degree of under-employment on the land. Over-population is accepted as a characteristic of the economies of India, East Pakistan, the Nile valley, the palm-belt of Nigeria and Ruanda Urundi, for example, all of which have population densities of a high order. But cultivable land is also in short supply elsewhere, as the wide prevalence of migrant labour systems suggests. In Africa the scarcity is only relative: it could be relieved if alternative techniques of cultivation could be devised to suit Africa's difficult conditions of soil and climate. Yet land left uncultivated is not always cultivable, as the C.D.C. learnt with the Groundnut Scheme and other similar experiments. Shifting cultivation, which is the perfect adaptation to these conditions, is extremely wasteful of land, requiring a fallow period of fifteen years at the minimum if soil erosion is not to result. Yet soil erosion is all too frequently seen, especially in East Africa and the Rhodesias, the least densely peopled part of the continent.[1] Soil erosion is less common in West Africa (although not absent): the sign of population pressure there is the prevalence of secondary bush and scrub, the fallow period permitted by population pressure being too short to allow the full regeneration of high forest, which is needed if soil fertility is not to fall.

In agriculture for the domestic market in Africa as well as in India we have the simultaneous occurrence of disguised unemployment and of inelastic supplies of agricultural produce, especially in the short-run.[2] The price mechanism in such circumstances cannot be expected to operate effectively in the allocation of resources, without the injection of additional capital[3] and the adoption of new techniques beyond the range of present possibilities.[4]

Lack of adaptability is also characteristic of both mining (inevitably) and of export crop production owing to the specificity of factors (in this case, land). An area in which cotton is being grown cannot be transferred to the production of groundnuts when their relative prices change because the climate and soil suited to the one are not optimal for the other. It is less easy still to transfer resources between permanent crops such as coffee, cocoa, tea, sisal and rubber, all of which take upwards of three years to come into bearing. Thus even in the longer run a fall in demand for particular commodities cannot be met by transferring land and labour to other types of primary production.

Nor can labour be transferred out of the primary sector without the provision of reproducible capital. The fundamental dilemma of the underdeveloped countries is that a transfer of labour out of primary production is proving difficult to bring about, although

1. Deserts apart.
2. I am not myself familiar with Latin America, but the same appears to hold true of peasant agriculture there.
3. E.g. in the shape of irrigation, fertilizers, expenditure on locust control, and so on.
4. Limits include lack of education.

returns to both labour and capital in other industries are much larger.

Is the transformation to be expected from the free workings of the market mechanism given prevailing economic structure and character of market institutions? Professor Viner[1] implies that this is so, when he says:

> "In a predominantly agricultural country, rapid growth of population unaccompanied by a proportionate growth in demand for its agricultural products will under free market conditions bring spontaneously into action forces tending to industrialize the country by making agricultural production less remunerative."

We must agree with Professor Gunnar Myrdal's mild comment[2] that "this is a very inaccurate description of what has taken place and what is taking place in the underdeveloped regions of the world".

This is not the place to examine the arguments for and against the doctrine of comparative costs with its emphasis on the freely working market mechanism. Suffice it to say that even Professor Viner has recently admitted[3] the necessity of interpreting comparative advantage in a dynamic setting in which the efficiency of production may change over time, external economies may exist and market prices of commodities and of factors may differ from their opportunity costs. With complementarities so important in both consumer and producer demand, current opportunity cost and market prices are insufficient, even theoretically, to determine where comparative advantage lies. Nowhere does this argument have more force than in the underdeveloped countries of today. While the price mechanism has its uses, especially on the side of demand, its functions as an allocative system should be recognized to have great limitations in that context. Myrdal goes on to dispute the validity of the theory underlying free trade doctrines by an appeal to history in the following terms:

> "It is an understatement to say that the theory of international trade does not furnish us with a model or logical mechanism representing a system of rational hypotheses which can be used

1. Viner, *International Trade and Economic Development*, p. 113.
2. Myrdal, *Economic Theory and the Underdeveloped Regions*, p. 150.
3. Viner, "Stability and Progress: The Poorer Countries' Problem", in D. Hague (ed.), *Stability and Progress in the World Economy*, London, 1958.

for explaining why and how the huge economic inequalities between different countries have come to exist and why they tend to grow . . . in recent decades while international inequalities have been growing . . . the theory of international trade has developed in the direction of stressing more and more the idea that trade initiates a tendency towards a gradual equalization of factor prices as between different countries."

If the conditions of the static optimum were all that the pure theory of international trade has to offer we might well hesitate to rely upon economics to contribute much to our understanding of such differences. We might, like Prebisch[1] and Singer, introduce perhaps a political or sociological element in contending that there is an asymmetry about productivity gains as between the prices of manufactures and the prices of primary products, which has caused a permanent lag to develop between them. Or we might adopt the view put forward by Western economists that the slow growth of underdeveloped regions is to be ascribed to the dualistic character of these economies, in which a sluggish traditional sector lives side by side with a vigorous market sector based upon the export trade.

Much energy has gone into explaining this lack of dynamism in non-economic terms, but before dismissing economics completely as an independent discipline or capturing it by incorporation in some wider scheme of interpretation, sociologically designed, we should pause to consider whether post-war developments in macro-economic theory offer any improvement. Yet the "dual" economy itself poses difficulties to a macro-economic interpretation.

"*Dual*" *economy and macro-economic concepts*

Can macro-economic concepts be applied in dual economies? If the price-mechanism operates only over a part of the economy, the remainder living in ignorance of, and unresponsive to, market changes, what meaning can we give to terms such as price itself, cost, and income? In such a situation there would be no market price for a part of the produce of the community and no meaningful way of aggregating the output of one sector with another to give the national product. Interaction between the sectors by definition could not take place and the economy could not therefore be considered as a whole.

1. See "Relative Prices of Exports and Imports of Underdeveloped Countries", U.N. 1948. Also Singer, *American Economic Review*, 1950, Papers and Proceedings, pp. 477–9.

This objection is more theoretical than real. For whatever may have been the case of Indonesia when Boecke wrote, or of Africa before the first World War, today each household sells some part of its produce in the market.

For even the poorest countries today are long past such a stage. At the first U.N. Conference of African Statisticians in 1961, for example, it was pointed out by the government statisticians representing the different countries, amongst which are some of the less developed, that no such duality exists today, whatever might have been the case fifty years ago. Today each rural African household sells some part of its produce for cash, although still producing a part of its own income by farming or other subsistence activities. There is no subsistence *sector* although there is subsistence income. The Conference recommended therefore that social accounts for African countries include an account for the rural sector (in which subsistence plays a large part) but none for a subsistence sector as such.

Nevertheless, are the difficulties of valuation of subsistence income such as to render its inclusion inadvisable? The volume of subsistence output is difficult to estimate where agriculture is based on shifting cultivation, and until recently there were differences in coverage and method of pricing in different countries. These difficulties have been partially resolved although the estimates made no doubt have considerable margins of error. The chief improvement is that the valuation of subsistence income is now based upon a generally accepted international convention.[1] Thus the pricing problem is no longer a barrier. Although the system of valuation used has the usual difficulties when international comparison is attempted, it is at least internally consistent with the valuation of other items in the national accounts of each country.

Is it valid to aggregate together output of goods and services produced for exchange, and therefore sold for cash, with those produced for own use? There are of course index number difficulties about aggregation, but even when there is no subsistence income they exist. These difficulties do not invalidate the conceptual use of aggregates for overall analysis given due sophistication in their use. Conceptually the case for its inclusion is strong, for subsistence

1. Proposed at the U.N. Conference of African Statisticians by E. F. Jackson and now generally adopted. The convention is to value output at ex-farm prices and consumption at market prices, the difference between the two aggregates being shown as imputed transport and distribution in the product account by industrial origin.

output occurs in all societies and some of it is included in the national income aggregate of developed countries (e.g. farmer's consumption of own produce, output of household allotments, even do-it-yourself decorating and building if there is some commodity flow upon which estimates can be based). Other items are not included (e.g. housewives' non-commercial services).

If the concept of income in the developing countries is to follow the international convention, subsistence income should accord with the first category above and some estimate of it should be included. For exclusion of subsistence income would materially alter the composition of domestic product by industrial origin and the structure of consumption, since it would exclude the bulk of domestic food production and consumption at a blow; it would also give strange orders of magnitude to parameters such as the savings and import propensities in macro-economic equations.[1]

Subsistence income and the parameters of macro-economic models

When we come to consider the parameters of our macro-economic equations the proportion of income arising as subsistence introduces some difficulties, not because of its size, for it is already well below 20 per cent of domestic product in most countries,[2] but because of the difficulties of measurement. Changes in subsistence output are unlikely to be recorded given the methods available for its measurement and are likely in any case to be well within the error of estimate. Thus subsistence income and consumption are usually treated as constant. Yet since subsistence income and consumption are self-balancing, this element in the totals does not introduce any bias into the *marginal* propensities to save, consume and import[3] providing net investment in subsistence production is negligible, as is usually taken to be the case.

The average saving, consumption and import ratios by contrast are affected by errors in estimating the value of subsistence income

1. See for example the accounts for Northern Rhodesia 1945–62.
2. There are a few exceptions, e.g. Tanganyika (36 per cent).
3. Let the subscript m denote monetary transactions and s subsistence transactions, while capitals denote aggregates, M = imports, C = consumption.

Given $\Delta Y_s = \Delta C_s = 0$

Then the MPC $= \dfrac{\Delta C_m}{\Delta Y_m}$ while the MPM $= \dfrac{\Delta M}{\Delta Y_m}$

and MPS $= 1 - c - m = \dfrac{\Delta Y_m - \Delta C_m - \Delta M}{\Delta Y_m} = \dfrac{\Delta S_m}{\Delta Y_m}$

and hence its share in aggregate income. Since *per capita* income comparisons with other countries suggest that subsistence income has, if anything, been undervalued, this means that both aggregate income and aggregate consumption should be increased by the same amount. If anything, therefore, existing estimates of savings and import ratios are too high in LDCs. Is it this aspect of universality that Dudley Seers[1] is criticizing when he says:

> "There are propositions of a very elementary sort which have some general validity (e.g. those showing the implications for prices if demand and supply curves have certain slopes and shift in one direction or another). But macro-economics is another matter. The burden is surely on those who claim that this is not highly specific to show how any macro-economic model fits various non-industrial economics, each with its own institutions and productive structure."

Yet, as phrases indicate throughout his text,[2] Seers does not seem to be criticizing the use of the usual aggregates in the developing countries. Nor does he appear to dispute the use of the usual parameters to define macro-economic relationships. He speaks, for example, of income-elasticities, the multiplier, the import "leakage". As I understand him, his criticisms are:

(1) the values given to the parameters (e.g. the multiplier), and
(2) the extent to which models of economic growth, the central concern of students of economic development, ignore foreign trade and payments although the underdeveloped countries themselves are heavily dependent on foreign trade.

Let us begin by looking at the extent of this dependence in the light of the national accounts aggregates which have become available since the war.

It is well known that many underdeveloped countries are highly specialized in exports. Of the thirty-one countries for which both exports and GDP are available from the UN Yearbook the number

1. D. Seers, "The Limitations of the Special Case", *Bulletin of the Oxford University Institute of Economics and Statistics*, May 1963, p. 83.
2. Thus he speaks of the "mechanism of income creation", of investment, exports, imports, consumption and so on. He also speaks of income elasticities $\left(\frac{\Delta Q}{Q}\Big/\frac{\Delta Y}{Y}\right)$ which inevitably imply aggregation of demand.

with 20 per cent or more of domestic activity generated by the export sector is as high as twenty-one. In no fewer than ten of these the share of exports is 30 per cent and in seven it is 50 per cent. Thus in two-thirds of the countries the degree of export specialization is 20 per cent or more, far higher than the corresponding figures for any except a few developed countries, such as New Zealand (24 per cent), Denmark (33 per cent), and the U.K. (20 per cent).

Another measure of the degree of export specialization is the share of special exports in the total export bill. A single commodity export is 50 per cent or over of the total for twenty-five underdeveloped countries. If we were to list the first three commodities, very few underdeveloped countries would show a percentage of less than 60 per cent and of those in which the share of the three leading commodity exports in the total is less than 40 per cent we have only India (25 per cent), Mexico (34 per cent) and Tunisia (39 per cent).

The underdeveloped countries are thus dependent upon foreign trade in a way and to an extent unknown among the developed ones. Their stability is dependent upon the market fortunes of one or two commodities. Productivity in the export sector is far higher than in those sectors producing for the domestic market, and there is often no market for the export or exports within the underdeveloped country itself. The export sector has in the past been largely dominated by foreign capital, whether in production or marketing or both. This dominance is still a feature of many underdeveloped countries today.

With these economic characteristics in mind let us consider the Myrdal–Seers criticisms of economic models.

Macro-economic growth models

Professor Myrdal's criticism of economic models related to the implications of comparative costs and the factor-price equalization theorem, but could it equally well have been made perhaps of Keynesian models, when these incorporate foreign trade? The literature[1] on international trade theory has grown rapidly in the last ten years, and there are models available in varying degrees of complexity. I shall confine myself to the relatively simple postulates by means of which H. G. Johnson has generalized the Harrod–Domar model to the case of an open economy.[2] Let us try to apply this logic to the interpretation of economic backwardness, as a way

1. See J. Bhagwati, "Survey of International Trade Theory", *Economic Journal*, 1964.
2. H. G. Johnson, *International Trade and Economic Growth*, ch. v.

of examining Seers's assertion that these models are misleading because they have been designed with the structure of developed countries in mind.

Johnson develops his models from the basic Harrod–Domar relationship:

$$(1) \qquad \frac{1}{Y} \cdot \frac{dY}{dt} = \sigma\alpha$$

where Y = national product

σ = output coefficient $= \left(\frac{1}{\text{capital coefficient}}\right)$

α = savings ratio

For the sake of consistency he assumes throughout that *either* the working population is growing at least at the equilibrium rate of growth of income, *or* that technical progress, of a type that leaves the capital coefficient unchanged, is going on rapidly and steadily enough to prevent the capital stock from outgrowing the labour force required to work it.

We begin with the simplest model: (1) in which there is no net flow of factor income to or from abroad, National Product being thus equal to Domestic Product, (2) in which the only imports are for direct consumption. Whereas investment is the only outlet for savings in a closed economy, in an open economy imports as well as savings constitute leakages from effective demand, while exports as well as investment fill the gap between domestic demand for and supply of home production at capacity output.

$$(2) \qquad (\alpha + m)Y_t = X_t + I_t$$

where m = import ratio

X_t = current rate of exports

whence

$$(3) \qquad G = \sigma\left((\alpha + m - \frac{X_t}{Y_t}\right)$$

which may also be written as

$$(4) \qquad G = \sigma(\alpha - b_t)$$

where $b_t = \frac{X_t - M_t}{Y_t}$

From these equations it may be seen that (3) G is higher the higher σ, α and m and the lower $\frac{X_t}{Y_t}$; *or* that (4) G is higher the higher σ and α and the lower b_t. By an extension of his model

Johnson is able to show that growth rates increase the higher the fraction of investment spent on imported equipment: where m′ is the fraction (assumed constant) of investment spent on imported equipment we have

$$G = \frac{\sigma}{1-m'}\left(\alpha+m-\frac{X}{Y}\right) \quad (5)$$

Or more generally he shows that the growth rate is higher the higher the import content (q) of domestic production: whence we have

$$G = \sigma\left(\alpha+m+qc-\frac{X}{Y}\right) \quad (6)$$

where q = constant fractional import content of domestic output and c = (1−α−m) = fraction of income spent on home produced goods.

Thus the role of foreign trade as an engine of economic growth can be spelt out by these models. While exports, if they absorb too much of the domestic product (in a fully employed economy), are unfavourable to growth because they limit investment, nevertheless they enable a country to pay for a high level of imports and this is favourable to growth. Given the gains from increased specialization, foreign trade is favourable to growth, though the distribution of these gains between trading partners depends upon the terms of trade established between them. Bearing in mind the extreme simplicity of these models, these conclusions are not without their value in teaching. But the logic hinges on the validity of the consistency conditions and the absence of difficulties in financing the surpluses or deficits in the balance of payments. For in these models Johnson is assuming that trade surpluses or deficits are financed in a way "that does not give rise to international interests payments—for example by unilateral transfers or by movements of international reserves".[1] Thus there is no balance of payments barrier.

Since the overall import propensity is (m+q)Y, the growth rate G is clearly limited by the volume of current receipts from abroad, given by x, the rate of growth of exports, and θ, the rate of growth of unilateral transfers (T) from abroad. When this is the case G will be higher the higher q relatively to m, because of the "import multiplier"[2] arising from q.

The models approach reality a little closer when the financing assumption is relaxed to allow for capital flows. On an alternative

1. H. G. Johnson, *loc. cit.*, p. 125.

2. J. Bhagwati, *loc. cit.*, p. 53.

assumption "that differences between receipts and payments on current account (including both the trade balance and interest on past debts) are financed by transfers of perpetual securities bearing a constant rate of interest i", we now have income arising from current production increased by interest receipts from or reduced by interest payments to the outside world. The growth equation (reverting to the assumption that all imports are for immediate consumption) then becomes

$$(7) \qquad G = \sigma\left(\alpha + m - \frac{X}{D} \pm \frac{cZ}{D}\right)$$

where D = domestic product = $Y \pm Z$
Z = interest income

The logic of this situation can be understood in two ways:

1. to quote Johnson himself: "Leakages from domestically earned factor income may be offset by consumption of domestic goods out of interest earned on foreign investments, as well as by exports and investment in new capacity; or such leakages may be augmented by the payment of interest to foreigners." This additional "leakage" is thus cZ in Johnson's model.

2. Alternatively we can arrive at the same result by treating Z as a receipt or payment for the use of factor services. If we begin with the National Product we shall then arrive at the same result

$$(\alpha + m)\,Y = I + X \pm Z$$

whence $(\alpha + m)\,D \pm (\alpha + m)Z = I + X \pm Z$

but since $c = 1 - \alpha - m$ we can write

$$(\alpha + m)D = I + X \pm (1 - c)Z \pm Z = I + X \pm cZ$$

whence (7) $$G = \sigma\left(\alpha + m - \frac{X}{D} \pm \frac{cZ}{D}\right)$$

The higher c, the propensity to consume domestically produced goods, the lower the rate of growth G when interest income is *received* from abroad. The opposite holds when interest payments are made abroad. The logic still rests therefore on the assumption of our consistency conditions (because it implies that consumption cannot be increased without curtailing savings or imports).

In underdeveloped countries interest *payments* abroad are the almost invariable rule[1] and equation 7 thus is

1. Exceptions include India, which receives interest income from abroad as well as migrant labour earnings. In most underdeveloped countries which receive factor income from abroad the inflow is exclusively the earnings of migrants, whereas the outflow is dividend and interest payments.

$$G = \sigma \left(\alpha + m - \frac{X}{D} + \frac{cZ}{D} \right) \qquad (7)$$

We now have all the same conclusions as before with the addition that the rate of growth of domestic product is the higher where Z is negative, i.e. represents the payment abroad of interest income. This somewhat paradoxical result is, within the assumptions so far made, formally correct. The larger the loans from abroad the larger the flow of resources available over time for investment, exports and consumption, and it is a balance of payments history of larger loans that is implied by a larger Z when i is constant.[1]

The equation tells us nothing directly about the rate of growth of national product (Y), nor does Johnson consider this question because he is interested primarily in developed countries where Z is small relative to D. Admittedly Y will grow faster than D, where Z is negative, because it starts from a smaller base and will approach D at the asymptote. But when Z is large relatively to D, as it has been in some underdeveloped countries at an early stage of growth,[2] the time taken before we can ignore the differences may be considerable.

So far the argument has been conducted in terms of the Johnson assumptions: the one most obviously discordant with the circumstances which prevail in underdeveloped countries being that of the full employment of resources. Do the conditions prevalent in LDCs affect our consistency conditions? With over-population on the land, there is no danger of the capital stock outgrowing the labour force[3] required to work it, so that it is only the first of the consistency options that is required. Since, however, it can certainly be assumed that the working population is growing *at least as fast* as income, the consistency conditions are fulfilled. Nor do the other assumptions of the separate equations present difficulties, as stages in abstraction, except in the assumption of homogeneity made in respect of the parameters

Does the situation alter if we modify the parameters of the equations to accord with the structure and institutions of underdeveloped countries? Can we assume that the propensities to consume domesti-

1. Amortization does not arise on the assumption of financing by perpetual securities.
2. See Appendix, Table III, on Northern Rhodesia 1945–62. In this case there is of course no presumption that Z would remain constant.
3. Shortages of skilled labour are a bottleneck unless this can be imported from abroad.

cally produced goods, to import and to save, will be the same throughout the economy? This assumption, perhaps justified in developed countries, has to be modified in two respects in underdeveloped areas where there is (1) a large population of foreign though resident managerial and technical staff, and/or (2) a high proportion of foreign financing of domestic capital formation over the past and in particular of foreign equity in the ownership of productive capital. Let us consider these two aspects in turn:

(1) The presence of a large foreign population in a country introduces one type of non-homogeneity, if the tastes and incomes of this group are markedly different from those of the native population. C in our simple model relates to the consumption of domestically produced goods and services, and changes in C thus will be determined both by changes in aggregate income and changes in its distribution between these disparate groups. This poses problems in policy making in respect both of growth and of stability. These problems are different in kind from those of communities in which there is a rich native minority, which can perhaps be taxed without leaving the country, and which in any case might represent no important loss of resources if it did emigrate. From the accounting point of view the resident foreign population is treated as constituting part of the "nation". It is valid to aggregate these groups together, but for some purposes it would be better to show them as separate household sectors within the "national" economy. These differences should not be concealed by our accounting methods, which I should prefer to see developed along the pioneering lines of the Rhodesian system, with some further disaggregation to provide the components of an integrated set of domestic and national accounts.[1]

(2) A high proportion of foreign financing introduces a fundamental difference into our equations by making Z larger relative to D, and in borrowing countries such as underdeveloped areas Z is negative. Z will be the larger at any given rate of interest the higher the proportion of the stock of domestic capital which has been financed in the past by borrowing abroad. It is also larger the larger the share of that foreign capital which represents direct investment in productive enterprises. On Johnson's assumption[2] of homogeneous consumption and import functions, we have seen however that Z is favourable to the growth of domestic output. How does the situa-

1. Along the lines suggested by G. Stuvel, *Economica*, 1959.
2. This assumption is plausible of developed countries because foreign held equity and debt is small relatively to that owned by residents.

tion alter if we modify this to the view, more plausible in underdeveloped countries, that interest payments abroad represent savings and imports forgone? If we turn back to equation (7) above we see that Z drops out of the constellation of growth factors if expenditure on domestically produced goods out of Z is zero.

The size of Z makes no difference to the rate of growth of D, which is once again given *either* by equations (3) and (4) when domestic output has no import content *or* by equation (6) if we consider an economy in which the import content of domestic output is q. From the equation (4) if we take the situation in which $b_t = o$ we have again the model for the closed economy, with the difference that b_t now equals $\frac{X-(M+Z)}{D}$.

Nevertheless the model tells us only that D grows irrespective of the size of Z, or the way in which it is changing:[1] it does not tell us what is happening to Y (nor within Y, as we have seen, to the income accruing to nationals proper or at least to permanent residents). As before, however, we can expect D and Y to be positively correlated except in the unlikely circumstances that Z is growing sufficiently faster than D to cause Y to fall.

If Z is large relative to D and represents savings and imports forgone, the propensities to save or import at any given level of national income will be that much smaller. The national propensity to save may also be somewhat unstable since it depends upon the dividend distribution policy of the foreign companies operating in the country.

Since Z drops out of the equations these now take the earlier form subject to the fact that they are describing the equilibrium path of domestic as opposed to national product, and some of Johnson's earlier results now become of interest. I shall draw attention only to three: those in which, taking the rate of growth of exports $\left(\frac{dx}{dt}\frac{1}{X}\right)$ as constant, Johnson shows that if this rate exceeds the rate of growth of income, (i) the latter is falling over time, viz., that domestic income is increasing but at a decreasing rate; (ii) there will be the

1. On his homogeneity assumptions Johnson has investigated the effect of changes in Z. He says "the behaviour of the equilibrium growth rate over time depends on its relation to the rate of growth of interest payments as well as its relation to the rate of growth of exports".

Johnson investigates a number of possibilities (see pp. 127–8), but if we assume that $cZ = O$ then Z drops out of this system. Z can thus move independently of D.

eventual emergence of an export surplus and net foreign lending; (iii) the ratio of the export surplus to total production will rise over time.

The economic meaning of these relative rates of growth is that if a country's equilibrium growth rate is lower than the rate of growth of demand for its exports, it must grow at a decreasing rate if its effective demand is not to outrun its capacity to produce. If it is higher then it must grow at an increasing rate if effective demand is to keep pace with its capacity to produce. Since exports constitute such a large component of final demand in underdeveloped countries, these propositions have more force in their context.

Uses of macro-economic models

Given adjustment of the parameters macro-economic models do not appear to run up against any particular conceptual difficulties in their application to underdeveloped countries. They are couched in real terms and there are, of course, particular difficulties about deflation in countries highly specialized in exports and whose export prices are highly unstable. For many purposes, both practical and conceptual, disaggregation is essential. Nevertheless as a first stage in analysis, such models are conceptually useful at three levels: in the analysis of stability and design of counter-cyclical fiscal and economic policy; in the longer period analysis of recent economic history; and in the design of the broad strategy for economic growth, viz. planning.

Time will not permit the discussion of the first of these, though it should be stressed that exports are still by far the biggest generator of changes in income in this group of countries which is so highly specialized in exports. Investment in the sector producing for the domestic market is still a tiny fraction of total investment in most of these countries and it is a still tinier fraction of final demand. Most underdeveloped countries have taken measures in one way or another to insulate their economies from short-period fluctuations in world demand and world prices[1] of their exports, changes in which now have little direct effect upon supply of the primary products concerned, although they do have considerable impact upon the finances of development.

Nor shall I spend much time on the second, since this will be of

1. E.g. through Marketing Boards, variable export levies, multiple exchange rates, etc.

relatively little interest to those who are trying to change the future of their countries. Nevertheless the models do provide some interesting clues to questions about relative rates of growths, as I shall try to show by taking a few examples from the history of the last 100 years or so. They can also be useful in crystallizing the nature of certain broad planning choices in an open economy of the kind with which we are concerned. In what follows there is no intention of suggesting that economics can explain everything. I offer my few examples to sustain the view that it can nevertheless take us a long way. It will be noted that these models do not derive from principles of comparative advantage, although there are economists[1] who consider that they are not incompatible with a modified doctrine of some such kind.

Examples from recent history

What does all this tell us about differences in country rates of growth? These models are only capable of giving a qualitative interpretation of historical situations because the constants of the equations (σ, a, m, q and z) cannot be presumed to have remained the same over long stretches of time. x, the rate of growth of exports, is in the case of primary producer countries closely geared to the rate of growth of the world economy, but as each new tropical country entered upon world trade in the last decades of the nineteenth century the impetus given to its exports must have been specially great for one or two decades.

The course of events in any particular country must therefore be interpreted with its own historical circumstances in mind (e.g. timing of entry into world trade, type of commodity exported, conditions of production, and so on), but also with booms and slumps in world trade as a background influence. While the rate of growth of exports of primary products as a whole was high before 1914 and even up to 1927 and 1928, it fell in the 1930s to a low figure, with consequent deflationary impact upon the economies of countries highly specialized in the export of primary products.

The advent of mass production in the twentieth century also increased the scale of industrial operations sharply, making the costs of entry higher and limiting profitability of investment in producing for the domestic market in small underdeveloped countries when these were open to competition from abroad.

1. See, for example, H. B. Chenery, *American Economic Review*, 1961.

Similarly the propensity to import consumer goods (m above) was much lower before the advent of cheap sea transport and the opening up of the Suez and Panama Canals in the last decades of the nineteenth century. Although in Japan the rate of growth of exports of silk[1] was phenomenally high for three decades, imports of consumer goods (m) remained lower than imports of raw materials and equipment for domestic manufacture (q). Before 1900 the value of m is likely to have been low in new countries.

Differences in rates of growth between countries cannot be ascribed to individual economic factors when there are so many parameters to take into account. Nor are economic factors the only ones to be considered as we began by saying. Yet it is of interest to ponder two whose influence is only implicit in our equations: (*a*) the part played by foreign though resident populations, and (*b*) foreign (i.e. non-resident) capital and enterprise.

(*a*) *Foreign populations*

Whereas up till 1900 high transport costs made for colonization or settlement of immigrants in developing countries, the twentieth century saw the emergence of a class of immigrant skilled workers and managers who resided in the foreign country only for the period of their employment there, and that interspersed with long leaves at "home". Both these classes of foreigners brought to the countries concerned a higher level of technical competence and, as they came from countries with a higher standard of living, both tried to maintain their old standards in their new surroundings. In the new countries of the nineteenth century this had to be done by increasing C, the output of domestically produced consumer goods, whereas in those entering world trade after 1890 it could, because of low transport costs, be done by increasing the import of consumer goods. The settler populations of the nineteenth century were also willing to invest in production for the domestic market, because they were content to enjoy their increased incomes within the country of settlement. Scale being much less important, they were also able to do so successfully and by ploughing back their profits were able to increase C. We should expect therefore that with all these factors in mind countries[2] colonized before 1900 would show self-sustaining growth as indeed they did.

1. Because of a variety of favourable circumstances, such as the coincidence of silkworm disease in France and Italy with the opening of the Suez Canal.
2. The Regions of Recent Settlement, as Eugene Staley termed them. These include the U.S.A. and Canada, Australia, New Zealand and South Africa.

Although Japan had no settlers her growth is to be explained along similar lines, with the additional influence of a vigorous government intent on fostering the development of increasing technical skill at home and on building up the capital stock of the country as far as possible out of domestic sources of financing. We may say that the Japanese tried to keep low m relative to q and both (m and q) low relative to c.

We may well ask why it was that India did not make similar progress. Export specialization has always been small in India, even after the tremendous expansion of exports following Suez in 1867, and the natural protection of high transport costs still operated to limit imports. Why did this not lead to an expansion of investment in production for the domestic market? Was it because European settlement in India was negligible? Some expansion there was,[1] but Indian technical and managerial skill was limited and was supplemented by immigration of temporary residents who preferred British imports to Indian manufactures and spent a large fraction of their earnings on services from abroad.[2] India, at the stage when transport costs still offered some natural protection, itself lacked a government bent, like the Japanese, on fostering domestic production at the expense of imports.

The other dependencies of Europe were also allowed by passive administrations to develop into the export-import economies with technical and managerial skill supplied by immigrants. By this time import costs were falling further through improvements in shipping services and later through the advent of mass production. Thus political factors must be adduced as well in order to account for the vigour with which the governments of Australia, Chile, Argentina and Brazil turned between the wars to fostering industrialization for the domestic market when the fall in the rate of growth of primary product exports threatened deflation at home, while countries less vigorously governed by contrast suffered the deflation passively to be caught in "a low level equilibrium trap". There are many other elements in the history of the period before 1939 to which attention must be given, but the failure of this last group of countries to industrialize between the wars was partly

1. The family enterprises of both Tata and Birla date from the late nineteenth century.
2. Such service imports include tourism (home leave) and expenditure on children's education. These immigrants also made transfers to dependants abroad.

due to the changed technical conditions[1] of the twentieth century which kept m high relatively to c and hence to q, and by failing to increase the growth of domestic production outside the export-sector, thus maintained a high ratio of $\frac{X}{D}$.

(*b*) *Foreign capital*

The other respect in which the nineteenth century differed from our own was in the much higher proportion of private capital from abroad which was available at fixed interest. In the Regions of Recent Settlement both the new settler governments and new enterprises were able to borrow from private investors abroad at fixed interest to finance the import of capital. The ownership of the equity of new enterprises remained therefore in settler hands, and expansion was financed largely by reinvestment of profits. The rate of interest paid on foreign borrowing in the nineteenth century was thus much lower than that which was earned on private investment in twentieth-century colonies, since so much of the latter has been on an equity basis.

Further, reinvestment of the profits of domestic enterprises adds less to the balance of payments burden when the equity is owned by nationals than when the equity is held abroad. For in the latter case the aggregate profit available for distribution grows with the growth of the capital stock[2] even if the profit margin is moderate and dividend distribution limited to some fraction of net profits. In the European dependencies of the twentieth century direct investment has played a major role while the national or even residents' share of the equity was small. While the share of profits in domestic product may well have been no higher than usual, their share in the national product was small.

Z is thus likely to have been large in relation to D and may have

1. E.g. the greater scale of operations required by best-practice techniques when domestic production was left to face import competition with neither natural nor artificial protection, and the high levels of technical skill required both in management and operation of industrial enterprises, and necessitated the presence of migrant skilled labour.

2. Australian experience with General Motors–Holden illustrates this point. In 1953–54 the profits of this one company, although only 14 per cent of sales, and 24 per cent on funds employed, ran at 39 per cent of shareholders' equity and 560 per cent of General Motors original investment. Dividends paid abroad amounted to 11 per cent of funds employed, 18 per cent on shareholders' equity, 260 per cent on the original investment and 8 per cent of Australian dollar receipts in 1954–55. Cf. Penrose, *Economic Journal*, 1956.

been growing in the twentieth century. Though Y must also have been rising, at least until 1929 when world depression altered all trends for a decade, it is not possible to say how fast it (Y) was growing. Nor is it possible to say whether the export surplus on merchandise trade so characteristic of many underdeveloped countries before 1939 was due to the persistence of a higher rate of growth of exports than of domestic product[1] or to the high level of Z, or both. The last of these three explanations is perhaps the most plausible, since exports undoubtedly grew faster than domestic product and since they were foreign financed, factor income paid abroad would have been positively correlated with them till 1929 at least. In the slump years of the 1930s when current profits fell the persistence of an export surplus perhaps indicates an outflow of capital.

Models and the strategy of planning in an open economy

Recognizing once again that highly aggregated models are only useful as a first stage in the definition of planning objectives, let us examine some brief examples of their possible use. In what follows we must distinguish between models based upon the assumption of unlimited financing by incoming transfers from abroad and those with a balance of payments barrier to face.

Let us begin with the cost and benefits of employing skilled labour from abroad. If this labour has to be remunerated entirely from national resources its costs are the imports (and savings transferred abroad, if any) forgone, while benefits reside in the higher techniques which their presence makes it possible for a country to adopt. Only on the assumption of financing the increases in payments abroad by an inflow of transfers can an underdeveloped country ignore the rise in m which accompanies the rise in σ. Where the skilled personnel are employed by public authorities in the developing countries this cost has been recognized by schemes of international or bilateral technical assistance,[2] but the contribution to the total supply of skill financed in this was has not been very large (nor is its impact on σ always identifiable).

When it is a question of skilled personnel in productive enterprise such services do not rate for international subsidy and the balance of

1. The export surplus on merchandise trade was too large a fraction of the export bill to be accounted for by service imports in most of these countries. The difference after allowing for insurance, freight and other items is thus due to factor income paid abroad and the export of capital.
2. E.g. U.N. Technical Assistance Administration, Colombo Plan.

payments elements become critical. Underdeveloped countries are apt to consider the costs of hiring such labour excessive. Nationals are cheaper as far as import cost and transfers are concerned, but in the short run they may have adverse effects on efficiency (σ). Refusal to use foreign technicians may also slow down the rate of importation of new techniques. Many countries are seeking a way out of this dilemma by using skilled labour with a lower requirement in consumer imports but similar levels of technical skill, e.g. Japanese, Israeli or Italian, while they use the foreign exchange thus saved upon training of their own nationals.

A similar analysis of costs and benefits can be applied to the financing of economic development. The national product will constitute a higher fraction of domestic product the higher the financing by nationals (including the State), next best comes financing by loans at fixed interest, and last comes direct investment from abroad. However, the domestic product is affected in exactly the reverse order, foreign direct investment being most likely to import new techniques and to find the managerial and technical skill from abroad that may be required, and thus the most likely to produce the greatest expansion of the domestic product. While one system of financing may be preferred to another when transfers from abroad are ample, the order may change sharply if a balance of payments barrier exists.

The ordering of benefits also changes if we consider the balance of payments consequences of a given total investment: where this is done by nationals there is no addition to foreign exchange resources; if by fixed interest loans, the foreign exchange credited is the full amount of the loan, but a subsequent deduction must be accounted in for payments of interest and amortization; if by private direct investment, the foreign exchange contribution depends upon the import content of the original investment outlay, firms borrowing as far as possible locally to pay for local resources in order to keep the capital at risk at a minimum, subsequent outpayments by firms depend upon rates of profit and distribution policy, on the one hand, and the rate of reinvestment and of capital export on the other.

Since the profits of enterprises do not enter into the growth equations the choice of financing, insofar as this lies with recipient countries, can be taken *inter alia* in the light of its effect upon the other parameters of the equations.

This brings out the point, often misunderstood by foreign economists in underdeveloped countries, that economic policy cannot solely concern itself with maximizing the rate of growth of domestic product. It is the producing of a high self-sustaining rate of growth of national product with which the governments of underdeveloped countries are concerned and perhaps more particularly with that of the income accruing to nationals proper.

It also indicates that, in the absence of ample financing by transfers from abroad, there is a limit to the part that can be played by foreign direct investment, unless this leads directly or indirectly to a fresh increase in exports.

There is little need to carry the examples further, in order to make the point that the use of macro-economic models in planning brings home the interdependence of our economic transactions in a way which it would be impossible to achieve otherwise.

Conclusion

In teaching economic development I have tried to show that there is a great deal to be gained by making use of certain parts of orthodox economic theory. The parts selected are widely accepted, whatever the nature of the allocative mechanism which is held to lie behind them by the different schools of economic thought.

All the analysis has been couched in the language of orthodox economics, leaving open the issues so much still in dispute as to the functioning of the allocative mechanism. The models I have used do not involve the assumptions of classical trade theory which requires that the effects of changes in the supply of factors be reflected in the market mechanism over time. To adopt comparative advantage as a principle of planning does not involve time in the same way, as this can be done within the framework of comparative statics.

The limitations of the price mechanism as the sole allocative device, particularly severe in underdeveloped countries, do not invalidate the use of macro-economic growth models in such areas. In growth models the emphasis is upon the sequence of expansion of production and upon factor use by sector instead of upon conditions of general equilibrium. Nor is there any inconsistency in turning again to the price-mechanism for use in planning, whether the "prices" used in the model are "shadow" prices or market ones.

This should not be taken to imply that economics can "explain" everything. Behind the values given to the different parameters of these economic models there are institutional, sociological and even psychological factors. Like all technicians working in underdeveloped areas economists may find themselves forced to become Jacks-of-all-trades. The temptation to adopt "psychosomatic" interpretations of "backwardness" is very great, but in my view economists, like doctors, have a duty to subject the patient to a thorough physical examination before pronouncing him to be a psychological case.

A training in the techniques of physical examination (economic analysis) is in any case the only discipline that we are qualified as teachers to pass on. Teaching economic development should not be read as telling the people of the underdeveloped countries what they must do, as this involves action upon a number of different levels, political, institutional, sociological and psychological, as well as economic. What we are equipped to teach is the nature of the economic system in which they live and the degree of interdependence of economic action. If they learn techniques by which to study not only the direct but the "feedback" effects of economic choices they will have been well trained.

Teaching Economic Planning at the Institute of Social Studies, The Hague

L. J. ZIMMERMAN

1. The Institute of Social Studies—The Hague, Netherlands—aims at promoting international research and training in the social sciences, with particular emphasis on problems of rapid social change and economic development. The Institute, which was established by the Netherlands Universities Foundation for International Co-operation in 1952, offers at this moment a great many Diploma Courses, e.g. in Public Administration, Economic Planning, Statistics and National Accounting, Comprehensive Planning, Social Policy, National Development, and some Degree Courses, e.g. one for Master of Social Sciences and one for Master of Public Administration. Two new Diploma Courses, one in International Relations and one in Industrial Development, are planned for the near future.

2. In 1957 the Institute launched a Course in Economic Planning and National Accounting. In 1962 this was split into two new Courses, one in Economic Planning and the other in Statistics and National Accounting.

It is my intention to deal here mainly with the course in Economic Planning. So far 168 participants have been enrolled in the course, 40 per cent of whom came from Europe (mainly from the Southern and Eastern part), 30 per cent from Asia, 20 per cent from Latin America, and 10 per cent from Africa. A few came from Oceania and from the U.S.A. The course aims at mid-career training (the average age of the participants is between 30 and 35), and assumes a good training in economics (an M.A. economics is a prerequisite) and experience in a planning agency. However, occasionally students are admitted who have just finished their University studies.

3. Because we know from experience that in low-income countries it is very difficult to send good mid-career people on leave, we decided immediately that the course should not exceed half a year. I am still convinced that a mid-career training course should not last longer than six months, because otherwise it is impossible to get good people.

4. Starting a course in Economic Planning in The Hague has of

course the consequence that the course is immediately associated with the Dutch Central Planning Bureau with its econometric approach towards planning problems. From the very beginning econometric model-building has played an important role in the course, but this implied that a certain knowledge of mathematics was considered one of the prerequisites for admission to the course. It turned out rather soon that mathematical knowledge was unevenly distributed over the course participants and that a refresher course in mathematics and model-building was needed.

We also learned that some of our course participants were mainly interested in national accounting and had only a slight interest in econometrics. Since the lack of statistical data is one of the great bottlenecks in development planning, we decided to divide the course into one in Statistics and National Accounting, laying special emphasis on the question: how to develop statistics; and another in Economic Planning, where the availability of statistics is assumed.

Nowadays in the Economic Planning Course only a general introduction to national accounting is given; the problem of how to make up national accounts is dealt with in the course in Statistics. These classes are optional for the participants of the Planning Course.

Apart from the refresher course in mathematics, tutorials are given to those lagging behind. Generally speaking, about 10 per cent of the participants are not able to master the econometric approach: for those participants special programmes have to be designed, because we are all convinced that somebody can be a very valuable planner without a mathematical background.

5. When we started the Planning Course we assumed that a good planner should understand the philosophical background of planning and also the social implications of planning. We therefore in the beginning included some classes dealing with those topics, e.g. "The principles of social justice" and "Prognostication and social consequences of economic measures". Although I still think that this assumption is correct, I came to the conclusion that those topics should not be included in a *training course* in Economic Planning. Today I am convinced that "widening of insight" should come after "deepening of insight", and that therefore such topics can much better be dealt with in a seminar at the end of the course. We are aiming now at multi-disciplinary seminars at the end of the course, together with participants of other courses, but I shall come back to this topic later.

6. I believe that during the first few years our course concentrated too much on Dutch experiences in planning, which were much more

in the field of short-term (business cycle) planning than in long-run (structural) planning. Although I have been asked to speak here about our experiences in teaching economic planning and therefore want to discuss only where and how we gradually changed the course, let me nevertheless say here that I do not think that our course five years ago was all that bad. We gave our participants a good deal of training in economic theory and econometrics and we certainly deepened their insight into those fields. However, the problem of the applicability of the theory in their own countries was somewhat neglected.

Let me emphasise here that this was not particularly felt by our course participants; they wanted to learn all the "new techniques", perhaps more because they assumed that that would increase their status at home than because they thought that they would be able to apply them in the near future (this certainly holds true for linear programming).

But the *Faculty* in charge of the Economic Planning Course (and especially those members who had experience of planning in low-income countries) became more and more convinced that it was necessary that the course should specialize more on the conditions in low-income countries.

7. First a few words about this Faculty. The Institute works with a very small permanent staff and staff members act as the Chairmen of the various courses: they organize the courses and invite the lecturers. Now we all know that University people are awfully difficult to organize: they know their topic, they know how to deal with it and they know how to lecture on it. But rather often, the most beautiful courses on paper turn out to be completely different things in reality, because, once before the class, every professor mounts his own hobby-horse. There is today—at least in many of the continental universities—still much truth in Omar Khayyam's complaint:

> Myself when young did eagerly frequent
> Doctor and Saint, and heard great Argument
> About it and about: but evermore
> Came out by the same Door as in I went.

My greatest headache for years therefore has been to mould the Faculty into a team capable of dealing with the topic of economic planning in a comprehensive and consistent way.

I think that in the end we have found a solution, and although I certainly do not claim that it is the only one, I think that it might be useful to discuss it here.

8. The idea is a rather simple one. Take an underdeveloped country and assume that an economic development plan is needed in that country. Now ask the faculty to make the plan. This implies that the work has to be divided between the various faculty members, but because all elements are now interrelated, national accounting, input-output analysis, structural and short-term planning and fiscal policy (to give only a few examples) are no longer taught independently, but as elements of the general planning process. The method has the great advantage that the participants understand immediately why the individual classes are given. I do not mind if it is argued that this is nothing but applying the case-study method. Although I think that there exists a fundamental difference, I really do not claim any originality.

9. The great difficulty, however, was to select one particular country, for two different reasons. Every country has certain quite unique features and it is not of much use to deal with them in a general training course. In the second place, most of the participants get bored after a certain time when in all classes only one particular country is dealt with. Further, the occasional participant from that country would be placed in a rather awkward position, especially when political problems are involved, as they always are.

I therefore decided that the best solution would be the creation of an imaginary country in which all kinds of underdevelopment features could be found.

10. I based my conviction that it is possible to create such a country on the fact that I have found rather close correlations between the *per capita* incomes of a great many (thirty-five) countries and certain socio-economic variables. Thus by taking the theoretical values of those variables at a certain income level one is able to construct the ideal type of say a $200 *per capita* income country. Some of those data, together with the correlation coefficients, are given here:

	Per capita income		
	$200	$800	R
Percentage employment in the secondary and tertiary sector	48%	78%	0.92
Energy consumption (coal equivalent, kg.)	340 kg.	2,550 kg.	0.95
Motor cars (per 10,000 inhabitants)	70	780	0.94
Newsprint consumption (kg.)	1.8 kg.	13.3 kg.	0.93
Working hours per week	55	43	0.90
Hospital beds (per 1,000 inhabitants)	4	9	—
Doctors (per 100,000 inhabitants)	40	100	—
Taxation as percentage of national income	13%	24%	0.82
Direct taxes as percentage of total tax revenue	23%	55%	0.89

We decided to construct a country with a *per capita* income of $250 (Greece, Spain, Brazil, Mexico, e.g.), because in such a country one may assume enough statistical data for planning purposes, and one may further assume that at such an income level enough qualified people are available to set up and execute a plan. We called the country "Utonia", and assumed that it had 10 million inhabitants.

11. We started with the construction of a system of national accounts, an input-output matrix and a family budget survey. By doing so, we had thus determined total consumption and investment, production in the various sectors, imports, exports, etc. But of course much more data on agrarian production were needed and an Industrial Census and Foreign Trade Statistics had to be worked out. But because it was also intended to make use of Utonia in other Institute Courses, many data on the history of the country, its social conditions (e.g. education) and its administrative structure had to be added. This opened the way to multi-disciplinary seminars, mentioned already in section 5. Our Public Administration people, for example, have already discussed with our Social Policy people the setting up of a Community Development project in one of the regions of Utonia. Here indeed the widening came after the deepening and the discussions turned out to be very useful.

12. When all the data were collected and their consistency checked (although even in Utonia statistics are not infallible) a Social-Economic survey of Utonia was written. This survey contained all data needed to set up a system of national accounts so that one of the first exercises of the course participants could be the construction of this system. The survey also provides the data for long-term and sectoral planning (the input-output matrix is given), and therefore it becomes easy to demonstrate the method of "planning in stages" and it is also easy to show how much trial and error accompanies the planning process.

13. As far as the Faculty is concerned, the response has been very favourable. For them it meant much additional work, but it turned out to be a fascinating job. Let me only mention here that the long term plan asked for a system of 100 equations that had to be solved with the aid of a computer. But because the final results of one stage had to be used in the next one, the Faculty became a much greater unity: everybody understood that he had to continue where his predecessor had left off. It also became clear to the organizer of the course that so far certain aspects of the planning process had been neglected and we had to introduce a few new series of lectures in order to fill those gaps.

14. How did our course participants react to this new approach? I have to distinguish here between two types of participants. One group, generally speaking a minority but often the very good ones, has been sent to us by their respective offices in order to study a very specific question for their own country. They normally concentrate on that topic from the very beginning. The others do not come with specific questions and about half of them start working on our project. Problems like regional development, the association of Utonia with the Common Market, the projection of the electricity consumption and the improvement of the existing port facilities are a few of the topics dealt with in Diploma Theses. We have especially sponsored feasibility studies and have studied the fertilizer and cement industries.

At regular intervals we hold meetings of the "Planning Board" where the outcomes of these studies are discussed. Especially when somebody is defending *his* project, these meetings become rather realistic, and we have often had strong disagreement about project priorities.

15. Because six months is a very short time in which to deal with all these topics, we have to take care that the participants work as hard as possible. I think that the best way to "squeeze" them is to introduce tests at rather frequent intervals. It is sometimes assumed that it is difficult, if not impossible, to "test" somewhat older people, especially those from underdeveloped countries, because they cannot afford the "loss of face" when they fail. We came to the conclusion that this depends entirely on the way in which the idea of tests is introduced to them and how the results are communicated to the class. Of course we cannot avoid occasionally having real failures, i.e. people who cannot be awarded the course diploma. So far I have managed to avoid *formal* failures, because I know that the majority of our participants are sent to us by their offices in the expectation that they could be promoted after having followed the course. A formal failure would ruin their prospects. In the very weak cases we tell the people that they have not yet fulfilled all the requirements and that they should improve their diploma thesis after their return home.

16. This year we are using Utonia for the second time and I expect that in about a year's time our final results will be ready. I hope by then to be able to publish the first report on the conditions in Utonia and to initiate a prize award for the best development plan for Utonia. I think that the publication of a few of these plans will be an interesting contribution to the theory of planning.

Appendix: Survey of the classes given in the Economic Planning Course, 1964

1. Introduction
2. Refresher Course in mathematics
3. Mathematical Statistical Techniques
4. Systems of Equations
5. Long Term Planning
6. Short Term Planning

7a. Concepts of National Accounting
7b. The Making of National Accounts (optional)
7c. National Accounting and Planning
8a. Input-Output Tables, concepts
8b. Input-Output Tables, analysis
9a. Organization of a Planning Office
9b. Administrative Aspects of the Implementation of a Plan: the Case of France
10a. Theories of Growth, Development and Progress
10b. New Developments in the Approach to Planning
10c. Manpower Planning
10d. Sector Models
10e. Monetary Policy for Economic Development
10f. Taxation Policy for Economic Development
11a. Investment Priorities
11b. Balanced Growth and Agriculture
11c. Institutions Financing Economic Development
11d. Physical Implications of Planning
12a. Infrastructural Projects
12b. Agricultural Projects

13. Regional Planning
14. Planning in the Soviet Union
15. Planning in India

(This survey does not indicate the strict chronological order of the classes).

Someone may be interested in how we set up the Course for the first year:

Survey of the classes given in the Economic Planning and Social Accounting Course 1957:

1. Comparative Economic Systems
2. Theory of Economic Development

3a. Outlines of Social Accounting

3b. Industrial, public and social accounting
4. Statistics
5. Theory of planning
6. Social psychology of opinion formation
7. Principles of social justice
8. Social Accounting under conditions of a rapidly expanding economy
9. New techniques of comprehensive development planning, with special reference to the allocation of priorities
10a. Post-war planning for reconstruction in Europe
10b. Planning in the European Coal and Steel Community
10c. Planning in the U.S.S.R.
10d. Planning under conditions of a rapidly expanding economy: special cases
10e. International economics and planning
11. Social research methods, with special reference to the preparation of economic development plans
12. Prognostication of social consequences of economic measures
13. Political implications of economic development plans, case studies
14. Case studies in long-term planning:
14a. Netherlands
14b. Yugoslavia
14c. Southern Italy
15. Administrative preparation and implementation of comprehensive development plans.

Teaching Economic Development at Manchester

KURT MARTIN

TRAINING or study courses in the field of economic and social development have sprung up all over the world in the course of the last ten years or so. In this country and the United States the predominant tendency has been to set up such courses within the structure of the university where this new speciality—if that is the right word for it—is grafted on to the regular courses. In other countries the more frequent practice has been to create special institutions, sometimes governmental, and in addition there are training programmes and institutions under the auspices of the regional Commissions and specialized agencies of the United Nations.

The various courses have in common their concern with those parts of the social sciences that are thought to have a direct bearing on the problems of developing countries. But there is great variety regarding the substance of teaching programmes, the duration of courses, and the selection of participants. Some courses are multidisciplinary, others are more highly specialized. A course in economic development which tries to convey "basic principles" to civil servants with no or little formal training in economics (such as the course run by the International Bank), is obviously very different from a course designed to train economic planners in programming techniques. Again, there are short mid-career courses lasting at the most six months, and longer courses extending over one academic year, or more. University courses usually are of the one-year type; nevertheless they may be designed for, or attended by, people who have already begun their career.

The following observations refer to our Manchester Diploma Course which was set up in 1960 on the initiative and under the direction of Dr. John Mars and was gradually expanded to its present size with the aid of a Ford Foundation grant.

The course is designed for graduates and most participants have a degree in economics: holders of degrees in other subjects are a very small minority and non-graduates are admitted only in exceptional cases. Applications mainly come from people in developing countries: in the current year (1963–64) there is only one student from the U.K. among the eighteen people whom we admitted.[1]

About half our students are young economists employed in planning offices or other government departments in developing countries; they are sent here for a further period of study. Most of the others want to prepare either for a civil service or a university career. In age our students usually range between 23 and 33.

The course we offer is divided into two parts, each taking one year. The first year is devoted to preliminary work at undergraduate level. We find this arrangement necessary because many of our Diploma students had a rather poor previous education in economics, even though they hold degrees. But we do permit people with a good record to go straight to Part II; where we are in doubt, we make our decision dependent on an entrance test. Currently about one-third of the newcomers are excused from Part I.

The Diploma is awarded on the basis of a written examination. Those who do well in the examination are allowed to proceed to a one-year M.A. course (if they wish), and our experience is that at least a third of the Diploma students actually stay on for higher degree work.

The composition and content of the teaching programme are different today from what they were a year or two ago, and will be different again next year. The following is a description of our plans for the forthcoming session:[2]

Part I

(i) Mathematics for Economists
(ii) Economic Statistics
(iii) Theory of Economic Development—I
(iv) Workshop on Empirical Aspects of Development Problems

Part II

(v) Theory of Economic Development—II
(vi) Statistical Techniques and Sources for Development Programming
(vii) *Two* further subjects chosen from a list of options (including Agricultural Development, Industrial Development, Case

1. (Postscript) Our present (1966) admission rate is between twenty-five and thirty, of whom four or five are from the U.K.
2. This description differs slightly from that presented at the Conference, when our plans were not yet final.

Studies in Economic Development, Comparative Economic Systems, Quantitative Economics, Transport Economics, International Economics, or some other approved subject).

The *curriculum* of Part I is quite rigid and offers no choice. The Workshop is for Diploma students only (see later), while all other courses in Part I are also taken by undergraduates, either as compulsory subjects or as options. All courses in Part II are postgraduate courses, except for some of the options.

There are two general comments on our teaching programme which I wish to make here. First, it is evident that this is not a multi-disciplinary course. We all appreciate that many disciplines have relevant things to say about development, but do not believe that a proliferation of courses across the disciplinary boundaries will help. The so-called non-economic factors ought to come in at each *stage* of the argument, rather than discipline by discipline. We therefore define the economic subject matter of development very broadly, but admit that problems of administration, for instance, do not receive the informed treatment they deserve. We hope to make up for this by inviting members of other Departments to take part in our Workshop and shall also experiment next year with an inter-disciplinary research seminar at staff level. Secondly, I wish to stress that, although civil servants working in planning offices form the largest single group among our students, we do not regard the course as a vocational training programme for planners. The course is more broadly based as we want to provide a *general* education in economics relevant to developing countries. Programming is an important *part* of the teaching in the second year; it is a compulsory subject which occupies 2–3 teaching hours a week covering—(i) the study of the anatomy of the economy (different systems of national accounting), (ii) the study of programming techniques (input-output, linear programming, simulation method, etc.), (iii) the formulation of planning models, and (iv) problems of application. These topics are part of present-day knowledge, to which our students ought to be introduced. But the instruction is kept at a relatively elementary level, and the *curriculum* as a whole, as it now stands, marks a certain shift away from the very strong concentration on mathematical analysis, which dominated the course in the earlier years.

May I now say a few words about the *Theory course* which, extending over two years, is devoted to the central theme of our programme: the study of growth and change in pre-industrial economies. Very briefly, the present plan of this course is as follows: our starting-point is the description of a pre-industrial economy, where there is a large amount of subsistence production. The economy may be more or less stationary—or stable with respect to average income—as it contains strong forces working against changes. The initiation of development and the problems surrounding the incentive to invest are among the first questions to be raised, but we soon shift to the problems which growth is bound to *create* in such economies, to the path that it may take and the chief constraints to which it is likely to be subject. At this stage in the argument it is possible to outline a broad scheme of analysis which can be applied to a wide variety of development phenomena. But as the argument proceeds it is necessary to be more specific about the initial conditions. Our main concern is with the development of the late-comers (which involves a comparison with the pioneers), and we find it useful to analyse first the development of countries where there is no pressure of population on agricultural land or where there are rich specific natural resources. This covers sequences of the kind described by Myint (1958), where peasant units with surplus capacity of labour and land are seen to move into the money economy (for exports) while retaining primitive handicrafts; it also covers the emergence of wage employment in export sectors and the phenomena of dualism in such economies. The relations between an advanced industrial sector and the traditional economy becomes the dominant theme when we go on to the study of growth in overpopulated peasant countries. A large part of the discussion under this heading is devoted to the elaboration of the Lewis model and its various extensions and applications.

By the end of the first year we have completed a series of analyses which do not add up to an all-embracing theory of development, but give some insights into the working of a pre-industrial economy and into the main determinants and historical patterns of economic growth.

There is no sharp break between Part I and Part II of the Theory course: there is a gradual shift in emphasis, which in the second year is on the problems of public policy, i.e. on the role of the State, the effects of different types of interventions and reforms, and on the questions of an investment programme and of efficient accumulation. This part of the course is complementary to the study of programming techniques in the second year.

The Theory course plays an important role in our programme.

It provides the unifying theme and introduces the participants to the existing body of knowledge, much of which is classical in ancestry. It serves as a revision and critical review of economic theory as one tries to apply the formal apparatus of economics to the phenomena of development. But a course of this kind, which is bound to stress the general rather than the particular, can never be wholly satisfactory, and we have therefore decided to introduce a Workshop in order to strengthen our teaching programme on the empirical side.

The *Workshop* is a weekly seminar devoted to the examination of narrower or more specific issues: we take the structure of foreign trade of a particular country, or its fiscal (or tenure) system, or study a river project, a regional plan, a stabilisation programme, and so on. No more than four or five topics are selected each year so that they can be examined in some detail. In doing such empirical studies one is forced to ask what figures really mean, how they were collected, how to make use of makeshift data, and so on. This is an essential part of the training.

A Workshop is not easy to run. It requires much preparation and it is rarely possible to pursue case studies on the basis of published material only: one needs additional documentation and possibly field experience. We are only now approaching the stage where we can hope that this part of the programme will be effective.[1]

We know of the work which some of our former students are now doing in government departments at home and in one country have actually participated in their work. What we have seen has convinced us that the course has helped to strengthen the analytical ability and professional competence of the participants.

To sum up: our teaching programme includes a number of subjects which are part of the normal syllabus of any student of economics. Our main interest, however (in this particular course), is in

1. (Postscript) Our actual Workshop procedure, as it has developed in the years following the Conference, is that each student takes up one topic only, which is chosen from among the problems of his own country; he concentrates on this topic throughout the year and at the end of the year delivers a research paper based on his findings. Students are encouraged in advance to bring relevant empirical materials with them from their home countries. The group meets every week to discuss the method of approach to work and the results as they come along. For administrative reasons the Workshop is confined for the time being to the first year; it is followed in the second year by a seminar conducted on different lines. But in future we hope to be able to extend the Workshop into the second year.

the problems of pre-industrial countries. This is a field where textbook economics does not take us very far and may even be an obstacle to understanding, certainly in inexpert hands. Taking an analytical approach, we have to reconsider a good many conventional theorems and notions.

It is also true, however, that in lectures and discussions we find it necessary, again and again, to go back to certain axioms or basic tools of economic analysis: to the concept of opportunity cost, the idea of a market, or to propositions about supply and demand. We do not teach these principles *ab ovo*, but it is one thing to have heard of them and quite another to get used to thinking in these terms. We are all very impatient, I suppose, with traditional equilibrium analysis which, to paraphrase Seers, is the economics of *No* real case. Yet there is embedded in it something that ought to be part of the "trained instinct" of an economist. A course in economic development which fails to convey or transmit this cannot be counted a success.

PART TWO

Oral discussion

Part A. The State of Knowledge

EDITED BY JOHN KNAPP

Opening Remarks

JOAN ROBINSON

WHAT have we got to offer to a student who comes to us from an underdeveloped country to learn economics?

We cannot tell him the answer to what he wants to know. His preoccupation is primarily political. "Which way should my country go?"

In general terms, the case for private property in the means of production cannot be made to appear as strong as the case for socialism and thorough-going planning; but it is not our business to tell our pupils that they ought to go home and make a revolution. On the other hand, it is not our business to tell them that they ought not.

We must try to teach them that part of economics which is generally true and can be helpful in any political setting.

What can be helpful is analysis, not doctrine.

Neoclassical economic theory was built up around the presumption in favour of laissez-faire. It was, therefore, very little concerned to produce operational concepts.

Moreover it was concerned mainly with the allocation of scarce resources with alternative uses. It, therefore, had little to say about development.

The Keynesian revolution finally shattered the presumption in favour of laissez-faire, which had been already riddled with exceptions, and introduced national-income accounting, which prepared the way for modern conceptions of planning.

But, looking back, it is astonishing how little consideration was given to the problems of long-run development before the war.

To find the economics of development we have to go back to the pre-neoclassical theories—that is to Ricardo and Marx—and forward to the post-Keynesian which is only now coming into being.

To take an example, when the second five year plan was being discussed in India the economists, who were mainly not yet even Keynesians, had very little to contribute. It was Mahalanobis who put afloat a version of the Harrod formula in terms of the share of investment in national income, the capital-output ratio and the rate of growth.

This way of thinking is of course only the very first beginning. A crude aggregate approach is useful only as an escape from the shackles of neoclassicism.

In fact the Indian plan suffered very much from being insufficiently disaggregated.

It is just as important to warn our pupils against new bad mental habits as against the old ones.

In particular, global thinking leads to overlooking the differences in treatment required for agriculture and industry.

To take another example, economists trained in the neoclassical tradition feel obliged to excuse the use of import controls in a developing country through some tortuous application of the Bickerdicke argument.

It would be better to start from the observation that the situation happens to be such that the purchasing power of foreign exchange over equipment and know-how for investment is far higher than the purchasing power of home resources; therefore none of it should be wasted on inessential imports.

All the same we must not lose sight of what was valuable in the old orthodoxy. In the U.S.S.R. the laws of supply and demand had to be learned the hard way.

The law of comparative costs must not be forgotten when the development of new export industries is being discussed. And the free trade doctrine still shows that the wider the area over which development can be planned coherently the higher the level of productivity that can be attained.

All this, of course, is only common sense. But common sense can be bamboozled by economic doctrines and strengthened by training in economic analysis.

Mr. Streeten

Mr. Streeten said that he entirely agreed with what Mrs. Robinson had said and would only like to supplement her remarks with a brief gloss on the salient points of his own paper.

It is, Mr. Streeten thought, not only the liberal laissez-faire doctrine that has been unhelpful in the formulation of operational concepts about planning for development. Marxist theory, as it is often presented, has not been very helpful either. There is a very important distinction between Marxist theory and Soviet practice. The Soviet practice is not in conformity with what many Marxists profess. In Marxist theory there is incorporated a particular version of one of the systematic biases which, Mr. Streeten said, he had called the *ceteris paribus* bias in his paper. In the laissez-faire theory, this bias takes the form referred to by Mrs. Robinson, of assuming that certain initial conditions are given and adapted to the economic variables. It then simply becomes a question of accumulating capital and reaping the returns. In Marxist theory there was the frequent suggestion, apparently accepted by the people who use the theory, that the institutions and attitudes which the liberal theory assumes to be given are a function of economic conditions, that is, that they are adjusted to the required extent if one changes the economic variables. Although not adapted, they are adaptable, not requiring specific planning. The superstructure adapts itself to the infrastructure. Of course this is only a schematized way of presenting Marx because Marx has said very many things—one can use his own writings to disprove him, and he even said that he was not himself a Marxist. It did therefore seem to Mr. Streeten that both the liberal laissez-faire theory and the Marxist theory failed to provide helpful theories for planning, since they both tend to lead to the conclusion that it is either unnecessary or impossible to operate directly on certain so-called non-economic variables, such as land reform, the breakdown of caste and class divisions, education, credit systems, the provision of information, the reform of the Civil Service, the enforcement of effective taxation, and so on. Mr. Streeten thought that the true situation may in fact be the reverse of what Keynes said when he maintained that the actions of practical men merely reflect what the academic scribblers said some years before. It may be that in some respects our theory is only beginning to catch up and to formulate what in fact any country which has successfully tried to plan for development has done in practice. To take one example, what Stalin's system of industrial planning has done is not simply to raise, in a Harrod–Domar growth fashion, the savings and investment ratio, and thereby with a given capital/output ratio, the rate of growth. Stalinism reinforced what one might call the investment savings *squeeze*, keeping consumption down and keeping investment up, by a consumption *twist*, reinforcing and encouraging those branches of "consumption" which contribute very importantly to development and growth, such as workers' health and education. But Mr. Streeten said, we have not really got, so far as he knew, a theory which shows that it is certain elements in consumption, combined with certain (but by no means all) types of investment, which contribute to growth. We either tend to concentrate on the fact that it is investment and investment only which contributes to growth, whereas consumption is somehow only current enjoyment, which destroys resources without contributing to their growth, or we get people suddenly picking up one item in the consumption bundle such as education, or health services or whatever the fashion may be, and concentrating on this item in isolation, in another type of systematic bias which he had tried to identify in his paper by calling it "one-factor-analysis", a special case of "illegitimate isolation".

Then again, inherent in our ways of formulating some of these concepts is the tendency, on the one hand, to aggregate along misleading lines, that is, to put together in concepts and models things which should be kept separate, and on the other hand to isolate along the wrong lines. Where one should combine certain types of activity—for example, in the investment field—with certain types of consumption activity, with certain policies aimed at reforming social institutions, human attitudes and cultural factors, we tended, Mr. Streeten thought, to cut across the relevant divisions. In his paper he tried to illustrate this by two concepts only, but he thought one could go much further than this. One concept was that of employment, where there is a tendency to use the concept developed by Mrs. Robinson for slumps in developed countries, that of disguised unemployment, of the match-seller in the Strand. He had re-read Mrs. Robinson's essay to see how it fitted into the context in which it had recently been employed by a number of people, namely the context of rural non-employment in underdeveloped countries. If one thought about it, everyone could see that the concept "disguised unemployment" did not apply to underdeveloped countries, but it was frequently used in the literature. Mrs. Robinson, herself, had drawn a distinction between unemployment and non-employment, but Mr. Streeten thought that even non-employment does not go far enough. For, while the concept of non-employment draws attention to the fact that not only effective demand, but also equipment is necessary to provide work opportunities, numerous other factors are left out. Caste attitudes, objections to women's work, the ability to keep certain hours, to co-operate with others and to keep discipline, to follow orders, to acquire and use skills, and many more conditions, affect the utilisation of labour. This means planning, and operating on the kind of variables which do not as far as he knew appear at all in our economic concepts or in the models which relate employment (or capital) to output.

To sum up, the first part of his paper, which many people would not have had time to read, was concerned with trying to isolate these four systematic biases; first the assumption of *ceteris paribus* (adapted non-economic conditions), or *automatic mutatis mutandis*, which means that institutions and attitudes get adapted and adjusted to the economic factors, in particular, investment activities without direct policies. Secondly, there is *one-factor-analysis*. Although we ought professionally to be trained to visualize interdependence, we nevertheless try to focus on one factor, such as investment or land or labour or education or whatever the case may be, and we tend to forget that certain actions and certain activities are only successful if they are complemented and supplemented by other types of activity. Then, thirdly, there is *misplaced aggregation*, lumping together all forms of investment irrespective of whether it is in palaces or embassies or in equipment and irrigation, without regard to land reform or to education of the peasants to use the waters properly. The same is true of "employment", "output", and many other conventional concepts and relations.

Finally, there is *illegitimate isolation*. One-factor-analysis is a special case of this and refers to the process of using certain types of action, certain types of concept and policy, without making it clear that their success depends on what other activities they are linked up with.

In the second part of the paper, however, Mr. Streeten said he had to some extent retreated from the position of the first part and committed some of the sins which he had been criticizing. In this part he had attempted to suggest how one could meet his earlier complaints. But he was fully aware that this had not been an entirely successful way of doing it, and perhaps the only useful thing about this part of the paper was that the attempt had resulted in a kind of *aide-mémoire* and a shift of emphasis. It also points to the limitations of the traditional approach. Finally, he had tried to illustrate his points by two concepts, the concept of unemployment or under-employment and the concept of the capital/output ratio.

PROFESSOR HAGEN

Professor Hagen said that the central problem everyone was

implicitly or explicitly talking about when discussing the problem of growth of low-income countries was: what are the factors that determine how fast output per worker or output per unit of income is increasing in such countries? Why does it increase faster in one than in another? What can be done so that it will increase at a faster rate in a given country than it is increasing?

He proposed to put the points he wanted to make about that in terms of applying the same question to the United States. In Japan, output per worker has been increasing on an average over the last decade or so by 6, 7, or 8 per cent *per capita*. Why hasn't it been doing so in the United States? If one says that productivity in Japan is rising rapidly because Japan can simply imitate, this answer no longer sounds as plausible as it used to. Japan's productivity in agriculture is increasing, he said, at a tremendous rate, and not by imitation. On farms of two or three acres in size, they certainly are not imitating American methods or British methods of increasing agricultural productivity. Nor are they imitating any longer in many of the industrial fields in which they are forging ahead.

Productivity in the United States is not rising at a slower rate because of shortage of capital. In general, with some few exceptions, private enterprises in the United States are now investing all the resources each year that they find it useful to invest. They are not short of capital. They are paying out quite generous dividends. They could easily retain more of them for capital formation, and they can easily float securities on the open market. They are not investing more than they are because they cannot think of additional good investment projects.

It could of course be said that the United States Government ought to be spending more for urban renewal, for housing, for schools and for other such social capital, and also for the current costs of education. With that Professor Hagen was very much in agreement. But if anyone suggested that increased investment of the Government would directly or indirectly raise the rate of increase of output, from say 2 per cent *per capita* to 4 per cent *per capita*, then Professor Hagen would say, on empirical grounds, that he thought this awfully implausible.

Professor Hagen suggested that the difference between the United States and Japan is most plausibly explained not on any grounds of economic policy at all, but simply on the ground that there is, relatively, a larger flow of creative innovational activity there than in the United States. Because this is true there is use for Japan's high flow of saving. None of the conventional economic theories has anything to say about how fast an economy transforms its production function. They certainly have a great deal to say about increases in productivity per person through capital formation, but implicitly or explicitly, this concerns moving to more capital intensive methods on a given production function.

Professor Hagen added that in these references to conventional theory he was not including discussions of the last few years, such as those by Mr. Kaldor. Although Mr. Kaldor refers to the question of why one country advances faster than another, he does not really, Professor Hagen thought, attack this problem of differential innovational capabilities. Certainly, conventional macro- and micro-economics does not attack this problem. Some writers seem to think it to be a sort of natural fact of the world that productivity would increase at some "normal" rate in any country if economic policies were right, but Professor Hagen wanted to suggest that there is no such natural fact. The amount of creative energy which flows into technological advance is largely determined by factors concerning which economics has nothing to say. One can say that making resources available for capital formation up to the limit set by this given flow of creative energy can be useful. Also, government policies which determine the effectiveness of the allocation of resources and government policies which will provide the necessary complementarities in infra-structure and so on will accelerate advance in productivity. But even if government policies are ideal, if there is not much creativity being exerted in economic innovation, then there will be no reason to expect a very rapid rate of growth. So really his argument was this: the most important factors determining the rate of economic growth of low-income societies are not economic at all. As economists we have nothing to say about them, and we should not assume automatically that economic policy has the answers, for this is not what the economic policy we have developed in our discipline concerns itself with.

Dr. Balogh

Dr. Balogh said that Professor Hagen's contribution amounted to saying that conventional economics, both in the short run and in the long run, is applicable to the analysis of reality. His argument implied an acceptance of views which had been effectively criticized by Mr. Kaldor. As in the case of other recent discussion, in a related field concerning education, the critics' contribution had been ignored, even though it was clear from the context that there was no excuse for overlooking it.

MR. SEERS

Mr. Seers said that it was very tolerant of the organizers of the Conference to invite him to Manchester in view of his rather rude and carping paper, written from beyond the academic fringe, which started off this exercise. He wanted to explain that the tone of the rather excessive number of papers which he had been producing recently was not just due to natural bloodymindedness, but to some impatience at being confronted with conventional Anglo-Saxon economics after working for a number of years in Latin America.

He wanted to quote one or two examples: two Latin American students at Yale, perhaps the brightest members of the Yale Graduate School, were recently spending large amounts of time working on a Latin American economy, one of them setting up a dynamic input-output model and the other testing the Hicks trade cycle model. Now the Hicks model may be an excellent one for a developed economy, but in the case of a Latin American economy one has to say something about export prices of leading commodities, for example. Turning points are not wholly, or even mainly, determined by excess or shortage of capital.

Secondly, he was astonished at the boldness of economists from Europe or North America who work overseas. Many of them have hardly arrived in a country before they are saying: "Well, what is wrong with this economy, of course is . . . ", or "What really needs to be done here is . . . " or "We find that such-and-such a policy works in the United States (or Britain or France)". This came out very clearly in the case of the Rio Conference in January 1963 on Inflation and Growth. Quite a large fraction of the most eminent economists in the world were present, but a large fraction of that large fraction had never set feet in Latin America before or apparently read any Latin American journals. This did not prevent them, however, laying down quite considerable generalizations about what needed to be done in Latin America, generalizations such as "What is needed is shock treatment". In many cases they spoke as if the same policy would suit each of the twenty Latin American republics. (Even psychiatrists are expected to make a detailed diagnosis of each case before they recommend shock treatment.) The implicit model of several speakers, such as Sir Arthur Lewis, included trade union pressure, for example, but only in a few Latin American countries are trade unions a significant force.

Thirdly, some leading economists use the same capital-output ratio for all the countries in the world. This raises serious questions:

What sort of a profession is the economics profession? Why is it so little interested in facts?

The subject of this session of the Conference was the state of knowledge, but this, Mr. Seers thought, was not really the problem. A certain amount of experience had by now been acquired in economic development. The channels by which this becomes available to the profession are by no means adequate, but it is the lack of interest which is alarming, the belief that one can make recommendations on the basis of very little study of the local situation.

Unless one finds out the political objectives of the government being advised, for example, one is bound to attribute to it one's own value judgments, usually implicitly. Unless one studies the structure and functioning of the economy concerned, one must assume some model drawn from elsewhere in the world.

Here we reach the heart of the problem. An economist is not trained to analyse eonomies. Most graduates can produce a study on the fiscal structure, say, or marketing policy, but not on the economy as a whole. They have great difficulty in explaining how and why the Brazilian economy functions differently from that of Argentina, or in contrasting the Ghanaian economy with that of Nigeria. This is the key to the general failure to see the need for constructing a model appropriate to local needs.

It is sad that students and graduates fail to ask themselves why they should expect to be able to transfer propositions from developed economies to others. As a working rule one could almost say that if a proposition applies in a developed country, the opposite will be true in an underdeveloped country. Someone who read Peter Ady's paper[1] might conclude, Mr. Seers said, that he was doubtful about the value of macro-economic models. Actually, he thought they could be extremely useful, as means of pulling together different parts of the economy, of seeing the inter-relations and therefore of getting consistency in policy recommendations. After all, a model is implicit in anything that one does. What he queried was the appropriateness of the types of model which are in use.

Paul Streeten had raised far more far-reaching questions, essentially about the concepts and categories which we are using. He could well be right, but at the moment many of us have to work with "employment" as a total category, particularly when working on practical development problems. We are unable to carry out the sort of reconstruction of working categories which is necessary, partly for lack

1. Cf. pp. 107–132 above.

of time and partly because we are ourselves held in the vice of conventional concepts. But, Mr. Seers said, he hoped that Mr. Streeten and other people would continue with this critical work, and make us think again and again about what we were using.

Mrs. Robinson had asked whether Mr. Seers was not tacitly accepting models in use, especially the neoclassical models, as accurate and useful for those working in *developed* economies. As a former pupil of hers, Mr. Seers felt he must have been successfully inoculated against doing this; he simply preferred to fight one battle at a time. There is a very strong case against the application in Latin America of traditional financial policies. (Another example of the transfer of policies without adequate analysis.) This case should not be confused with the issue of whether or not such a policy had any function in developed countries.

As someone working on development problems, Mr. Seers wanted to suggest, with due humility, that the profession should free itself from supposedly general theories like those of Keynes and the Harrod–Domar model, and acquire some relativity. It was time for a more stringent approach to economics. Speaking from the outside, it would be useful if those engaged in teaching tried to instil in their pupils a sceptical, comparative attitude, rather than constructing and conveying great models. We need in fact a Hume or a Moore rather than a Hegel. After removing the junk which is cluttering up the subject, the next phase would be the construction of models that would be relevant in non-industrial countries. And of course this last task would be formidable and unpopular; it involved thinking.

Mr. Worswick

Mr. Worswick said that he knew little about economic development and less about the teaching of economic development. He had been put in a pessimistic frame of mind by the discussion up to this point, the tendency having been to say that economists had next to nothing to offer. He therefore proposed to launch a counter-attack to get the discussion going.

He proposed to take up some points from Mr. Seers's original paper in the University of Oxford *Institute of Statistics Bulletin:* "The Limitation of the Special Case",[1] which had been described by the Chairman as making Mr. Seers the "father" of the present Conference. He would also refer to one or two points which Mrs. Robinson had made.

1. Cf. pp. 3–29 above.

Mr. Worswick said he thought that Mr. Seers was asking for something which was not to be found. Mr. Seers gave the impression that students from developing countries went abroad, read Samuelson, went back home and applied what they had read, and this was all wrong. Mr. Worswick further got the impression that Mr. Seers was saying that if the economics profession in Britain, America, and elsewhere would only buckle down to it, they could produce an ideal book, visualized by Mr. Seers, which would contain the truth. If only one could teach *that* and give *that* to the students from developing countries, they could return home, and fast development would start everywhere. All this Mr. Worswick was not prepared to believe for a moment. It seemed to him that the real problem was that the young men who came to our universities for no more than a couple of years found themselves, upon their return home, in a short time confronted with a much higher degree of power and responsibility than they would immediately find in an advanced country. That being the problem, he did not think that a great deal of difference was going to be made by whether the young men were reading about production functions or whatever else was considered inappropriate. The real difficulty was that their education for the responsibilities to be placed on them and their experience was much too short. There was, he thought, really very little in Mr. Seers's problem. The same misconception or a similar one underlay Mr. Seers's remarks referring to the silly things done both by foreign-trained local economists who have returned home, and by foreign economists going in. What economist, Mr. Seers had asked, had ever been any use in an underdeveloped country? If Mr. Seers had in mind academic economists, all Mr. Worswick could say about that was, what academic economist was any use in our own country, or in the United States? Being an economic adviser for a big business or for a government was a specialized, highly skilled occupation. One could think of dozens of members of our profession, all men of great distinction, whom one would never dream of asking to be economic advisers. If the Ford Foundation and other bodies made the mistake of asking the wrong people, Mr. Worswick thought the blame should not be placed on the profession as a whole. How to stop the selection of the wrong people was a different question altogether.

On a more general point about the state of knowledge, Mr. Worswick found himself not entirely in agreement with Mrs. Robinson. He thought that there was one aspect of the state of knowledge in economics which was rather encouraging, even on the American side. It concerned the question of the need for a theory or doctrine in the broad sense. Talking to his contemporaries generally, he did not find that they had the same kind of need for doctrine or theory that people seem to have had in the past. Mr. Seers was asking for a new post-Keynesian theory of development, but Mr. Worswick did not know whether that was the right kind of thing to ask for at all. He thought, by the same token, that perhaps Mrs Robinson did not give enought weight to one contribution to economics being made in this country, namely, the emergence of a shift of emphasis, among some economists anyway, away from pure theorizing. These economists abstained from engaging in theorizing about how the system works without first looking at it, and also from the kind of abstract theorizing which consisted in trying to work out from some ideal planning or policy point of view how the system ought to work. The distinction here was that, in a case like competition theory, these economists would ask what it is about: is it an explanation of what we actually see or is it a set of instructions concerning what we ought to arrange? Is it that the real world is like that or is it that it ought to be arranged like that? This to the present generation of economists is an obvious point, which it perhaps was not fifty or sixty years ago. There is some progress in this. There is further progress, he thought, in contemporary economics in its tendency to study more closely what actually does go on. In terms of what we can contribute, the new emphasis on the process of ascertaining what goes on and studying facts, as well as theorizing about them, is something which one should not be too pessimistic about. The real difficulty here from Mr. Seers's point of view was, Mr. Worswick could see, that he apparently wanted to bring students here but then to teach them about their own countries and their own problems. This, Mr. Worswick thought, we certainly were not particularly fitted to do. We might be able to teach them how to study problems. Whether or not the particular *method* of study, which would inevitably draw examples from our own experience near at hand, was something that could be transferred to Argentina or India, could only be ascertained by experience of working in these economies.

Mr. Worswick entirely agreed that it was obviously unwise for people to walk into a developing country and then to pontificate within twenty-four hours. He hoped nobody present at the Conference did that kind of thing. He concluded that there had perhaps been too much pessimism about the state of economics. If one set out consciously to seek for some new theory of development which was going to be an all-embracing theory of a kind which one could rely on throughout and which would tell one exactly how development ought to be done, pessimism about the state of economics might be warranted. Mr. Worswick did not think it possible to do it, but he was not so sure that this was not something which others were mistakenly attempting.

MR. KNAPP

Mr. Knapp proposed to address himself to the questions raised by Mr. Seers concerning the degree of adequacy of our present body of doctrines.[1] He also proposed to make references to the papers submitted to the Conference by Mr. Myint and Professor Hagen, and to the preceeding oral discussion, in the course of doing so.

Mr. Seers had posed the question of whether we have a coherent development strategy, and if not, whether this is impossible in our lifetime. Mr. Knapp stated that his hopes in this matter were a little more optimistic than the remarks of Mr. Worswick suggested Mr. Worswick to be. It was, Mr. Knapp said, evident from Mr. Myint's admirably organized critical survey of the critics of older doctrines, and also from Professor Hagen's hilariously crisp massacre of the more recent rationalizations of development strategists, that we do *not* now possess a coherent development strategy. By a development strategy, Mr. Knapp took Mr. Seers to mean a range of optimal policies based on well-tested theory of a kind which Mr. Worswick noted with approval is now developing in applied economics. Such policies would of course have to be suited to the different combinations of circumstances which may be expected to exist in different economic, social, and institutional environments. Of course, if one meant by a coherent strategy not policy which is based on a body of tested knowledge, but merely policy proposals based on consistent but untested sets of ideas, then it is clear that the difficulty is not that we do not have such strategies, but that we still suffer from far too many of them, in spite of efforts such as those of Mr. Myint, Professor Hagen, and most notably of Mr. Seers. Mr. Worswick is sceptical about the prospect for arriving at a widely acceptable and relevant general theory, but Mr. Myint wishes us to persevere even though he expects that the fruits of our efforts in this direction are likely, as he puts it, to lie in a somewhat indeterminate future. If Professor Hagen were right about what matters in growth, namely, creativity determined by non-economic forces, then of course the prospect would depend on two things: the rate at which economists can be made to hand over to social

1. Cf. Mr. Seers's Questionnaire, pp. 31–2 above.

psychologists, and on the prospects of agreement on strategy among members of that profession. For his part, Mr. Knapp wanted to resist this takeover, for the time being at least, because he thought that the fun is only just starting in economics itself.

Mr. Seers had raised the question of what was the most productive way forward: to try to generalize economics or to develop doctrines appropriate for different types of economy? He had also asked whether Keynesian economics was now an obstacle in the subject's development, because of its highly global approach, its emphasis on the demand side, and its failure to specify basic assumptions or to assess their relevance? As regards the first of these questions, Mr. Knapp thought that the dichotomy Mr. Seers's question raised is not a genuine one in theoretical terms. One is unlikely to be able to generalize economics except as a result of reflection on the deficiencies of existing analysis as they appear from considering their applicability to reality in different types of economy. If one refuses to go along with Professor Hagen, because one insists that there is a breakthrough to be achieved in economics, one is left with choosing between the three approaches to advance discussed by Mr. Myint. These are: (1) extension and adaptation of the static optimum theory; (2) macro-economic approaches including the macro-growth models; (3) "the new dynamics" including micro-structural and historical-dynamic approaches.

Mr. Knapp thought that Mr. Myint clearly has a soft spot for what he calls the "extension and adaptation of static optimum theory", and he repeatedly asserts the present relevance and importance of this for policy, even in poor countries. It seems that Mr. Myint regards this as something safe to be going on with until we have a tested new dynamics in an indeterminate future. Mr. Knapp said that this may conceivably be good advice in practice, at least in some countries, since having some rules for decision is essential in real life. However, analytically speaking, this attitude is surely question-begging, and moreover may be as completely wrong as writers such as Gunnar Myrdal have suggested. Mr. Knapp wondered how Mr. Myint thought he knew that paying attention in policy making to our present static optimum theory does not produce misallocation and preventable waste even in the short period. How would Mr. Myint test the matter? In his paper Mr. Myint had referred to an episode of muddle in Burmese rice distribution in the later 1940s, but this is not, of course, a thorough test. Until we have a tested dynamic theory as well as some agreed operational criterion for a dynamic optimum or a set of dynamic optima, Mr. Knapp said, it was impossible to see how either Mr. Myint or anyone else could know. A related point was made by Mrs. Robinson: it is not clear how far Mr. Myint, and indeed Mr. Seers, do regard existing economic theory as adequately relevant even in the context of trying to understand growth in advanced economies. In his original Oxford paper, Mr. Seers certainly appears to imply (although he had given an explanation of that point in the discussion at the present Conference) that our existing theory does apply to advanced industrial economies. Professor Hagen appears to share that view. Mr. Knapp suggested that they might all have a look at Profesor T. W. Schultz's *The Economic Organization of Agriculture*. This book, while a product of the University of Chicago, represents nevertheless a most impressively agnostic attitude to the problem under discussion here.

Mr. Knapp said that, far from being an obstacle to the subject's development, he felt that the best chances for a new dynamics may be looked for in a further extension of post-Keynesian analysis. To say this was not inconsistent with sharing Mr. Myint's and Professor Hagen's scepticism of the "big push" analysis, and it was misleading of Professor Hirschman to identify that analysis with Keynesian ideas. Mr. Knapp hoped that when the break-through he was looking forward to did occur, it would absorb conventional price and welfare theory, branches of economics which are still implicitly or explicitly based on Say's Law. As to preliminary signs of such a break-through, Mr. Knapp thought that colleagues might like to re-read Mrs. Robinson's *Exercises in Economic Analysis*, in particular the chapter on the capitalist firm, as being one point at which one can start. He also said he had been very excited by the last eight pages of the Hart–Kaldor–Tinbergen submission to the recent United Nations Trade and Development Conference in Geneva.

Finally, Mr. Seers had asked how much of existing so-called "pure" theory will be left when the subject is generalized, and he also wondered whether the significance and meaning of such major concepts now in use as "National Income", "Capital", and "Employment" will need modification when one considers their general applicability in the world, that is when one also considers non-industrial economies? Mr. Knapp said he thought that, *in its present form*, rather less would be left than Messrs. Myint, Seers and Hagen appeared to believe, at least judging from the way in which they have formulated their positions in the papers that they had submitted to the Conference. In some reassembled form, however, perhaps a very great deal will turn out to be relevant, as rebellious writers such as Myrdal had of course also suggested. As to the question of whether the meaning and significance of concepts will change, the answer is surely that this is merely a semantic matter. Their significance certainly should change if the change in theory turns out to be as large as Mr. Seers appeared, quite rightly, to expect and hope. How far the meaning of concepts changes will depend on the elasticity of definition of conceptual terms that will come about in actual usage.

Mr. Eshag

Mr. Eshag said that economics being a subject which is very closely related to practical life, unless what we teach is useful we are really wasting our time. If one took Mr. Worswick's suggestion that most economists are not useful either in developed or underdeveloped countries seriously, it should be realized that acceptance of this view would entail that economists had no reason for existence as a profession.

Mr. Eshag thought that Mr. Seers's Oxford Bulletin paper[1] was very useful in bringing out two important things. One of these concerns the limitations on the usefulness of what is taught in economics. If one can constantly bear in mind that the purpose of economics is to be useful, then one is likely to be automatically forced into what one might call a common-sense humility in teaching the subject. One will then be inclined to stress the qualifications to its applicability, whether in relation to actual conditions in developed or underdeveloped countries. In relation to conditions in underdeveloped countries macro-economic models have great applicability. In micro-economic analysis, the need to qualify will be more frequent, but so long as one keeps explaining to students that the models are principally concerned to give a general idea, then it could, he thought, be left to the students to sort matters out.

Another point in Mr. Seers's Oxford Bulletin paper, which was also touched upon in Mr. Streeten's submission to the Conference, is of particular importance to underdeveloped countries. The point concerns the need to explain the proper scope of the subject and also the need to observe a right order of priorities in explaining it. This is more important even than stressing limitations on the applicability of analysis, and this is where, Mr. Eshag thought, our teaching really fails. He doubted whether these last matters fell within the curricula of teaching the subject at Oxford, Cambridge, London, or even Manchester. As some of the papers, notably that of Mr. Seers,

1. Cf. pp. 3–29 above.

had stressed, the important factor in development or growth is not what we call economics at all. It is really institutional and political. This is borne in on one if one looks at the history of the underdeveloped countries or if one studies them closely and lives in them. Mr. Eshag thought that unless what is propounded concerns itself in the first place with institutional, political and historical matters—in other words with the sort of things that old-fashioned Marxism is concerned with—one's study becomes meaningless in terms of understanding development.

MR. BECKETT

Mr. Beckett thought that the appearance of a multiplicity of conflicting theories in the economic development field probably reflected the fact that each theory has relevance to some places or aspects of problems at some times but not to other places, or other aspects at other times. The need now was for keeping a continuous review, for seeing what is happening in particular places and relating this information to our whole list of concepts and theories.

MR. KALDOR

Mr. Kaldor explained that he had come without having seen any of the papers in advance, but he was going by what he had heard in the preceding discussion. He felt that speaker after speaker had somehow managed to give, at any rate collectively, a rather pessimistic impression of what economics can do with regard to the problem of economic development, especially in underdeveloped countries. He felt somewhat like Mr. Eshag did about this.

Mr. Kaldor said he agreed with Mrs. Robinson's strictures against the traditional doctrines of our textbooks. He thought that when one is confronted with an underdeveloped country, none of our elaborate theories seem really useful as such. That was so if one is trying to answer the kind of question which Mr. Hagen had raised, why it is that some country will grow at one rate and some other country at some other rate. Furthermore, Mr. Kaldor was ready to admit that he knew of no single textbook on the question of economic development with special reference to poor countries that he would confidently put into the hands of students from these countries and feel able to say: now you read that book, and when you read it, it will help you to make up your mind on specific matters when you get home and are trying to do something. Mr. Kaldor added that he would certainly not include his own theoretical writings in the list of things he would advise such a student to read in that spirit.

Nevertheless, Mr. Kaldor felt that, in his own opinion at any rate, his training as an economist did help him when he went to underdeveloped countries. He did feel that he was able to approach the problem more fruitfully than he would have done if he had had a training as a lawyer or a philosopher or something else. One could not deny, he said, that economics does something. When he went to underdeveloped countries in Asia and Latin America it seemed to him that although the problems of these countries and their situations were different, one's approach as an economist to problems of growth certainly proved fruitful in trying to get some concrete answers or in trying to select the specific areas which were critical if growth was to be accelerated. He did not find that the difficulty was that, as an economist, one was not able to find the cause of the trouble. The difficulty, he found, was not in diagnosing what was wrong, but the difficulty of putting things right. In this one was up against tremendous social and economic forces. Anybody who had been to Chile, for example, would not be at a loss to say what is wrong with that country or in telling them what needs to be done. But this does not help, Mr. Kaldor said, because the obstacles to the necessary reform are political and institutional in character. Lack of good analysis or advice is not the primary obstacle.

Now, in many underdeveloped countries, though not in all, Mr. Kaldor said, he would regard land reform as an absolutely essential precondition for economic development. Yet, wherever it was proposed, it was often flatly resisted.

Unlike Professor Hagen, Mr. Kaldor said, he did not believe that economic growth is simply a matter of creativity conceived as some mysterious substance of vitality in the human population with which some countries are richly endowed and others are poorly endowed. Despite all the things he had written about the nature of technical progress and the importance of the technical progress function, Mr. Kaldor said, he did not believe in this whole antithesis between moving production functions around and leapfrogging them, and so on. All this, he said, was an artificial creation. The problem which Professor Hagen had posed was, he thought, a problem drawn from the textbooks and not a problem drawn from anything that one encountered in reality. In the textbooks one is confronted with some completely unproven and unidentifiable hypotheses about linear and homogeneous production functions which necessitate the assumption of diminishing returns to particular factors of production. When, on empirical investigation, one did not in fact find diminishing returns, the economist falls back on a residual explanation—he attributes increasing returns to technical progress. When, going further, he finds that productivity grows fast in some countries and slowly in others, the next thing to say is that some countries have high rates of technical progress, and other countries have low rates of technical progress. However, this is not very illuminating either. So the next stage is to go into creativity. It may be true that the populations of some countries do have more vitality than others. Climate is no doubt of some importance. But it would really, he said, be a counsel of despair simply to say that that is the ultimate reason why some countries are rich and others poor.

Mr. Kaldor said that he believed that there is much in a particular version, at any rate, of the theory of balanced growth, which says that the expansion of any crucial sector of the economy is conditioned by, and at the same time contributes to, the expansion of the others, and that the economy as a whole cannot grow faster than that particular sector which has the lowest growth potential. That low growth potential may be, as in the case of land and agriculture, simply due to the existence of outdated social institutions which have not yet been changed because there is too much social resistance to change them. If one has a completely backward and undynamic agriculture, then all the plans and programmes of industrial development, etc., are bound to remain abortive. This was just one example. Continuing, Mr. Kaldor said be helieved that effective demand on a world scale rather than on a national scale was a most important determinant of the rate of growth of the underdeveloped countries. If a far more expansionary policy could somehow be contrived among the advanced countries in the West, he thought that would in itself help to remove all kinds of obstacles in the path of development, which now appear to be structural bottlenecks.

Mr. Kaldor said that he would regard a useful economist as being one who has had a sound training, who is not particularly wedded to any one rigid body of doctrine, has an elastic mind, and a keen interest. If such an economist goes out to an underdeveloped country and sets the right questions – namely, what is it that really prevents this particular community from progressing faster – he did not think he would need to be a genius to find out what concrete courses of action are likely to be the most conducive to this end. These may of course vary between countries and situations. His training as an economist should enable him to analyse the situation and to give a diagnosis that is definitely superior to what it would have been if he had not had that training. In that sense, Mr. Kaldor said, he would not share the view that economics is completely useless. He did feel though—and this seemed to be a general point, not confined to economics—that in second-rate minds any mental discipline becomes an orthodoxy and therefore tends to be barren. Whether this happened more often in economics than in other subjects he did not feel competent to say.

Mr. Little

Mr. Little said that he had been inspired to speak by Mr. Kaldor partly because, like him, he had not had time to read any of the papers and partly because he too had invented a progressive land tax for a country, some time before Mr. Kaldor as a matter of fact, in India. Unlike Mr. Kaldor, he would guess, looking back on it, that he would be pretty frightened to see it introduced. One often does not know what the full reactions might be to one's proposals and in this sense he professed himself to be very sceptical. He had become much more sceptical as a result of going to Africa.

In a sense, as Mr. Kaldor had said, it is very easy to put one's finger on what is wrong, but what is wrong may be very general indeed—and here he was supporting Professor Hagen, he thought. There may be little that one can do effectively in many of these countries, except to try to change people and their behaviour, which would include agricultural extension, education of all kinds, birth control, and so on—and it was in these fields, Mr. Little felt, that we know very little.

Suppose one imagined oneself to be in a position of economic adviser in Nyasaland. What really had one got to offer? Very little, because practically everything that they might do were things that economists know very little about. Mr. Little said that he felt that in such countries the main thing that economists had to offer was that they were interested in growth and could try to make others like-minded. Many of the questions to which answers are needed lie in other fields, but a lot of professionals in these fields are not basically interested in growth. Doctors have their own ideas of what is the right thing to do, for instance, which is to save life. This is all very well, but it does not necessarily make for growth. In the field of education there are still a great many things that we do not know. We do not really know a lot about the effects of Africans being educated in the way they are. We do not really know quite simple things, like the effect on the rate of urbanization of this kind of education—a pretty important thing to know. Doctors are not really interested, and educators are not really interested, in the long-run effects on growth rates; and, he suspected, not many anthropologists were really interested either—they like to leave things as they are. He thought there were quite a lot of sociologists in America who were interested, but very few in this country.

Mr. Little thought one of the positive things that we can and should do is to try to get some of these other disciplines more interested in economic development and really make a start on curing the deep basic ignorance which, it seemed to him, prevails concerning the basic causes of development.

PROFESSOR HAGEN

Professor Hagen said he thought he agreed with everything that Mr. Kaldor had said. He wished to speak for a few minutes to see if he could solve some purely semantic differences, not between Mr. Kaldor and himself, but, judging by the papers, among the group at the Conference in general.

Professor Hagen thought that the economic theory that is applicable to economically advanced societies is applicable to underdeveloped societies in senses such as this: if in an underdeveloped country it appears that there are uses for more investment—which is rather likely to come out of the operations of the private part of the economy—then conventional fiscal and monetary theory, which indicates policies to be followed in industrial countries, would also indicate the fiscal and monetary policy that is applicable in the underdeveloped country. The policies would differ, because of different circumstances, but there is not a different theory to be applied.

Another example: marginal analysis does not say that in deciding whether a given investment project is desirable one should consider only the expected marginal productivity of the capital in that project. Marginal analysis says that this is the proper theoretical way to approach the problem if one has a right to assume that nothing else in the situation is changing during the time one is considering it. If one uses the conclusion without remembering the assumptions, then one is going to get some wrong conclusions when the assumptions are not applicable. If a comprehensive development programme is proceeding in an underdeveloped country, then of course the assumptions are not applicable. One may well want to consider the linear programming of the matter, and that is not contrary to the theory we teach in advanced countries. What he was therefore suggesting was that we remember the assumptions underlying our theory and ask whether these assumptions are applicable. If they are not, we must ask what our theory will teach us with the necessary change of assumptions.

However, no economic theory is applicable to some of the problems faced. If in an underdeveloped country the advice tendered by a flexible, sensible and imaginative economic adviser was ideal policy and was being perfectly followed, even then one would find, Professor Hagen suggested, that in Nyasaland or Bolivia or the Congo—either Congo—the rate of development with these ideal economic policies was not going to be as high as it was going to be in say Yugoslavia during the forthcoming decade. He suggested, further, that this difference is due to factors that economic theory is not able to cope with. That however does not mean that there is no theory that is able to cope with them. There are advances in personality theory and sociology and social anthropology—though Professor Hagen agreed with what Mr. Little had to say about the attitude of many sociologists. But to say that another kind of theory is very important in explaining the differences certainly should not lead us to say that economic theory does not count. Professor Hagen concluded by saying that although clearly Mr. Balogh would disagree and insist that our theory does not apply, Professor Hagen nevertheless asserted that many of the differences among those present were of a semantic character and that there are fewer substantive differences than people think there are.

Mr. Balogh

Mr. Balogh said that the awkward fact for him was that he really so much agreed with, and so much liked, Professor Hagen's new approach to some of these problems that he was therefore really the more irritated by his stubbornness on this question of economics. What did Professor Hagen mean by "the economic theory"? Mr. Balogh said that if Professor Hagen meant by economic theory that one tried to look at certain motivations on the economic plane, and looked at what their probable consequences would be; and if he thought that if we took the economic theory which we had been taught, this will teach one to take into account certain factors which other people would not take into account, so that in this sense economic theory is applicable; and that, therefore, to be an economist might be better than not to be an economist—his own view would be that, in general, he did not know. One could think of some economists who if sent to some countries might do worse than a non-economist in terms of their usefulness, and this is in fact the problem.

For instance, Professor Hagen had said that if we find in an underdeveloped country that savings are too low, the sort of economic policy, the sort of fiscal and monetary policy which our theory teaches us will be applicable. He proposed to look at this point because it can perhaps explain the difference of approach between Professor Hagen and himself and can also throw light on certain problems of what the methodology of economics involves.

First of all, Mr. Balogh said, he did not know what Professor Hagen meant by developed theory, because Professor Milton Friedman's monetary theory is very different from, say, Mrs. Robinson's. Secondly, suppose one took the Robinsonian theory, the difficulty would arise that this theory can obviously only be applied in a system in which one has a market, but, Mr. Balogh said, in these countries one has not got a market and the motivations in these countries are completely different from the sort of motivations one would encounter where markets are well developed. The response to increases in the rate of interest, for example, in the sort of penumbra one encounters in these countries, is nowhere near what would be required to make the theory applicable. One finds, for example, that there are four capital markets, in one of which the rate of interest was about 50 or 60 per cent p.a. This prevails for agriculture. Then one has a 25 per cent market for entrepreneurs in the traditional sector, e.g. lorry owners. One has something like a 15 per cent market for the very few bigger entrepreneurs, and then one has a 6 per cent market for the expatriate industry. What applies to expatriates does not apply to the rest of the agricultural sector. And vice versa.

Or take the sort of impact which fiscal policy would have—here again, our theory would not apply. For instance, most of the development economics textbooks say that a greater equality of income increases imports. This is the opposite of the truth in most underdeveloped countries. The rich people import Cadillacs, and the poor people buy the home-produced textile goods.

When Professor Hagen and Professor Solow go and do certain things, they are the sort of people who might not make mistakes through believing in traditional thought because they also have common sense, but if the Solow type of approach were mechanically used by the average economist, obviously complete nonsense comes out of it. He thought Professor Schultz's book on education was an example of this.

MR. STREETEN

Mr. Streeten said that although what Mr. Kaldor had said sounded very considerate in tone, it was nevertheless probably the most pessimistic speech that had been presented so far. His own view was that economic doctrine, as exemplified by the theory of perfect competition and the theory of prices, has been defended on three successive barricades. The first of these is to say that this is a true analysis of the facts and that it gives one a correct description of what is happening. The critics then point out that this is not so. People then sometimes retreat and say that although this theory may be quite untrue as a description, it is a very good basis for making recommendations—shadow prices are used to approximate perfect competition conceived as the ideal. Then people discover that there are certain reasons—externalities, indivisibilities, complementarities, etc.—why the doctrine is neither a correct description or a good analysis of the facts, nor a sound basis for recommendation, and then one says that it is a good training of the mind. But how something that is neither true as a description nor valid as a basis for policies can be a good training of the mind, he did not understand, Mr. Streeten said.

When Mr. Kaldor had gone on to illustrate, he provided a very good example of exactly what Mr. Streeten was suggesting. We really have three types of theory of capital now and Mr. Kaldor himself is responsible for at least one and perhaps two of them. The traditional textbook theory of capital, on which we had been brought up, proceeded on the basis that there is capital investment and a given "state of the arts" or technical knowledge. On this basis we can of course have inter-disciplinary cross-fertilization and we have some people talking about how the arts develop, others about how capital accumulates. But no inter-disciplinary cross-fertilization will produce the technical progress function that Mr. Kaldor introduced when he propounded the notion that you introduce or infuse knowledge through new equipment. This is quite contrary to the way we have been taught capital theory. The Kaldor theory, that one introduces new knowledge through new capital while knowledge grows independently, and the Arrow theory of learning by doing provide testable hypotheses, and this is exactly the kind of disaggregation combined with new combinations which, Mr. Streeten thought, the theory of economic development and of planning for development requires. The fact that Mr. Kaldor had said that this is what ought to be done proves that the existing textbook theory, at least the pre-Solow–Arrow–Kaldor theories, has not produced the goods.

The same point also implies a criticism of the idea put by someone else, that one can make progress by having seminars on education or on the state of knowledge with experts in special fields. There was really no possibility of marrying economics with these other fields by cross-fertilization in seminars which bring together specialist knowledge, because each specialist thinks in terms of his own models. It has been rightly said that the only fruitful cross-fertilization occurs under one skull—for it takes a model to defeat a model—facts by themselves are too weak. The need is for ingenious new theories, for building up new concepts and new types of functional relationships.

Mr. Streeten continued that he did not see how Mr. Kaldor's theory of balanced growth proves what Mr. Kaldor appears to want it to prove. It is now apparently clear to everyone that agriculture is a lagging sector and that what one wants to do in underdeveloped countries is to increase agricultural production and productivity per acre. But a cursory survey of writings on economic development even quite recently does not reveal that anyone then knew that agriculture would become such a serious bottleneck. Industrialization was almost identified with development and emphasis on agriculture was considered reactionary. It was successful industrialization and *unbalanced* growth which focused attention on the high priority of reform in agriculture.

PROFESSOR HANSON

Mr. Hanson said that as there had been so much talk about other disciplines, he thought it appropriate for a political scientist, so called, to intervene.

There had been a great deal of self-flagellation by economists in the proceedings so far, but he had heard this with some surprise because he felt that really economists ought to be whipping somebody else. It seemed obvious to Mr. Hanson that the study of economic growth is essentially inter-disciplinary, but he did not think that economists have as yet received the sort of assistance that they need or even the sort of assistance that they deserve from the practitioners of other disciplines. Although he was not an expert, he thought economists were doing a good job on planning, if only for the reason that their growth models could, he thought, save people from the more obvious forms of inconsistency. The difficulty arose when numerical values were inserted into the abstract growth models, because in doing this one is building into the models a whole range of social, political, administrative, psychological and even religious assumptions which, in the majority of cases, have by no means been adequately examined. It is at this point that the whole thing begins to fall to pieces.

For some time now Mr. Hanson had been looking at the process of planning in India and although he had done so from a political and administrative rather than an economic point of view, he necessarily had to look just a little bit at the economics of it. Looking at the figures in the Mahalanobis plan frame and finding out the source of those figures he found himself in for a bit of a surprise. Although the plan frame had been presented to the Indians as something totally scientific which would ensure that within the limits of human error their plan would achieve success, figures such as that for six million tons of steel had been obtained from an announcement by the Ministry of Industry, which in turn was obviously based on certain completely false assumptions, hopelessly optimistic about the administrative and managerial capacity of Indian society. The agricultural targets were based on quite mistaken assumptions about the capacity of the community development projects to raise the rate of agricultural growth, and so on. One can take one figure after another in the Mahalanobis plan frame and find built into it a number of assumptions which for administrative or political reasons are entirely unrealistic. Mr. Hanson thought this was partly due to the fact that knowledge was insufficient, it was partly due to the fact that the knowledge that was there was not properly used, and partly due to the deliberate distortion of the knowledge that was there for political purposes. But he did not think that one could blame Mahalanobis for what happened, for the fact that the second five-year plan went very sadly astray. The blame, he thought, is to be very much more firmly attached to the politicians and the administrators and those who were concerned with the study of politics and administration and society. This is why it seemed to Mr. Hanson that there is no need for excessive self-flagellation on the part of economists. Whether an economic model works out well or badly, largely depends, he thought, on various assumptions of a non-economic character which are built into it. Surely, therefore, the main job is to ensure, by increasing inter-disciplinary cross-fertilization, that these assumptions are a great deal more realistic than they have been in the past.

MRS. ROBINSON

Mrs. Robinson intervened to say that she just wanted to say a word to drive a wedge between Professor Hagen and Mr. Kaldor. They appeared to be trying to bridge the gap, but Mrs. Robinson felt that the difference is what needs to be emphasized. She did not think that there is any economic theory. One could not find any result which can be applied in any circumstances. All economic theory can do for one is to show one the right way to set out the questions, and we are learning, and, she hoped, improving our method of doing this by having more experience of different questions. She thought that the kind of approach which Professor Hagen was putting forward is extremely dangerous and pernicious, because we are teaching our young men such things as correct monetary policy or the rules of fiscal policy, or something of this sort, and they go back to their countries thinking that this is what they have learned. Yet it is anti-educational to teach them that. What we must teach them is how to look at the questions and what considerations ought to be taken into account. When Mr. Kaldor was saying that economics does do some good, he meant that kind of economics, but Professor Hagen was trying to pick it up the other way in order to say that we do know something about fiscal policy. This, Mrs. Robinson thought, is a wrong way of teaching and does a great deal of harm.

MR. SINHA

Explaining that he belonged to an underdeveloped country, but was trained in this country, Mr. Sinha said that, regarding the state of knowledge, he had the feeling that there is no reason for too much lament if economists in this country did not have knowledge about underdeveloped countries, since in some cases there is not sufficient knowledge even about economically developed countries in their primary stages of growth. He thought that the most important problem facing underdeveloped countries is the problem of population, but until recently most Western economists were themselves not agreed on probable trends of population growth. Until 1953 or 1954 Professor Lewis had been stressing that in the earlier stages of growth the birthrate remains constant; but then Professor

Habbakkuk suggests that even in the U.K. the birth rate actually did rise in the earlier stages of growth.

MR. CLARK

Reference had been made at the Conference to inadequate knowledge and understanding of agriculture in low-income countries, and Mr. Clark wanted to make the case that some reasonably stable and concrete economic relationships did exist in subsistence agriculture.

Mr. Clark said that on the importance of agriculture in low-income countries he is an absolute and dogmatic physiocrat. Nothing, he thought, could be more important. He felt it to be rather ironical that he has to divide his energies between telling people that they pay far too much attention to agriculture in countries like our own and pay far too little attention to it in the other half of the world. The reference to half of the world is almost literally exact. The families who live by subsistence agriculture, whose main efforts have to be devoted just to producing food for their families, still constitute half of the world's population.

(Mr. Clark and Miss Haswell distributed half a dozen diagrams relating to some of the most striking empirical findings of their forthcoming book[1] *The Economics of Subsistence Agriculture*.)

Commenting on the charts he had distributed, Mr. Clark said that Japan was a fascinating model case illustrating the crucial causal role of the growth of agricultural productivity, in enabling her to feed each generation of Japanese rather better than its predecessor, and at the same time enabling her to raise the non-agricultural proportion of the labour force from the original 30 per cent up to 70 per cent by the 1930s. In doing this, Japan undoubtedly had benefited not only from its very interesting social structure but also from a remarkably low income elasticity of demand for food, which Mr. Clark thought had probably a sociological origin.

In general Mr. Clark and Miss Haswell had found some surprising facts about the income elasticity demand for food in the course of their studies. They started off, as most people do, from the concept that people who are very close to the physiological limit of hunger will have a highly voracious and more or less predictable demand for food as their incomes increase. This conception is by no means confirmed. In general, the results indicate rather that, especially among urban populations, there can be strong demonstration effects of a desire to eat European foods, although this is not always

1. Now published. (Ed.)

true of urban populations in Asia and Africa. Other, more austere communities like Japan show little by way of a demonstration effect and display a low income elasticity of demand for food, which has the effect of releasing resources to accelerate the industrialization of a country. Mr. Clark said that there is a lot of misinformation on this subject which arises out of a curious statistical bias in Indian studies, most of which are based not on per head figures, but on per family figures. The difference which this makes arises from the fact that if an Indian acquires an income, half a dozen additional relatives promptly turn up to live with him, and this gives a very strong upward bias to the per family food consumption figures. If one works them out per head, great differences appear.

Mr. Clark next referred to a logarithmic relationship between agricultural productivity regarded as the causal force and proportion of the labour force in non-agricultural employment. Japan is again an exception, having industrialized a good deal faster than this relationship would indicate. Mr. Clark stressed that, although qualifying the purely physiocratic case, and therefore with reluctance, he had to admit the finding that the relationship was significantly improved if one included mineral and forest productivity with agricultural productivity, insofar as they led to exportable products.

Mr. Clark next discussed some diagrams relating to marginal productivity in agriculture. The figures for Gambia had been prepared by Miss Haswell in the most careful detail, family by family, checked hour by hour throughout an agricultural year. Other data related to Nigeria, China, Yugoslavia, Japan and India. The general conclusion was that marginal productivity in agriculture can fall to zero; but it certainly is wrong to say that it is always at zero in subsistence agriculture countries. In India, for instance, and in some parts of Africa, the marginal productivity of agriculture can be high. There is also evidence that the amount of labour input possible before marginal productivity falls to zero is influenced by such factors as the amount of livestock kept.

There had been some rather metaphysical discussions as to whether anything whatever can be done to improve agricultural productivity, or whether it is a thing which happens of itself. On this, Mr. Clark wanted to be materialistic; he thought there are certain very concrete things which can be done to improve the productivity of subsistence cultivation. Quite in a class by itself, more urgent and important than anything else, is transport. This arises from the nature of the case. So many villages, even in Asia, are completely isolated from

N

transport except by mud tracks. If there is no transport a sensible man will remain a subsistence cultivator. He says: "If I try to produce a commercial crop I won't be able to transport it to a market, except at an enormous expense." As Sargent's interesting researches in Borneo show, in a really primitive country, once you provide a road, the marginal returns to your investment are very high indeed. The only difficulty Sargent found in Borneo was lack of population to exploit the roads which are being built.

With roads, there are two other things which one must provide. One must provide reasonable marketing facilities, and one must provide reasonable terms of trade. The latter is the point that Lenin forgot when he set out to plan Soviet agriculture in the early 1920s. The peasant may not be able to read or write, but he knows when he is being offered bad terms of trade, and he declines to increase production any further. It is the first duty of economists therefore to find him good transport, markets and terms of trade. After that one goes on to fertilizers, and after that to education, followed by all the further stages in economic development.

MR. KALDOR

Mr. Kaldor said that he thoroughly agreed with Mr. Clark's emphasis on the primacy of agricultural productivity. He had been emphasizing this for the last ten years and so had many others.

He wanted to add a footnote to what Mr. Clark had said, on the income elasticity of demand for food in Japan. He had been told—he was not a professional Japanese expert by any means—that in Japan this was very largely the product of universal education. They very early introduced, with universal education, school meals, of a very peculiar kind, which were invented in Japan, consisting of raw fish and soya beans and a few things which add up to the right sort of combination of proteins and calories, the cost of which is extremely low. What is true about the Japanese is that in childhood they acquire a taste for this peculiar food, which is cold, and is supplied from little standard paper baskets. In matters of taste, everything is a matter of learning. They learn to like this very cheap and very wholesome food of such peculiar taste that once acquired it is very difficult to disacquire, and as a result they spend a very low proportion of their income on food, even when grown up. If one looks at the Japanese compared with any other nation, the striking thing is that for the level of real income per head the proportion of income spent on food is low. Apparently this was the result of a deliberate policy, although he could hardly believe that the people who started it were so intelligent as to foresee its very far-reaching consequences. But the typical Japanese like to eat raw fish from little paper baskets —they can't see the point of spending more money on food.

Mr. Kaldor said he also agreed with the emphasis Mr. Clark placed on other things. He thought transport is very important and is very often overlooked. The inaccessibility of many agricultural regions, from the point of view of marketing, is one of the really important factors in these countries in preventing an increase in the marketable surplus of agriculture.

Where Mr. Kaldor found himself in disagreement was when Mr. Clark turned to the marginal product of labour in Indian agriculture. If Mr. Clark were right, then surely Indian agriculture should suffer from under- rather than over-population, and we should then plan to transfer the population from the urban areas to the rural areas rather than the other way round. Every Indian is brought up on the doctrine that India has about 150–200 million of surplus people on the land, who cannot be effectively employed in agriculture. There is no country in the world where the ratio of cultivable acreage to the population is so unfavourable as it is in India. The total number of potentially cultivable acres in India is only 300 million and this is for a population which is now 450 million. If one looks at the figures, he thought, even for Japan, one does not find such a low ratio. He was not sure about Japan, but for China he was sure the ratio is much less unfavourable than for India. So when Mr. Clark tells us calmly that in India the marginal product of labour is not zero as we have been teaching all this time, but that it is high and higher than the wage, he would really like to know what sort of calculation underlies this estimate.

Mr. Clark

Mr. Clark said that he had not made himself clear: he had said *in certain circumstances:* there is great diversity in India. He would agree in general; as one could see in his diagram he had shown marginal productivity falling very sharply when a certain critical limit was reached. In Southern India there is a chronic over-supply of labour throughout the year. In Northern India the analysis was made on the basis of annual labour input, in relation to marginal products. The analysis here is more complex. If one made a monthly analysis one got the rather surprising result that there is a definite *labour shortage* in the short monsoon season. It is possible, in the monsoonal areas of Norther India, that this labour shortage can only be overcome by mechanization. But this would still leave one with surplus labour during the nine dry months. There are however certain parts of India, and certain farms within each village, where the marginal productivity of labour is high.

DR. MYINT

Dr. Myint said that he would like to hark back mainly to the earlier discussion about the applicability of economic theory, but he was also pleased to hear that some of the later discussion by Mr. Clark and Mr. Kaldor was rather relevant to the point he wished to stress.

The paper he had submitted to the Conference was really concerned to make two points, the first and more important of which related to the question of the significance of studying the market mechanism, while the second and relatively less controversial one related to a plea for not being dominated by models of a particular type of underdeveloped country, such as India.

Taking the first point, he had noted that people criticized the market mechanism either because they thought that the free play of market forces would not lead to an optimum allocation in any way that one wishes to define an optimum, or were criticizing it on the ground that the optimum itself was too static and would therefore not give any guidance to the theory of economic growth. Since in fact the controversy about the applicability of economic theory to underdeveloped countries is linked up, below the surface, with the controversy about planning and free enterprise, it seemed to him that the best thing to do is to try to discuss the question of the applicability of economic theory to these countries in terms of a classification of the various types of criticisms of the market mechanism. He, himself, was not concerned to be ambitious in his claims about the applicability of economic theory as a whole to these countries nor was he concerned to settle the issue of whether we should or should not go on to social psychology. He was interested in the more pedestrian task of seeing which parts of economic theory were relatively more applicable to underdeveloped countries than others. He had made a plea that the static or optimum theory is perhaps as applicable as any other part of theory and that, before we have any more satisfactory theory, we should make do with this.

Dr. Myint said that the point here really is that whether we are in favour of planning for economic development or not, whether we prefer direct planning or indirect planning and so on, we ought to look at the working of market forces in underdeveloped countries for the simple reason that the state sector occupies a smaller part of income generated than the private sector, including the subsistence sector. Dr. Myint said that he therefore believed that the functioning of these economies should be studied by looking at the mode of operation of market forces in them. In particular, while he would agree that one cannot generalize, one may nevertheless want to place one's analysis in different boxes. And while one may be unable to fill the boxes he thought they can best be made up of the sort of thing one encounters in market theory. He was particularly interested in how far market imperfection theory should be applied. His argument was that some people simply say that markets are imperfect or inefficient or ineffective, and ignore market imperfection theory. He himself, on the other hand, was not saying that the market was quite perfect or good or anything, but simply that this is one way of, and an instrument for, studying underdeveloped countries and how they function. This was really his central point.

Of course, Dr. Myint added, one has to confess that when one starts talking about studying the market element of a mixed economy, this may be an exhibition of bias in favour of solutions by way of the market. That may be so and he did not deny that various people have got biases, and he himself may have a bias also. His own bias probably arises from looking at South-east Asian countries. If one looks at the post-World War II performance of South-east Asian countries, one finds that the most prosperous ones, or those which seem to be doing well, are the Philippines, Thailand and Malaya. These are not laissez-faire economies. They are controlled economies. But—leaving out Hong Kong—they are economies which do rely on indirect control by way of the market and on encouraging foreign enterprise to come in. The less prosperous countries, on the other hand, Burma and Indonesia, they have different conditions, which are roughly the same, and they have roughly the same history and so on. Now, although he was not generalizing and was not suggesting that this can necessarily be extended, he did find these associations rather suggestive. It did lead him to say that if one has got small countries with export ratios which are high, and which are not suffering from population pressure in the Indian sense, it might well be worth looking a little more at the market element.

A further point in this connection, which would perhaps link up quite a bit with what Professor Hagen had to say, was this: he thought people tended to look upon the market mechanism too much as a way of allocating existing resources, whereas he was wondering whether it is not possible to look upon the long term effects of the market as an effect on the supply of factors.

Professor Hagen

Professor Hagen said that he wanted to make a few comments directly related to what Hla Myint had said, but he wanted to introduce his comments by coming back to what Mrs. Robinson had said earlier. She had said that they are not really in agreement, that what Mr. Kaldor said is good, and that what Mr. Hagen said about theory being applicable is dangerous. In fact—with the qualification that, as an adviser to an underdeveloped country, Professor Hagen thought he would not be as imaginative in thinking up policies as Mr. Kaldor, because he did not regard himself as imaginative a person as Mr. Kaldor—he thought that they would give much the same advice. This raises the question of what is meant by theory being applicable. Thinking about it and talking to a few of the people at the Conference, and using the vocabulary that he thought most of them would use, he would *now* say that large amounts of economic theory, as we teach it about advanced countries, are *not* applicable. Nevertheless, he would be saying the same, in substance, that he intended to be saying previously.

For example, interest-policy conclusions as commonly taught in elementary courses are certainly not applicable in an underdeveloped country in the same way as in England, if there is not a reasonably integrated capital market. Professor Hagen did not think of that as saying that the theory is wrong. It is saying that the assumptions are different, so naturally one arrives at a different policy conclusions. But he suspected that the usual vocabulary is to say that therefore the theory isn't applicable. He agreed. Again, he thought that where subsistence agriculture is important, some of the policy conclusions we draw from our theory, which implicitly assumes a money market, need to be modified to be effective in such a country.

He wanted to cite one more example. In Burma he had recommended (without any effect at the time) certain high excises collected at source. Now, any tax theorist knows that this is the worst possible type of taxation. One ought to have progressive taxation. If one insists on having excises, one ought to have them at the final point so that they won't be pyramided. In fact, he felt that income taxes would not be collected in Burma and that the excises would not be collected if levied at retail. Those he had proposed were on luxury goods that by and large were consumed by high income groups, and he thought that these excises collected at source were a rather progressive tax, and more progressive than what one could get in other ways. He didn't think of that as meaning that the theory wasn't applicable. Others thought it did mean this. The difference results mainly from the fact that when some persons refer to theory, they mean only the general postulates, while others think of theory as comprehending also the specific conclusions. Many of those present may be closer together in substance than our vocabulary indicates.

PROFESSOR KAHN

Professor Kahn said that at this point he really wanted to ask what this Conference was all about. He had come to this Conference thinking that they were going to discuss the problems of teaching development economics. But it seemed to him that the Conference so far had been mainly concerned with the question of how people with first-class minds, although they may be suffering from the handicap of having had a traditional education in economics, are nevertheless able to give good advice in developing countries. Professor Kahn said that he was perfectly prepared to believe that people with first-class minds—which included most people, in fact, everybody at the Conference—can overcome the defects of their education and, when it comes to the point, can be sensible. But he thought—and this was, he thought, the point of what Mrs. Robinson had been saying at the last session—that what they were concerned about in this Conference was what we teach to people who have not got first-class minds. He thought that the prior question, and certainly after the preceding discussion it was a question very prominent in his own mind, was whether one should try to teach them anything at all?

MR. KALDOR

Mr. Kaldor said that he would like to follow up the last two speakers, Mr. Hagen and Professor Kahn, because he was in some ways in an intermediate position. He did believe that a great deal of what we learn about the economics of developed countries is either very important or useful in understanding the processes which go on in underdeveloped countries yet, at the same time, these processes themselves are often fundamentally different between different underdeveloped countries.

He wanted to illustrate by means of an example, since speaking in general will never get one anywhere. Inflation is something that has worried people in all sorts of different countries, including England, for a number of years. Inflation is far more prominent in the countries of Latin America than here. There is something in the processes of inflation in all these countries which is in some sense common, and some understanding of the nature of the wage-price spiral is, he thought, illuminating in both contexts. If Professor Kahn, who has done a great deal of work on wage inflation, went to the Argentine and Brazil, he would be in a very much better position to pronounce on the situation than somebody who has not gone through the controversies on inflation in the Western countries. But at the same time if, as many people going from America or the International Monetary Fund do, one goes to the Latin American countries and tells them in a most dogmatic and mechanical way that they must apply the same remedies which the Federal Reserve Board in Washington thinks are appropriate for dealing with inflationary tendencies in the U.S., they can go absolutely wrong. The trouble here is not in the method of analysis, or in the theory, if one uses the word theory in any fundamental sense. The trouble simply is the mechanistic application of results which have some validity at any rate in some contexts and have very little validity in others. In Latin America the *causes* of the wage-price spiral are completely different: inflation there is due to structural factors, which he did not want to spend too long in going into. These factors have nothing to do with excessive credit creation as a causal factor, and therefore cannot sensibly be remedied on those lines at all. The thought and ideas one has devoted to the study of the mechanics of inflation in advanced countries can certainly bring light to bear on the situation in these other countries, but they are only important and useful so long as they are brought to bear in a flexible manner and without an insistence on rigid application of the kind of policy conclusions which one may think appropriate in developed countries.

PROFESSOR ZIMMERMAN

Professor Zimmerman said that the gist of what the Conference had been hearing was that it is not so much economics as such that is the problem, but the economists who apply it in a wrong way. He agreed entirely with those who had been saying that our methods of analysis can be applied in any country in the world, so long as we are studying economic problems. The trouble is that the results of analysis obtained for policy purposes in the West are sometimes illegitimately used for policy purposes in other parts of the world. This points to a definite need for an interdisciplinary approach. Political situations and sociological conditions are often completely different from those in our countries. This does not mean that the economist has to change his theory: Professor Zimmerman thought Mr. Hagen was going a little too far in that direction. The need was for working in teams composed of people from different disciplines, who must, after they have made their various analyses in their own fields, together work out a general policy.

PROFESSOR NOVE

Professor Nove said that he wanted to take up one problem, or one way of looking at a certain kind of problem, which he felt possibly underlay some people's dissatisfaction with certain economists' way of looking at things. He was referring to instability and its consequences. Somehow a very large number of theories, models, approaches to economic development, seem to make no assumptions whatever about this rather key subject, although most of us know that political, social and economic instability is a common feature of developing countries. This is not something external to the development problem. It is not like the consequences of an earthquake. It is a part of the problem that we are studying. This brought one to some of the work of Mr. Hagen, with which Professor Nove said he would like in part to agree, and in part to ask that it be taken further. Obviously, development involves a challenge to traditional ways of life, and possibly to traditionalist governments. This is a part of the instability-generating processes that we were talking about. We were also uncomfortably aware, from time to time—this has been said, by Joan Robinson among others—that industrialization and the spread of democratic institutions go ill together.

The point that Professor Nove wanted to appeal to Mr. Hagen to take further, as being an important part of the study of development, was his analysis of the role of the "authoritarian traditionalist". In his very interesting book, Mr. Hagen had talked a great deal about this type. What Mr. Hagen did not seem to realize is that in this situation there often emerges an "authoritarian reformer". The problem of the authoritarian reformer is worth stressing and worth thinking about. It is a major part of the phenomenon of catching up: the conscious replacement of spontaneous processes by a forced process directed from above. Peter the Great, Stalin, Kemal Ataturk are obvious examples. The ideology may be Marxist, it may be nationalist, it may be all kinds of things. This is rather an important point because their *modus operandi* in politics and in economics is worth pondering.

Some may say that this is no doubt true, perhaps, but what has it to do with us economists? Professor Nove thought that we must take this into account not only in giving advice in unstable countries, where of course people are conscious that the political situation is what it is, but, possibly, we should also take into account in our theorizing because the economic consequences of instability are many, and they differ greatly in different countries. He was not suggesting that this kind of extension of theory was easy. Nevertheless it may be quite feasible. It could, for example, be that economic instability is partly caused by land reform, with certain effects on the politics of the country, on the off-farm surplus and on the possibilities of accumulation. There may be a threat of rebellion and confiscations, of disorder, inflation, or balance of payments crises accompanied by necessary but unpredictable changes in import controls. All these things have a number of effects, which are sometimes predictable enough to warrant being theorized about. One such effect is surely that a high degree of uncertainty is likely to influence the direction of private investment. The rate of interest is likely to be rather high. The risk element of doing anything involving several years' foresight is extremely high, so that it is in these circumstances not irrational either to send money to Zurich or New York, or to use it, as many business men in these countries do, for land speculation, for short-term trade deals, and so on. There is no need to make any assumption about "underdeveloped" entrepreneurial attitudes in order to obtain this kind of prediction. But all this in turn has a deep and, Professor Nove thought, predictable effect on the functioning of the market mechanism. It means that although there is a market and although for certain purposes it can and should be used, there are certain market indicators which go wrong in these circumstances, which are distorted in particular ways. The argument does not depend on market imperfection. The effects of the underlying instability, or the effects of the State's efforts to struggle with the unstable situation, which is apt to cause it to intervene in all kinds of ways, are bound to result in distortions of prices and of rates of return. These distortions are the outcome of quite rational ways of acting, but once the market indicators have become twisted out of shape as a result of the underlying instability of the situation, it becomes genuinely very difficult to use them as a guide either for private or indeed for public decisions. This, Professor Nove thought, is a part of the essence of the problem. It is not external to it, it is not an accident, it happens rather often. If one were fortunate enough to find a country free of such phenomena, then the problems are of course very much easier to solve.

A problem which makes development economics both fascinating and extremely difficult is to decide what it is that one is optimizing, Professor Nove continued. Here, he thought, Mr. Streeten's paper was extremely valuable with its emphasis on the interconnected character of the processes of advance in social, institutional and other changes. The wider institutional consequences of dam building projects in Persia were an example of a case where the strictly economic direct rate of return was relatively small, but the effect of the resulting irrigation arrangements in breaking up the share cropping system in agriculture were of a fundamental importance for the whole economic advance of the country. By what sort of economico-socio-political criteria can one advise a government in such cases? How does one know when one has hit on the right solution?

Indeed by what criterion would one approve, as a citizen, of what a government does in such a field? It is a very difficult problem, but it is a problem which arises often and it does so in a highly unstable, changing society. A very similar situation in North-east Brazil led Professor Hirschman to argue in favour of dams, praising in particular the work of Celso Furtado, who is very conscious of this problem. The latest that Professor Nove had heard was that Celso Furtado is dismissed by the new Brazilian regime. This merely underlines the fact that economics in developing countries is emphatically political economy.

PROFESSOR HANSON

The important thing in what Professor Nove had said was that this is essentially political economy. He was quite certain, Mr. Hanson said, that the first thing an economist who goes to a foreign country has to do is to familiarize himself with the political system of the country in order to understand both the opportunities and the limitations which it imposes on the advice that he can usefully give. It may be, of course, that the country requires a revolution, but it is not, he thought, for the economist to say so. After all, the economist goes to advise a particular government on its economic policy and therefore he has got to accept, *pro tem.* in any case, the limitations which are imposed by the constitutional system and by the political structure of the country. Professor Hanson became very acutely aware of this when he was looking into the problems of Indian economic development, particularly the question of the location of new projects, such as multi-purpose river valley projects, and industries, and so on. It isn't difficult, he thought, for the people in the Planning Commission, with the sort of information they have at their disposal, to decide on what would be an economically optimum location policy. But one of the principal facts of Indian political structure is that political power is divided between the centre and sixteen states, which are becoming more and more politically conscious, and very often don't regard Delhi with any particular favour or affection, and so often the Planning Commission has to allow mere economic rationality to yield to strict political prejudice in order to preserve the unity of the Indian Union. This seems to make economic nonsense, but ultimately it doesn't. If one insisted that India ought to remain the kind of federal democracy that she is, then, if one is going to place strains on the political system which results in a tendency for the states to contract out of the whole thing, one is going to degenerate into political chaos in which any kind of economic development is going to be very difficult indeed.

Another example of the same sort of thing was strongly impressed upon Mr. Hanson when he read an article by Mr. Balogh on the Five Year Plan in the Indian journal *Capital*. Mr. Balogh was strongly urging that the Third Five Year Plan was too small, that it ought to be considerably bigger, and that if it wasn't bigger, then the improvement in the Indian standard of life would be so slow that one would pretty soon have political trouble. People's expectations were at such a level that they would not be prepared to stand for so slow a rate of advance. Consequently it was necessary to speed up the pace of development and to squeeze out more resources for capital formation and so on. The point that struck Mr. Hanson in reading that article was that if the policy which Mr. Balogh was advocating had been adopted, then one would pretty soon have a completely different kind of political strain, which might have been equally disruptive to the interests of the political system, and that the Planning Commission was in the extremely unenviable position of having to decide upon a pace of advance which was sufficiently fast to avoid the kind of political strain which Mr. Balogh had in mind, but not so fast as to create a completely different and equally disruptive kind of political strain. It therefore seemed to Mr. Hanson that unless this political situation was understood and unless the economist was prepared to work within the limits of the political system of the country concerned, his advice would be automatically rejected by the government. Alternatively, being accepted, it would quite possibly be fatal to the government concerned.

MR. RADO

Mr. Rado said that he wanted to clarify one or two points which the discussion had raised, and, in particular, to revert to some matters arising from Mr. Balogh's paper.

Mr. Rado thought that we may be leading ourselves into unnecessary difficulty, by placing quite unjustified expectations on what economics can or should achieve. It was useless to seek for a panacea of what makes some nations grow and not others. There was not any kind of medicine which was going to make all economies grow equally. The present Japanese rates of growth and the present U.S. standard of living were probably not within the reach of most countries in the foreseeable future.

The search for a panacea arises, Mr. Rado thought, because people confuse economics as a method of approach with economics as a body of conclusions which can be "applied" to "solve" specific practical problems. It is in the latter field, when it comes to applications, that it is not even worth attempting to find results which will be valid for all time and for all economies.

Educational planning is fashionable nowadays in underdeveloped countries. Huge plans are being prepared in isolation from attempts to determine what the rest of the economy is going to do. Mr. Balogh was perfectly right in criticizing non-operational approaches to planning education, such as the "residual approach". The "rates of return approach" is almost equally non-operational, but the real difficulty arises when one gets past the destructive phase of criticizing illegitimate approaches. He did not think that anyone could quarrel on methodological grounds with the approach that Mr. Balogh brought to the question of what kind of education underdeveloped countries need. But when one tries to translate this approach into the actual reality of how many schools are needed for how many pupils and how much of one's resources should be applied to education, the "correctness" of one's approach and the "correctness" of one's methodology cannot guarantee that *therefore* one's recommendations will turn out to have been right. He agreed with the approach that Mr. Balogh suggested, and at the same time one may have doubts about whether his particular practical recommendations were going to be as feasible and desirable in the circumstances of one country as they happened to be in another. The kind of agriculture combined with the kind of education he suggests may be absolutely right for Algeria but not feasible for another country. This is not to say that his economics is wrong. It is right. He had illuminated the irrelevancies, he had concentrated on those things that are important. He had asked the questions which economists should ask. But beyond that his practical conclusions may be right or they may be wrong. No amount of correct methodology is going to guarantee that, by the purity of our approach, our conclusions are also going to be correct. The only thing the truth of which is guaranteed by the assumptions is a syllogism. If one tried to be comparatively modest and did not expect or hope to prove that by economic analysis—which is based on intelligent application of the syllogistic approach—one can also build up a universally acceptable body of applied knowledge, some of the disappointments with which people have been castigating themselves in this conference would be avoided.

Mr. Seers

Mr. Seers said that he wanted to raise what seemed to him quite a central issue. This was what we meant by saying that a certain theory was appropriate. Mr. Hagen's remarks about the uses of traditional fiscal theory in suggesting ways of closing the *ex-ante* gap between savings and investment brought out the essential questions.

Supposing one wants to raise the ratio of investment to the domestic product from 5 to 10 per cent, and one is looking for the savings to offset this. To start with, one can hardly treat savings or investment as "globally" as one can in developed countries. Investment in mining, for example, is financed by savings which are earmarked for the mineral sector, namely profits of certain companies; if one does not use these savings for mining, one cannot necessarily make them available for something else. They cannot be expected to flow round into another sector of the economy. Then, when one comes to deal with the final gap, which has to be closed by government savings of some kind, the nature of the taxes is of prime importance.

In this respect, there is some difference in emphasis between different parts of the world. Working in a developed country, one would consider various ways of closing the same gap—increases in cigarette taxes, or in import duties, or in direct taxes. One would probably conclude that if income taxes were used, a higher increase in revenue would have to be aimed at because of the effect on savings. But in the first stage one is looking for (say) £200 million from the budget; this is the important thing, the implications of different ways of doing it are of a second order of importance. In underdeveloped countries, however, if direct taxes are raised, the negative effect on private savings may be almost as great as the positive effect on public savings, because of the inequality of income distribution. What is more important, whichever the taxes that are increased (though this applies specially to a regressive tax), the result may not be to transfer resources from inessential consumer industries to capital investment. It may be to release resources which are then not used at all, but simply stand idle; this is because of the immobile and highly specific nature of resources in underdeveloped countries.

The same problem arises in the case of *big* shifts in developed countries. The 1951 economic programme for the United Kingdom ran into difficulties because the government was trying to achieve not just a marginal shift, but a big transfer of resources from consumption to military expenditure. The result was a steel shortage on the one hand, and on the other inadequate demand for textiles, with unemployment in Lancashire. Of course in mobilisation for war, the shift is even more difficult to achieve by purely fiscal means.

There is really only one way in which one can shift resources by taxation in underdeveloped countries, and that is by using taxes to reduce the demand for imports, so that foreign exchange is released for capital goods; this after all is the essence of most development plans. Foreign exchange is *the* mobile resource for development purposes.

What this means in practice is that one has to look much more closely at the *structure* of the required taxation than at its *total*; secondly, it means that one can expect much less help from fiscal policy for financing investment than in developed countries. (One could make analogous points, more sharply in fact, on monetary policy, which Dr. Hagen also mentioned.)

But does this also imply that conventional fiscal theory is useless in underdeveloped countries? The answer could be no, if the question is just: can we still use the conventional categories of analysis? The words he had been using are after all familiar to anyone working on fiscal problems. But if one thinks of the practical applications of fiscal analysis, considerable changes in the content and the policy implications have to be made to take account of the different structure of underdeveloped countries.

This of course raises the question of what is a "theory", which is, as Dr. Hagen had said, in large part a semantic issue. But to say this is to say that it is largely a matter of convenience. Now, one can argue that the same theory can be used overseas as at home, and that all one needs to do is to make one's assumptions clear and to stress the qualifications and to introduce social factors and so forth. But this procedure does impose on economists the responsibilitiy to stress these qualifications and these assumptions continually, so that in every lecture and every paper one keeps on saying "I am only dealing with the special and rather boring case of an industrial society." If economists are prepared to go one saying that, again and again, well and good.

Unfortunately, Mr. Seers thought, they were not prepared to do that, and consequently the student who goes to work overseas did so without adequate preparation for the magnitude of the leap which he had to make.

Mr. Seers stressed that he was talking of the inapplicability not merely of the Quantity theory but of Keynesian theory too; Keynesian economics was now, he thought, an obstacle to the understanding of development problems.

Perhaps, Mr. Seers said, the theoretical shift is possible for the "first-class minds" to which Mr. Kahn had referred. But Mr. Seers could not help remembering that first-class minds had done some rather stupid things when they were working overseas. The reason for this was that our cerebrations are not pure, they are determined by our environment, particularly the national customs and traditions of the country where we are educated. It is not just a matter of thinking one's way through. In fact it could be argued that the more brilliant the intelligence, after a certain level of I.Q. is reached, the less able people are at professional work overseas, because they come to rely too heavily on sheer mental power. The evidence for this is that very good minds of even the same political temper, from, say, France or the United Kingdom, come to quite different types of conclusion when dealing with the same problem; one sees this very often in African conditions. Of course, the difference between the conclusions reached by Soviet and British economists, or Chilean and British, is still greater. Mr. Seers said that he had tried to indicate some of the reasons for this at greater length in an article called "Why Visiting Economists Fail"[1] the title of which, he expected, was going to hang around his neck for the rest of his professional life.

The jump one had to make was perhaps comparable to attempting

1. *Journal of Political Economy*, August 1962, vol. LXX, No. 4.

to be an economic adviser to Cromwell or to Robespierre or to Lenin. He put it in these terms because (such is the nature of our education) we realize more sharply our social distance from Cromwellian England or the French or Russian Revolutions than from the present-day underdeveloped countries. So he believed it better to say that our theoretical structure, as taught, is *not* adequate.

MR. THOMAS

Mr. Thomas said that a good deal of criticism had been made of the applicability of traditional Western economics to problems of economic planning, without putting anything very much in its place. From limited experience of trying to do a planning job in the field, in a new irrigation project in North-west Syria, it did seem to him, and to some of the members of his department, who were also engaged in this, that parts of the theory anyway have real application.

On this particular project, the correct allocation of resources now could make the difference between failure and success of the project, a difference between a very low and a reasonably good rate of return on what is an enormous investment of capital. An adequate rate of return on investment would in turn affect the future rate of saving and of investment both within agriculture and in other sectors. That part of economics dealing with resource allocation was therefore of real relevance.

The difficulty that one finds is not so much in formulating realistic economic models for optimizing, but in finding the physical coefficients to feed into these models. Perhaps economists no longer insist, as Robbins once did, that technology is none of our business, but Mr. Thomas thought that too many of us still perhaps escape by assuming that technology is given, or perhaps by assuming it will change at some given rate derived from the experience of Western countries where development has been natural and not imposed. The fact is, of course, that in agriculture, even in underdeveloped agriculture, one is not dealing with one technology, but with a whole spectrum of technologies, each with its own resource requirement, and each with its own production function. The production possibilities depend very largely on what level of technology one assumes, or on what level or technology one thinks one can introduce within a reasonable space of time. The choice, for example, between two crops may depend entirely on the assumptions one makes as to what level of technology can be introduced by a multitude of small peasant farmers. In this particular project, one of the things that is under consideration is the development of a dairying industry. It would appear that the raw materials are there, by way of enormous crops of lucerne, and the availability of things like cotton cake *in situ.* The demand for livestock products in Syria is high and growing rapidly, so that, in a general way, the possibilities do seem to exist. But when one comes down to detail and looks at this question more closely, one finds that the indigenous cattle are so poor that they would not be able to make use of what are excellent materials, and convert them economically into dairy products. One can then think in terms, perhaps, of importing Dutch or Danish or British cattle, which is one step up the technological ladder. But the expertise for handling a dairy industry at this new level of technology also does not exist amongst the peasant farmers as they now are. One cannot rule the whole idea out on this count, however, because if we could, for example, evolve some system of co-operative dairying, under expert management of cattle and production of dairy products, one would be operating at another entirely different level of technology, which might be economically very viable and make all the difference between success and failure of the whole project.

Mr. Thomas felt that economists, working on development projects, could no longer avoid being concerned with technology, neither could they depend upon the agronomists or other physical scientists to provide them with the necessary technological coefficients for their models. In Mr. Thomas's experience, the physical scientists, the agronomists, the hydrologists, the irrigation experts and so on, think in much too narrow a range of possibilities; they think in terms of discrete ways of doing things, they think in terms of the perfect irrigation system, whatever it costs, they think in terms of, often, a very narrow range of crops, which is related to what they think about the ecological conditions, not to what economic circumstances in the country would dictate. For this reason, Mr. Thomas thought the economists on the Syrian project would have to search for their own coefficients to put into the kinds of models which they were building. They will try to do so by looking at experience in other countries, those which have recently developed in particular, or at similar projects within Syria, and in this way try to build up a body of data which can be used when optimizing for this particular project.

Of course, the level of technology which one assumes does in fact depend to a very large extent upon the economic and social institutions which one can also build up at the same time, and therefore he thought that there is a need for inter-disciplinary working on this kind of project.

The morals of the story are three: Firstly, this question of building up a fund of knowledge from recent experience of developing projects—and there now must be hundreds of them up and down the world. It does not seem sensible that each one of us who does this kind of work should have to build up one's own fund of knowledge. Why not have a clearing house, perhaps at F.A.O. or U.N. where the necessary fund of data could be built up, and from which we could select, with greater objectivity than is now possible, the relevant material for the particular purpose in hand? Secondly, since the level of technology does depend upon the kind of social and economic institutions which are feasible, and acceptable, there is the need, already mentioned, for developing some inter-disciplinary work. Lastly, and of relevance for teaching, all this may point to the case study approach, where one not only has economists and agricultural economists, but also sociologists, agronomists and physical scientists working together on the same project.

On rather a different point, Mr. Thomas thought that it had become fashionable to think of land reform as a sort of panacea for all the evils of underdeveloped agriculture, and reform had often been identified with the creation of freehold tenure, the advantages assumed being based mainly on the experience of Europe and North America. He was by no means certain that this is the right solution for many underdeveloped regions without, at least, considering some of the alternatives, such as co-operative farming, even state farming, or the gradual reform of tribal or tenancy systems. The things in favour of a freehold tenure system are so obvious that they have blinded us to some of the disadvantages of the system. The incentive to work and to innovate because it is your own land, which you can pass on to your heirs, is all very clear. What is much less clear is that the creation now of a large number of small peasant proprietors under freehold tenure may become a positive bar to development in the future. Economic development implies the transfer of people from agriculture to other occupations, a process which has been shown in some instances to be impeded by the rigidities introduced by the freehold tenure system. We are, Mr. Thomas thought, in danger of being blinded by what seems so simple and so obvious.

PROFESSOR GLUCKMAN

As the only pure social anthropologist present, Professor Gluckman wanted to clear up some misconceptions about anthropology which had been advanced by three speakers earlier and had provoked laughter in the distinguished audience.

Of course anthropologists have always been interested in problems of social change, and were writing about them at a time when most economists and political scientists hadn't realized that there were continents outside Europe. Professor Gluckman was not quite sure of the extent to which social anthropologists have been interested in what one might call the problems of growth, in the sense of trying to assist growth, because—since this is Shakespeare's year—"the galled jade winces". When your withers have been wrung you shun the hot seats of power, to mix the metaphor. But, in fact, anthropologists had made numerous studies of change.

What they rarely did was to give advice, and this for a very good reason. When they did give advice, they ran into difficulties with colonial governments who mostly didn't like the advice, and usually before that didn't like the findings. When Professor Gluckman was directing research in Northern Rhodesia, he went to considerable trouble to try to protect his staff, who were studying the growth of trade unionism, the position of African élites, and so forth. In fact in the end he issued an ultimatum to his Trustees, of whom the Governor was one, to the effect that he would not allow anybody to work in any of the urban areas unless a guarantee was given that if any allegations were made against a research worker, an enquiry would be carried out into the truth or not of these allegations. He had done so because already one man had been excluded from the mining compound on false allegations. And the Trustees would not give him that guarantee. The next man who was put in, after Professor Gluckman left, was excluded, and there was no enquiry into the allegations made against him. This is because when one has been dealing with people—and people are much more dangerous than statistics in countries which, both before and after the war, have been in an unstable political condition, as Professor Nove had said—when one is dealing with people as anthropologists do, one's behaviour is inevitably doubly suspicious. In fact, anthropologists were constantly dependent on the colonial governments for permission to carry out research, and also largely on mining companies, when working in the towns. They just kept away from giving advice, published their findings, and then were happy in the knowledge that nobody would read them, or very few would who had any position of power or influence. Since independence, of course, the position has been much more difficult, because anthropology has become a suspect word. This is because it has wrongly been associated with the study of so-called "savages" and "primitive society". This was clear at the Accra conference on African studies. Professor Gluckman himself was told by a friend of his, a Minister in one of the Central African countries, with whom he had worked and spoken on many occasions against the imposition of the Central African Federation, that anthropologists were no good because they had shown Africans to be savages. The opposite is true: anthropologists had either shown them not to be savages, or else had shown everybody, including Europeans, to be savages. The Minister asked Professor Gluckman for proof of this, and was sent a book of Professor Gluckman's on the judicial process of a tribe in Northern Rhodesia, in which Professor Gluckman compared this with the Western judicial process. This book was never acknowledged. Why?—because there is now a policy in that country to state that all chiefs were corrupt, undemocratic, bribable, giving false judgments: and Professor Gluckman's study proves this is not true.

Work is now being carried out in trickier circumstances. In the time of the Imperial government, no one really cared what anthropologists were saying. Thousands and thousands of books were published about the Commonwealth, and hardly any person in power read them. The books made no political impact. But in an independent small country, one book that criticizes the assumptions on which the government is working can possibly become political dynamite. Therefore again anthropologists don't give advice.

To Professor Gluckman, the most interesting problem, even allowing for all this, was why it is that when economists and political scientists since the war, and particularly since independence, began to be drawn into these countries, they have tended on the whole to ignore the years of experience and knowledge which social anthropologists have accumulated. In his own department, which is one of the newer ones, there is forty-four years of experience in a whole variety of countries. Nobody takes any notice of this. There may be good reasons for this, and maybe anthropologists know too much for some newcomers into these fields. But, he thought, a lot of it has to do with the present attitude of the newly independent countries about the work of anthropology and to the misconceptions on which this attitude is based. Some scholars jump off an unpopular bandwagon. But there is a lot of work done by anthropologists on problems of labour supplies, problems of marketing, and so forth, in these countries, particularly the peasant areas. They have studied the whole swing of labour between town and country, the difficulties that arise in the development of cash crop farming with the rise and fall of income in particular families caused by the cultural demands for sumptuary expenditure at certain stages in the life cycle of the family. They have analysed, further, the effect of the life cycle on supplies of labour for particular purposes, and again it struck him, going around Africa and seeing economists working on these problems (and not on the general national problems), that they don't read the anthropologists. They pick up their information about land tenure, as well as about general topics such as tribal cultures, by gossip which is biased and often prejudiced. Most of it is untrue. A lot of it seems to be derived from British-trained lawyers, who, though of the country, have not very accurate knowledge of what is actually going on in their own homeland and who produce unceasing litigation by pleading cases in a manner which has no reference to the facts of the situation.

He wanted to say, however, that it is quite true that a lot of anthropologists are much more interested in studying the old situation than they are in studying the new. And this for the very good reason that the old situation is going, and change, happily, will always be with us. Therefore anthropologists will always be able to study change. And they feel that they have a duty to these people and to ourselves to record their traditional cultures and their traditional forms of society before these disappear. The essence of anthropology is that it is a comparative discipline and the more varieties of forms of social organization they have for their theorizing, the better off they are. If one is interested in questions of both comparative law and the development of law in the history of Europe and other societies, comparative religion, psychiatric disorders, forms of family and kinship life, and forms of economic systems, then we have got to get these systems studied before they are altered, whether by authoritarian democracy or democratic authoritarianism. The only studies that have been made, covering a great range of economic systems, for instance, have not on the whole been made by economists. They have been made by anthropologists, and he wanted to suggest that this is a very important part of the study of economic society. Anthropologists want to get this done, and have a duty to do it. Anthropologists' resources in funds, and, more importantly in personnel, are much scarcer than economists'. His department, Professor Gluckman said, grows rather more slowly than that of his colleagues, because of the way in which Manchester students opt for economics and political science rather than for anthropology and sociology. Therefore he encouraged students to the study of traditional systems, as much as he could. Anthropologists work largely by direct observation of ongoing social life; and if that life is changing, they must study change. Therefore most students of anthropology in fact are studying problems of social change when they go out to the developing countries.

Anthropologists are not chary of studying growth and what has happened, but they are very chary of giving advice. It is clear that the training economists have had does enable them to point to specific differences and at least to focus choices. He took it that what Mr. Kaldor was saying about land reform in Turkey was really this: "If you want economic development, you must reform the land system. If you don't reform the land system, you won't have economic development. That's my advice. If you don't take that, get another economist and see if he can give you different advice." Professor Gluckman was sure that anthropologists can give equivalent advice: but their advice would be on issues which are even more obviously political. Hence, advice is best shunned.

Part B. Teaching Economic Development

EDITED BY KURT MARTIN

PROFESSOR ZIMMERMAN

Professor Zimmerman, introducing his paper on Teaching Economic Planning at the Institute of Social Studies at The Hague, said that the programme described in his paper was designed for mid-career people. He did not think that Europe was the place where undergraduates from developing countries should receive their basic education in economics. It was much better for them to be trained initially at home, and help could be given by way of assistance in the design of university programmes in these countries. The Institute at The Hague was aiming at people who had completed their studies at home and after several years of government service came to the Institute to review their experience and extend their knowledge. Such courses for mid-career people could not be run for more than six months because it was impossible for the governments of developing countries to release trained and experienced personnel for longer periods. High ranking officials could not leave their posts at all, and in some countries the possibilities of study leave were extremely limited even further down the chain. The Development Centre of O.E.C.D. was therefore sponsoring the idea of sending out small teams to conduct short courses and seminars on the spot.

After these introductory remarks Professor Zimmerman gave a brief summary of the main points of his paper.

MR. JACKSON

Mr. Jackson said he regretted that an unexpected mission to Iraq had prevented him from submitting a paper to the Conference. His intention now was to link up the previous discussion on the state of knowledge with the discussion on teaching.

When he was in Iraq advising on the collection of statistics he had looked into the reports and the recommendations on economic policy which the Government had received in earlier years from economists, first from Lord Salter and then from Mr. Balogh. Both had taken a very wide view of what it was proper for economists to talk about and had not hesitated to give something in the nature of political advice, while expressing an understanding of why it might be difficult for the Government to accept this advice. Their findings and proposals were broadly similar and had struck him as very sensible. In this particular case there was nothing economists had to be ashamed of for the advice they had given. International organizations might sometimes send out the wrong kind of economists; such mistakes were bound to occur, but provided no evidence for saying that the training of economists made them generally unfit for giving sensible advice.

Nevertheless, there might be a better route to realistic economics than was offered by the conventional textbook. He was in sympathy with the line taken by Mr. Seers in his article in the Oxford Bulletin, though he was more sceptical than Mr. Seers about the possibility of constructing a general theory of development encompassing all the variables. He was also in broad agreement with Mr. Streeten who had stressed, among other things, the need for some disaggregation of our conventional concepts. The Economic Commission for Africa had actually made a start in this direction in their statistical work.

But the question whether or not there was a better route to realistic economics was a long way from the sort of problems likely to face the members of this Conference. As teachers they were dealing with graduates from Africa or Asia and Latin America who had already received some basic instruction in economics along more or less traditional lines. Their task now was to offer these people something that made them more useful in their own countries, rather than to teach them economics from scratch in a new way. The remoulding of the courses was an important job, however, for university teachers in underdeveloped countries. Unfortunately, British universities had sometimes stood in the way of such reforms. At Ibadan, for instance, which had been a university college enjoying a special relationship with the University of London, he was told that they had tried to get away from the London curriculum and introduce a paper on economic development, but had encountered great resistance because at that time there were not enough people on the relevant committees in London who were prepared to admit that there was a subject called "economic development" that could be academically examined.

Turning to Oxford, Mr. Jackson reported on the decision to set up a new Diploma course in economic development, which would come into operation in 1965. This was planned as a one-year course with four compulsory papers: Principles of Economic Development, Development Problems and Policies, Statistics for Development, and International Economics. The first paper would mainly cover the various theories of development and growth, the theory of income determination, and the operation of the market mechanism, with special attention to the relationship between agriculture and the other sectors of the economy. (In his own view, there was too much emphasis on the Keynesian theory of income determination, which he thought was not very relevant to underdeveloped countries, but, of course, in a university one could not always insist on one's own views.) The second paper, Development Problems and Policies, was intended to be a very earthy paper dealing with the preparation and implementation of investment plans, domestic and foreign financing, taxation and control of government expenditure, land reform, the use of unemployed labour, and so on. The third paper, Statistics for Development Planning, was to be restricted to national accounts, demographic statistics, resource budgeting, monetary, fiscal and foreign trade statistics, index numbers, and methods of sampling, and was not intended to turn out professional statisticians but to produce people capable of understanding the importance of statistics and of using and interpreting statistical data. The last paper, International Economics, called for no further comment.

Under the regulations they could admit anyone who was thought worthy of admission by the relevant university board, but it was hoped that the Diploma would mainly attract civil servants with academic qualifications, particularly from African countries. The reason for making this a one-year course only (which in fact meant a nine-month course) was that governments were not likely to release qualified officials for a longer period of training. He agreed with Professor Zimmerman that it would be preferable to have a still shorter course, but it was extremely difficult to work this into the English academic year.

He had met similar problems last year when he and two colleagues had been appointed by the U.N. Special Fund to advise the managing director on a project for setting up a new African Institute of Economic Development and Planning at Dakar. When this project came to him, it was in the following form: the Institute was to offer two-year courses mainly for new African graduates. A committee of experts set up by the Secretary to the Economic Commission for Africa had recommended that the first year should be devoted almost entirely to mathematics; civil servants should be able to go straight into the second year to be taught the following topics (apart from a number of optional subjects): Intermediate Vector and Matrix theory; Linear programming, Simplex method; Sample evaluation tests; Consumption econometrics; Analysis of variance; Micro and Macro models; Leontief models, etc. He and his colleagues thought that this proposal was quite unsuitable and ought to be stopped. They visited some ten African countries to discover what sort of people would be available to be sent to the course, what their experience and educational background would be, and what they wanted and needed. In some of these African countries he found a very disturbing snobbism about advanced mathematical techniques and econometrics. In Tunis, for instance, the planning office had just been moved up into a limbo world where the head of the office had no access to any Ministry; yet, while their work bore no relation to anything that was going on in the civil service and the Government of Tunisia, their main worry at the office was that they had no econometrician on the staff capable of studying the elasticity of demand for food. In Morocco the complete lack of statistics on agriculture had not prevented the planners from compiling quite an ambitious input/output table (which, he was told, the French had inverted, for a small fee).

This excessive enthusiasm for the latest techniques, which he also found in some other countries, was often associated with a great admiration for French planning. The French planners were excellent mathematicians (Mr. Jackson said) who had learnt their economics by the back door. The fact that planning in France had started with the establishment of crude priorities in a few sectors and had only gradually developed further had not seeped through to the many African admirers of French planning, who were quite convinced that in order to do anything useful they had to become first-class mathematicians. This concentration on mathematics and highbrow techniques in countries which offered no scope for application was deeply disturbing, and he thought that it was their duty as university teachers to fight this tendency.

This is why he and his colleagues had recommended a curriculum for the Dakar Institute similar to that proposed for the Oxford Diploma and much less highbrow than the expert committee had suggested. He did not know what had happened to these recommendations, but wanted to emphasize that the objective of the Institute in Dakar, as he and his colleagues conceived it, and of the Diploma course at Oxford, was not to produce professional economists but people capable of thinking about the things that were relevant to planning in their countries. The time was so pressing in many of these countries that there was no choice but to take short-cuts.

DR. MARTIN

Dr. Martin, apart from introducing his paper in which he had referred to the impact of the state of knowledge on the content of teaching, went on to comment on some practical aspects of organizing courses in development.

On the question of length of courses both Professor Zimmerman and Mr. Jackson had suggested that only short courses were practicable for mid-career people. There was no doubt, Dr. Martin said, that the main demand was indeed for short courses. However, in Manchester only about a half of the students taking the course were in mid-career, and were in fact usually near the beginning of their career so that they could frequently be spared from their duties for longer periods. Most other students came straight from first-degree work and sometimes from postgraduate work in overseas universities. He was hoping that the number of British students taking an interest in this field would gradually increase.

With a relatively long course lasting two years, it was possible to introduce an element of flexibility, allowing some people with higher qualifications to take the Diploma in one year. This arrangement reduced the difficulty of having to deal at the same time with people widely differing in capacity and educational background.

Other difficulties of such a course are inherent in the subject matter itself, and in the imperfect state of our knowledge. Students always craved good textbooks, but they did not exist at present. A. J. Brown's *Introduction to the World Economy* although not specifically devoted to development, seemed to him more useful than most economic development texts. He also recommended to beginning students Arthur Lewis's *Theory of Economic Growth.* This last he regarded as systematic reflections on development rather than as a text. It was impossible to recommend a single text to students after the introductory stage. They were referred to selected parts of the books of Mrs. Robinson and, of course, to a wide variety of theoretical articles. He himself benefited a great deal from Bensusan Butt's small book on growth.

The balance of courses was always a problem. He had mentioned in his paper that mathematics and econometrics played a somewhat smaller role in the present course than in previous years. This was partly because he had become more sceptical about the present practical use, at any rate of the more advanced techniques, and partly for educational reasons. The students were more in need of a strengthening of their grasp of economics than of an increase of their mathematical dexterity.

It was also obviously important to maintain a balance between analysis and applied work. There were practical problems of securing materials for the workshop. This was being dealt with partly by encouraging students to bring empirical materials concerning their own country with them.

Concluding on a personal note, Dr. Martin said that he had initially some doubts about whether one could teach development. It was not until he found himself working with a group of former students in a government department that he had become convinced that, as Mr. Kaldor had put it, "economics does something".

Mrs. Penrose

Mrs. Penrose said that in the University of London economic development was taught mainly at the London School of Economics and the School of Oriental and African Studies. She was associated with both Schools but would confine her brief observations to the new developments at the School of Oriental and African Studies.

The School had traditionally been an institution where languages, law and history were taught for oriental societies in an orientalist tradition, but in recent years some new departments had been added: a Department of Anthropology and Sociology, a Department of Economics and Politics, and a Department of Geography, which was the most recent addition. The School, therefore, was a multi-disciplinary institution and was rapidly developing "Modern Studies", that is, studies of the contemporary economies and societies of Asia and Africa. They had an unusual opportunity because they had had generous foundation grants and enjoyed a substantial amount of autonomy in the development of their study and training programmes.

The Department of Economics and Politics was now in its second full year of operation. It was a post-graduate Department only, and, for the time being, the main emphasis was on economics rather than politics, and on Asia rather than Africa. Staff members and students were expected to specialize on particular areas. The aim of the Department was to train postgraduates who had a knowledge of the language (where desirable), culture, history, and economics of the countries they were studying as well as a sound knowledge of economics.

The first and biggest problem of the Department had been to collect a staff, and they were still in the process of building it up. Their policy was to appoint highly qualified young economists (preferably with research degrees), who were willing to specialize on particular areas, and to provide a "regional" training programme for them, including a year or more in Asia or Africa, to give them the opportunity to acquire field experience and a working knowledge of the language. The eight staff members appointed so far were all specializing on Asian countries—sometimes more than one on one country—but the Department had now also begun to take on people who would work on African problems.

As to their students, they all had first degrees in economics and were candidates for higher degrees of the University of London. The training of some of them included a period of field studies under the Hayter programme. The departments of the School concerned with languages, anthropology and sociology, etc., were contributing to their training and lecture courses at other colleges of the University were available. Course work was emphasized in the first instance, especially for overseas students, rather than research. Mrs. Penrose thought that one of the mistakes that both British and American universities had been making in teaching overseas students was to take people who had just obtained a first degree in their own countries, and put them straight on to research; what they first needed, in almost all cases, was a more solid basis in economics. It was for the same reason, Mrs. Penrose said, that she tried to dissuade students from their natural tendency to want to study problems of immediate economic policy in their own countries and to encourage them to investigate how the economy worked and the nature of the economic relationships that were important. Our own insight into the working of these economies was so far very weak indeed.

As part of its training programme, the Department put on an intensive qualifying course in economics which emphasized those aspects of economic analysis of special relevance to poor countries and their development. This course was designed for students whose basic economics needed strengthening, and since there was only a limited amount of time, it was important to decide which parts of traditional economic theory were most relevant for students of economic development and which could be dropped. Mrs. Penrose thought that a good deal of welfare economics, for example, and parts of the theory of the firm could be dispensed with without much loss. She would be interested to hear the opinion of other teachers on this matter.

In addition to courses in economic theory, applied economics and statistics, the Department ran regional seminars on the Middle East, China and South Asia, and were experimenting with an interdisciplinary, inter-regional seminar where people from several departments of the School working on different regions came together to discuss problems of common interest, emphasizing both the generality and the uniqueness of the difficult subject with which they were dealing.

Mrs. Penrose said that the Department was still at a formative stage and that there was plenty of scope for changes and new experiments.

Postscript: In 1965 the University of London abolished the old M.Sc.(Econ.) and substituted a one-year M.Sc. course by examination only; it also provided for a two-year research course leading to an M.Phil. In addition to the research degrees the Department now teaches for the M.Sc. by papers, to which only students with high second-class honours are admitted. Overseas students, British students whose economics is not quite up to this standard, or students wanting to change their field of study, may enter this course after a year of qualifying study leading to an examination at the end of the year, which they must pass at an upper second standard. The M.Sc. courses centre on the economics of poor countries and their development, for which courses in applied economics, economic theory, statistics, and regional economics are taught. The examination consists of three papers in these subjects and an essay. S.O.A.S. is at present the only College in the University offering this option for the M.Sc.

Mr. Berrill

Mr. Berrill said that until recently there had been no courses on the economics of underdeveloped countries at Cambridge. They had started in a modest way two years ago when a paper on this subject was introduced which undergraduates could choose as one of their three options in the Part II examinations. The purpose of teaching this subject was purely educational; there was no intention to train planners or people who would go out as economic advisers. It was one out of about a dozen options and there was no requirement for anyone taking it to have particular qualifications. In content the paper covered both general problems of development and problems of particular areas (mainly India, and to some extent the Mediterranean countries and Africa). Since this was only one of six examination subjects, students could hardly be expected to devote very much time to it. But the paper was fairly popular—it was chosen by about a third of the students in Part II—and having read the scripts in each of the last two years, he felt that the teaching of the subject had been of educational value to the students in that it had widened their horizon.

The more difficult problem was what kind of postgraduate education to provide for people coming from underdeveloped countries. As Mr. Jackson had said, they all wanted to learn the latest techniques and obtain a Ph.D. Most of them had taken their first degrees in their own universities, but often this had not provided an adequate training. They were resistant to taking any kind of qualifying examination, and although the best thing for many of them would be to improve their basic economics and take some of the Part II examinations before going on to research, it was extremely difficult to persuade them to do this. It was unavoidable that after three years or more of Ph.D. research some of these Ph.D. candidates had to face the risk of failure; in view of their family responsibilities and their commitments at home this often created very serious personal problems.

In order to have an acceptable alternative there was now a proposal before the university authorities to institute a postgraduate course in economic development leading to a certificate or diploma. The intention was both to provide a one year course which was useful and complete in itself and to stop those graduates from underdeveloped countries, whose previous education in economics was insufficient, from going to the Ph.D. until they had shown by passing the examination for this diploma that they had acquired the necessary qualifications. If they did go on to Ph.D. or M.Sc. the year's work on the Diploma course would count towards the higher degree. They were thinking of a one-year course with four papers—two of them theoretical, the other two applied—and a short thesis; but the full details had not yet been worked out and he had no idea how many students could be persuaded to take the diploma before going on to research.[1]

In addition to the undergraduate paper in economic development which he had mentioned earlier, there was at present at Cambridge only one other special course in this field, on which Miss Deane would report.

1. (Postscript). This Diploma has since been accepted by the University and courses start in October 1966. Numbers are initially restricted to about twenty a year and it looks as though this will be fully subscribed. Also, since the Manchester Conference the University has instituted three area studies centres (South Asia, Africa and Latin America) all of which are concerned with development problems and provide lectures, seminars, publications, and research projects which cut across the normal faculty arrangements.

MISS DEANE

Miss Deane reported that for many years there had been a course at Cambridge for people in the Colonial Service, mostly graduates of British universities, who were either colonial probationers about to go out to some administrative post, or people who had already been in such posts in a colony. In time the composition of this group had changed. At present most of the participants of the course were civil servants from newly independent countries, and insofar as they had academic qualifications, they had obtained their degrees at home. Only very few of them were trained economists. The course had now been reorganized to make it more suitable for officials from independent countries. Lasting one academic year, the course covered a variety of subjects besides economics. They had seminars on history and geography, public administration and politics, international affairs and law, as well as a fairly intensive five weeks' seminar on problems of economic development. The topics in the economics seminar ranged from national income to problems of fiscal policy, inflation, foreign trade, and so on. There was also an agricultural economics seminar and several study groups on the problems of particular countries. The intention was, not to train planners, but to show civil servants what was involved in thinking about economic problems. Miss Deane said that her impression was that the course was a success, but a more definite assessment could only be made at the end of the year, when they had seen the examination papers.

MR. BECKETT

Mr. Beckett said that the most common expression of opinion he had heard was that *economic growth* should be a postgraduate subject, taught to people who had read economics. Some economists held the view that economics itself should be a postgraduate subject. He had met very few economists who agreed that economics was a suitable subject for inclusion in G.C.E. His own view was that the study of *economic growth* is a suitable subject for school level, even for the Certificate of Secondary Education, the new examination for the use of non-grammar secondary schools. These views were based on his own experiences. Thirty years ago he found no difficulty in discussing problems of international trade and raw product prices, or such concepts as we now call the capital coefficient or the savings ratio, etc., with illiterate peasant farmers in the Gold Coast (now Ghana). In more recent experience with the one year postgraduate Diploma in Agricultural Economics, in Oxford, there were students from widely different backgrounds, who may have read economics, science, agriculture, geography, etc. With such a mixed bag the highest common factor for any particular discipline is low, and it proved necessary to arrange basic courses in mathematics, economic theory, etc. before the main body of the course could be proceeded with. Over the years an increasing number of students came from overseas countries and were more interested in the development side of agricultural economics than the more formal aspects of the subject. To provide the background for this Mr. Beckett has given a course of lectures for the last six or eight years on "Economic growth and agricultural development". Some students prefer a logical approach, some understand graphical presentations better and some a mathematical approach. However, provided that concepts and ideas are presented without the use of sophisticated statistical procedures, all students appear to be able to make progress, without difficulty.

There was, Mr. Beckett said, a need for publishing an agreed vocabulary of concepts and terms used in discussion of economic development. This could be used in school curricula, in mid-career training of people without an economics background, and in inter-disciplinary working groups of persons employed in practical development work. There could not be one body of economic theory which fits all economic development. There can be no single blue-print.

Teaching and the planning of courses should take note of this and the student be introduced to *all* the different theories and also to the different practices in economic development in both capitalist and controlled economies. He would then make his own choices.

PROFESSOR MUNTHE

Professor Munthe said that economic development was taught in Norwegian universities as part of International Economics, which was one of the specializations that students of economics could choose in Part II of their five-year degree course. However, there were few students from underdeveloped countries at Norwegian universities and only few teachers had direct experience in these countries. This posed a severe problem in teaching. It was necessary to provide students from Norway with sufficient background material without making the course a purely descriptive one: students rightly expected the analysis of development to be linked to the central body of economic theory. In the present state of knowledge this was a very difficult task. He thought that the paper submitted by Professor Hagen to this Conference was extremely fruitful in questioning some of the assumptions usually made in theorizing on development. Moreover, if development was defined as the transformation of peasant economies using handicraft techniques into industrial societies (as Dr. Martin had defined it), it was clear that a rather complex theory was needed and that highly aggregative models were or little use. He hoped that the many economists serving in various advisory capacities in underdeveloped countries would write up their experience for the benefit of those engaged in teaching this new subject.

Mr. Stewart

Mr. Stewart reported on the following developments at Edinburgh. First, undergraduates were now offered a paper on economic development as an option for the Honours degree in Economics. The subject was taught in seminars and by the usual lecture method, and he thought that this was working well. Secondly, Edinburgh was introducing an Intermediate Degree in Economics for which it was hoped students from overseas would enrol before proceeding to the Ph.D. This would normally be a two-year course, the purpose of which was to strengthen the knowledge of basic economics and statistics of students aiming at a research degree. The course work was to be adjusted to the requirements of each candidate.

Thirdly, under the Hayter programme a Centre for African Studies was established at Edinburgh. The Centre was accepting suitable candidates for a one-year course leading to a Diploma in African Studies, with specialization either in Geography, Anthropology, Economics or History. On the Economics side there was a slight bias towards West Africa. Students would take four papers (or three papers and a dissertation) of which one or two were selected from the senior undergraduate syllabus to suit individual candidates. The Centre was still in its infancy, and the main problem was to get the right sort of students in the right numbers. In its first year the Centre had accepted four or five candidates, but they were now offering 10–12 places for future years.

Professor Wilson

Professor Wilson said that he wanted to start with some general remarks about educational problems, not just about the teaching of economics. What he had to say was directly related to Nigeria, but he hoped that what he would say would not be entirely irrelevant to other underdeveloped countries.

He thought it fair to say that there was too much emphasis at either end of the educational scale: too much emphasis on primary education and too much emphasis on university education. Primary education, of course, was a matter of national pride. This was very proper, but questions arose as to how rapidly it should be extended and as to what the courses ought to be about. Here he found himself in agreement with what Dr. Balogh had said. He agreed that the content of primary education needed to be altered in certain respects. At the same time he thought that it was not enough to say that primary education is too literary because that is only part of the story; the other part is that the primary education is sometimes inadequate by any standard, partly because some teachers are inadequately trained. Then there was the most tremendous wastage. In Eastern Nigeria roughly half the children who go to primary school have left by the end of three years and, he supposed, about 40 per cent in the West. Quite a proportion of those who stuck it out will, in the end, be discontented and unhappy about returning to the family farm. Thus there was discontent and rural unemployment and the other things the Conference had been talking about.

There was much snobbery in these countries, as there was nearer home, and a consequent reluctance on the part of any reasonably intelligent child to undertake technical training that won't lead to a degree. He did not think it was fair to say that this was entirely the result of either the French or the British tradition. We rather enjoy this sport of self-denigration, as somebody had said. It was no doubt true that we had contributed to the snobbish attitude, but he was sure the snobbery was also deep-rooted and indigenous. He recalled a conversation in Nigeria with a Professor of Engineering who told him with what enthusiasm and, on the whole, with what success, his students tackled quite difficult mathematics. But he went on to describe the reluctance with which they would strip a machine.

In the teaching of economics, the emphasis had been faulty in some respects. It could be said in favour of London University that it had not only performed the difficult task of organizing examinations for colleges in many countries but also succeeded in maintaining standards. But there seemed to be agreement that the content of the traditional economics courses should now be altered. He wanted to say a little about the training not only of professional economists but also of future administrators. What sort of courses should we be giving them while they are abroad or in their own universities? Professor Wilson thought they all agreed that they will have little scope for using the more advanced mathematical techniques. These ought to be included as optional papers only. Perhaps there should be a little more attention in their courses to cost-benefit analysis. He did not say this because he was over-optimistic about what can be solved by that type of analysis, but it might help to sort out the issues. A critical question to ask was what these future administrators will ultimately do. They will spend most of their time, not in planning industry, but in coping with the problems of public investment and public consumption. This was the larger part of what, in practice, central planning means for these countries. All kinds of dreadfully difficult questions came up, such as how much it was sensible to spend on education.

In fact, in a country like Nigeria, comprehensive industrial planning was just not on—not at the moment. This for various reasons: there were no figures and there wasn't the staff. And as well as that, there was a great deal of uncertainty about just what industries would be represented in the country in ten years' time, especially when so many of these industries would come from abroad. This situation may change, but at the moment central planning meant above all the planning of public consumption and public investment. As well as that, there was the planning of some industries that are publicly owned or had derived their origin, or their expansion, from public initiative. There ought to be some attention paid, therefore, to project analysis. He meant, for example, the choice between thermal and hydro-electric power stations. Here is where capital theory could be so useful and the problem could be illustrated by reference to France or Russia or Britain or other foreign countries. Agricultural economics and transport economics were also obviously very useful.

Thus, if one began by asking what industries the future administrators were likely to have to deal with, it might be easier to see how courses for them should be devised. These should include some discussion of the problems of physical planning.

His last point was that in the underdeveloped countries the main lack was not plans; it was projects. It was not the devising of elaborate models that was needed as much as ensuring that particular projects were worked out in detail and implemented. What he had in mind was not simply, or even mainly, project analysis of a sophisticated type. He meant the work of deciding where, for example, a new agricultural college should go and how large it should be. He meant the purchase of the site, the engaging of the architect, the awarding and the progressing of the contract. This was another way of saying that the underdeveloped countries are short of administrators. Professor Wilson thought there was a need to consider a little more fully what should be done to train general administrators as well as economic planners. Then there was the vast question of industrial entrepreneurship. By this he did not mean exclusively private industrial entrepreneurship, but entrepreneurship whether the capital be privately or publicly owned. Would this emerge from the merchant classes in Smithian style of not? An interesting discussion of this question was to be found in an essay by Lange in which he posed the question: If there is a shortage of entrepreneurial talent, is it wise to centralize more or to centralize less? It was an interesting question which he would not now try to discuss. But he was a little surprised that so far no referencc had been made to training for management. Such training would provide at best only part of the solution, but it clearly needed to be discussed.

At Glasgow they were now expanding substantially the work on underdeveloped countries and had made some new arrangements which may be of help to students from abroad. Apart from a special paper in the first degree, the new B.Phil. degree can be taken with an emphasis on the problems of development. They had also devised a new diploma with two main specialities: planning techniques and agricultural economics. In one respect he thought they were in a position to carry out an interesting experiment, for Professor Nove would be able to approach these matters from the point of view of a student of the Soviet economy. It was going to be interesting to see how this will affect his attitude to the problems of the underdeveloped countries.

PROFESSOR ZIMMERMAN

Professor Zimmerman said that he agreed with Professor Wilson's remarks on the need for giving more attention to project analysis in a training programme. The Institute at The Hague was now introducing a course on industrial development which would be largely devoted to feasibility studies. Economic theorists, business economists and engineers would have to come together to contribute to such a course.

MR. BALOGH

Mr. Balogh said that he was completely out of sympathy with the present emphasis on mathematical and econometric model building. It would require long investigations into modern literature to find a single example of an econometric model that had come out right or contributed anything worth while to our insight or capacity for prediction. In the study of economic development, in particular, a historical approach seemed to him the only promising one. To aim at a general theory of development was begging for the moon; this was the only point on which he disagreed with Mr. Seers. Nor was it possible in his view to approach the study of development in a non-political way, in the hope that objective conclusions on economic policy would follow from pure analysis. Turning to Mrs. Penrose, he said that, if one began in this way, one would only end up with conclusions that were determined by the kind of prejudice one had put into one's assumptions. Economists trained along conventional lines were apt to misinterpret the situation in underdeveloped countries. Mr. Balogh illustrated this by reference to the role of entrepreneurship. A South American landowner, for example, who left his peasants completely untrained, was an "economic man" who was arranging his affairs in a way that helped to preserve the system in which he was doing well. It was not just a matter of political instability standing in the way of entrepreneurial activity, as Mr. Nove seemed to imply; the real point was that entrepreneurship had a different rationality in a different social setting. Development problems were always specific problems, and he agreed with what Professor Zimmerman and Dr. Martin had said about the importance that ought to be given in a teaching programme to case studies.

PROFESSOR NOVE

Mr. Nove said that he was in agreement with Mr. Balogh. His own reference to political instability was meant to provide one example of the influence of social factors on economic development.

MR. WORSWICK

Mr. Worswick (who had been invited to summarize the discussion and to reopen it with his comments) said that in considering problems of teaching it was necessary to distinguish between different types of students. Courses for undergraduates in British universities nowadays often included a paper on the economics of development. This had not been so ten or fifteen years ago and was worth noting. As to students from underdeveloped countries taking their first degrees here, he thought there would be little disagreement with

Professor Zimmerman's observation that they should learn their basic economics in their own countries; but the trouble was that the teaching of economics in these countries was often rather poor. This raised the question of the extent and the ways in which British universities might render technical aid to universities abroad. He knew that this was done already on some scale, but it was worth giving further thought to such arrangements. This was relevant also to the organization of courses for British graduates in economics wanting to go out to developing countries as teachers. He thought that courses of the kind described by Mrs. Penrose combining area studies with the learning of the languages might be a very suitable way of building up a supply of people for teaching and other work abroad. He hoped that Mr. Morris of the Department of Technical Co-operation would talk to the Conference on the experience of his Department in matters of recruitment, the qualifications needed, and so on.

Next Mr. Worswick turned to postgraduates from developing countries. This group, with which the Conference appeared to be mainly concerned, was made up of two fairly distinct types of students: those who were sent here by their governments to obtain a training in planning and administration, and those who for a variety of motives came here in search of further education without necessarily being committed to a particular career. The question was what these students really wanted (particularly the second category), what they needed and what we could offer them.

He said Mrs. Robinson in her opening talk had given one possible answer, but late in the discussion there had been other suggestions. In any event, it appeared from the reports submitted to the Conference that the various centres here and abroad were approaching these matters in different ways or were setting themselves different tasks. The Hague, for instance, was concentrating on the training of planners, while other centres were less specialized and more concerned with providing a further general education in economics. Whether these things should be kept in separate compartments or whether one should try to cater in one centre for both types of students (as appeared to be attempted at Manchester) was something that could be further discussed. Whatever the answer, it was important that the various centres kept one another informed about their intentions and the nature of their courses.

There was the further question whether British universities should make special provision, at graduate level, for students coming from countries with a poor standard of undergraduate education. He thought that, while universities might be prepared to design special courses, many universities would object strongly to any suggestion of double standards in the awarding of degrees and diplomas.

Turning to the content of our courses, Mr. Worswick said that the main issue, which had emerged from the debate on the state of knowledge, concerned the role of theory and the use of models; he referred in particular to the contributions by Mrs. Robinson, Mr. Seers and Mr. Streeten. His own view was that courses for graduates from underdeveloped countries, including planners, ought to have a high analytical content, for very often these students had had no proper analytical training.

Describing what he meant by an analytical training, Mr. Worswick said that the teaching of economics involved leading the student through three stages. The first step was to construct a simple model system, isolating the key factors of the problem in which one was interested. Such a system contained a number of variables, connected by a set of relationships, and what one tried at the first stage was to explain how a set of values of the variables might be found which satisfied all the relationships, given the initial assumptions about the things omitted from the model. Next, one assumed a change in one of the relationships, and examined the consequences of such a change on the "equilibrium" values of the variables. Once one had learned how the system or model "worked", one came to the third and most important step: the testing of the relevance of the model. There were many students who never got to this third stage where real economics began. To teach this kind of thinking ought to be the kernel of the theoretical part of our instruction.

Now, one of the questions he would like to raise for further discussion concerned the type of model that one should use as a teacher at a British university. His own preference was to use models that could be illustrated and tested with reference to easily accessible and familiar material which was readily available for the advanced countries. He would feel much less confident if, for teaching methods of analysis, he had to construct special models for underdeveloped countries on the basis of inadequate data and insufficient understanding. There was always the risk, of course, that students who had learnt their economics on the basis of the familiar "western" models might apply them mechanically to situations to which they were not appropriate. These were the cases that worried Mr. Seers. They showed up the shortcomings of students who had never reached "stage 3" of a proper theoretical training. He wondered whether the use of special models for developing countries would really advance the analytical education of such students. He understood that the key factors in economic development were subject to frequent and rapid changes: models, therefore, which appeared relevant at the time they were taught, might be just as misleading, when applied mechanically a few years afterwards, as the conventional western models. It was true that the shortcomings of students could be the fault of the teacher. Some economists were so enamoured of their models that they flogged and peddled them as though they embodied some absolute truth. In teaching how to think about economic problems one had to be detached and use a variety of models.

Mr. Worswick went on to express his reservations about the tendency to nationalism in theory. When he was in Argentina it often happened that when he had set out a simple proposition (about supply and demand, for instance) he received the knock-down answer that this might be true in other countries but not in Argentina. It was obvious, he said, that there were differences from place to place, but he felt uneasy nevertheless about having nothing but "lots of little local economics".

Referring to the discussion between Mr. Kaldor and Mr. Hanson on the role of economic advisers, Mr. Worswick said that whereas in advanced countries any recommendation made was thoroughly screened by civil servants and critics before action was taken, there was no comparable process of vetting and screening in many underdeveloped countries. Economists might therefore find their proposals quickly accepted, but it often turned out that their recommendations were impracticable without administrative reform. Ought not therefore the teaching of the economics of development be more closely linked with the teaching of public administration and applied sociology?

These, then, were the main issues which he thought the Conference might wish to discuss further. First, how can British universities help to improve the teaching of economics in the universities of underdeveloped countries? Related to this, what kind of courses would be most suitable for building up a supply of people for teaching and other work abroad? Secondly, what type of models should we use for teaching purposes? And finally, should not the teaching of economic planning and development be combined with the teaching of public administration and related subjects?

Mr. Morris

Mr. Morris said that some of the problems facing the Department of Technical Co-operation might be of interest to the Conference.

The principal task of the Department was to strengthen the administrations in a large number of developing countries, particularly but not exclusively in countries which were formerly British colonies. The Department was trying to extend the area of its activities, but it was extremely difficult to develop programmes, including the provision of training in the United Kingdom, for countries outside the traditional British nexus.

Last year about 3500 people were in this country—not all of them of course for the whole year—taking full-time courses of study under U.K. Technical Assistance; their numbers were expected to increase in the coming year to well over 4000. But only a small proportion of them—not more than perhaps 200 in total—were taking courses in economics or related subjects; these were mostly administrative generalists who wanted to acquire a certain amount of intellectual equipment in economics (or were sent by their governments for this purpose). It was the Department's job to find places for them on various courses. Many of them were sent to university courses, notably the Manchester course, as well as to courses at Oxford, London and Cambridge, that were designed primarily for administrators but also paid attention to economics and economic development. In addition there were special courses organized by the British Council—one every year on Central Government Finance, and one every other year on Economic Development—each taking about twenty people. Finally there were some individual students seeking training in economics at postgraduate level under government schemes. Their number was quite small, however (less than ten), and they were difficult to place because the qualifications of these candidates, whose names were put forward by their governments, were usually below the standards required for admission to postgraduate courses in British universities.

Moreover, while the quality of Asian and African officials sent to courses on Public Administration was gradually improving, the standards of those selected for specialized or postgraduate training in economics appeared to be falling off. This was probably due to the enormous pressures on governments overseas who were so short of competent economic staff that they were reluctant to release anyone with respectable qualifications for a prolonged period of training. His impression was that the situation was different in respect of students coming to British universities under their own efforts. Thus some time ago the Department had tried to provide through government channels a supply of students qualified to take a special course in Industrial Financing at the London School of

Economics; they had been unable to present a list of suitable candidates at a time when the London School had many applications from private students who appeared suitable for postgraduate work.

Mr. Morris added that in operating these schemes the Department was responding to requests from governments overseas. The Department was not in a position to take great initiatives nor could they always ensure that the best people were selected for training, or that the kind of training that was requested was always that which the country seeking assistance really needed most. Moreover, one had to keep in mind that there was competition in the field, such as the Institute at The Hague, the O.E.C.D. Development Centre, the Dakar Institute, and several others; unless the Department could do its best with the talent such as it was, this talent would go somewhere else.

In this context Mr. Morris mentioned that, following a recommendation made by a committee under Lord Bridges, the Department had been engaged for about a year in investigating the idea of organizing a special Institute as a focus of research and training in Public Administration and Development. He said that a decision of this matter might be expected in the near future.[1]

As to Mr. Worswick's enquiry about the possibilities of British universities rendering assistance to universities abroad, Mr. Morris reported that there was now a committee under Sir Charles Morris which was dealing with just these problems. If any member of the Conference knew of people who were interested in taking teaching posts abroad (in countries of the Commonwealth), it would be quite easy to put them in touch with the joint secretaries of the Morris Committee.

Mr. Seers

Mr. Seers said that this was a very satisfactory conference on which the organizers should be congratulated, because of the interest which had been shown and also because it had brought out the progress which had been made in this country in the teaching of development economics. If an effort had been made to hold a conference like this five years ago, there would have been little to report so far as teaching was concerned.

1. In October, 1964, the D.T.C. was absorbed within the newly formed Ministry of Overseas Development. Proposals for an Institute of Development Studies were approved by the government in 1965, and the Institute is being established on the campus of the University of Sussex.

In the account of the courses which now are being taught, there were some conspicuous gaps.

There had been very little reference to the world economy as a subject for study and teaching. This was not the same thing as International Trade. The subject of International Trade deals with the relationship between autonomous units in a more or less open environment, whereas the world economy is a closed system with certain internal structural relations and with its own trends, on which there is some material. This subject would provide the correct setting for teaching about development problems. Just as the starting-point in the basic undergraduate course was changed from the theory of value to the national income, so we could introduce a world economy approach. This too could be used in such a way as to raise conceptual problems, simultaneously introducing people to descriptive materials.

Secondly, there was not yet much provision for undergraduates to study development processes, only optional courses, which the majority of those reading economics would miss. There was so to speak a beachhead in the undergraduate syllabus which he hoped and expected would become enlarged. (It reminded him of the late nineteen-thirties, when he was an undergraduate at Cambridge; Keynesian economics was smuggled into Part II of the Tripos then under the Theory of Money.) We could try to persuade our colleagues to accept the proposition that nobody should be sent out into the world with a piece of paper saying he is an economist, unless he had some knowledge of development processes.

By "out into the world" he did not necessarily mean overseas. A student who received this type of instruction would be helped to deal with the problems of the United Kingdom, because the issues in development economics are issues which are relevant to this country too. It would in fact be interesting to study this country as a development problem, using the techniques which have been worked out in underdeveloped areas. This would mean estimating the institutional and physical requirements, including the manpower of different types, to achieve certain objectives in the future. No doubt parts of this exercise had been done, perhaps in "Neddy's" offices, but no serious comprehensive study of this kind had been published. As the fraction of the profession which at some time had dealt with development problems increased, and as the teaching in this field expanded, the attitude to the United Kingdom economy would itself change both in teaching and in professional work.

Mr. Worswick raised the question of what is an appropriate

model for teaching purposes. There seemed to be some slight internal inconsistency in Mr. Worswick's proposals. As far as teaching in this country was concerned, Mr. Worswick was saying that the correct procedure was for teachers to talk about the economy with which they were familiar, i.e. the local model, using national material for illustration. Yet he apparently wanted to deny his Argentinian students their own national model. Perhaps, Mr. Seers said, he had put this a little unfairly, but there was a real point here.

This raised the question whether one could talk of a "more general" theory. There was in the first place a world economy, with its own internal patterns of development which he had mentioned earlier. Beyond that, there were groups of economies which consituted model types, because they shared certain characteristics of structure and performance. A great deal of material was available on various economies by now, which shows how they function. These model types could be related to one another in teaching. For example, one could start with the industrial economy, and then remove some sector, say the capital goods industry, and show how it would affect the system's functioning.

He believed one could expect a "more general" theory of development to be constructed. The fact that we cannot anticipate the features of such a theory at the moment would not in itself be sufficient reason for saying that this will not or cannot be created. One can never forecast future theory—if one could it would be present, not future, theory! Again it depended on what one means by a "theory", but this would be a general theory in the sense that there would be some agreement on what questions are relevant, reflecting certain well-known causal links.

At the very least there was going to be a common set of questions which one would learn to ask about economies, such as the extent to which they are export-oriented or possess internal dynamic forces. There were already recognizable similarities in the patterns of development, running right across different types of country and different continents. One example was Professor Chenery's work on the structure of production. Perhaps as more was learnt other types of pattern would be found which will be more useful in explaining growth rates. One could also see, if only very roughly, institutional and social patterns which are associated with the productive patterns, and the size of the subsistence sector.[1]

1. Since Mr. Seers found the main stages-of-growth schemes (those of Marx and Rostow) unhelpful for work in developing countries, he had tried to sketch an alternative, showing the social and institutional implications, in a paper called

There were of course major differences in these patterns between underdeveloped countries. (He had suffered himself when first working in Africa from being too "Latin American", e.g. from putting too much weight on the foreign trade bottleneck and not enough on education, though this had been a less incurable fault than being too "Anglo-Saxon".) But one did not expect even a general theory to cover every single case, and the question why particular countries or particular types of countries are exceptions is itself interesting.

The next point he wanted to make was one that struck very forcibly those working under African conditions, namely that a transfer of human beings as well as of capital is needed from the developed countries to the underdeveloped countries. However one looked at the future, over the next twenty or thirty years one could not get out of the local education systems enough people to man a viable political and economic structure. He hoped that it will be increasingly accepted that a large fraction of each profession should be working overseas, especially in Africa.

This applied to economists too. For them, as for others, what was needed was machinery for giving a person a career consisting of work alternately overseas and in a university at home. Sabbatical years and occasional journeys overseas were not really satisfactory. The D.T.C. had already initiated a small improvement, with posts at British universities, involving work overseas. Another alternative would be to provide periods at a research institute in this country for those with jobs overseas.

One needed the combination. A career wholly overseas made one eventually very out of touch with the current of professional thought; a wholly academic career in a developed country must mean work divorced from economic reality. University councils in this country would no doubt come to accept this point, as they were increasingly accepting it in the United States.

His last point was that he hoped that this meeting would have some further implications. To repeat it in this form might not be necessary, at least until there is more experience of teaching. But there could be other meetings for those working on development problems, perhaps focusing on areas of the world; economists working on Africa, Asia or Latin America would contribute the main papers, but those working on other areas or other types of speciality would

---

"The Stages of Economic Development of a Primary Producer in the Middle of the Twentieth Century" (*Economic Bulletin of Ghana*, Vol. VII, No. 4).

also attend. After all, how could one teach development economics, or any branch of economics, unless one had some idea of what is happening in Africa, Asia and Latin America?

MR. CASSEN

Mr. Cassen said that he was very pleased to have heard the last few contributions. These had given him some grounds to believe that the Conference were not after all, as suspected earlier, going to fulfil the description of an academic as a man who is too smart for his own good and not smart enough for anyone else's. There seemed to be a large number of complaints made about the state of our subject, a lot of critical remarks made about what economists were doing, and not much in the way of constructive suggestions as to what they should do instead. He was glad to have heard that some people did have such suggestions, as he was sure even those who made criticisms had themselves. He wanted to cover two or three items which had been mentioned.

The first thing he wanted to talk about was the teaching of techniques of economics, about which there had been considerable complaint. He confessed that after conversation with the people who had made these remarks he realized that he had to some extent misinterpreted them, while they were speaking, but as the proceedings of this Conference were going to be recorded, he wanted for the record to prevent others similarly misinterpreting them. Mr. Jackson, in particular, had laid very proper stress on the excesses of enthusiasm for certain kinds of techniques, particularly econometric techniques. Whilst agreeing from his own experience that the students of economics in low-income countries do tend to have excessive enthusiasm for such things, he did think that the impression Mr. Jackson gave was somewhat dangerous—namely, that most advanced techniques available in economics should not be taught to the people who were going to work in these countries. There were a lot of reasons for thinking that even where the basic data did not exist for employing these up-to-date techniques, there was still a great deal of virtue in teaching them to people. Take for example input-output analysis. It may not be possible to construct a table in a country. This did not seem to him a good argument for failure to teach people about input-output analysis, which gives a very good intuitive understanding of how these economies might work, even if one actually could not ever build an input-output table in them. The same would be true for a large number of things—the need, for example, to understand income elasticities of demand. He did not see how anybody could hope to have any kind of sophisticated knowledge of what these things meant unless they had had a certain amount of training in statistical technique. He was not saying that Mr. Jackson or anybody else would disagree and he only wished, for the record, to correct the impression that these techniques should not be taught. After all we did not really know what was going to happen in the next ten years and he suggested that Professor Hirschman's notion of forward linkages may be a relevant analogy here. As to the complaint that certain kinds of data are not available in low income countries, it may well be that they would never become available unless one had planners in planning offices who knew that they wanted a certain kind of data and created pressure to get it. Similarly, one had, for example, knowledge of computer programmes that were able to select a set of projects from a whole collection of interdependent projects. Now many countries were not yet in the happy stage of having worked out projects, but if they had and if computer programmes existed which enabled one to make an intelligent selection from these projects, the fact that there may be nobody in a planning office who knew what a computer programme was seemed to him liable to be somewhat reprehensible. It seemed to him that what was really needed was some kind of balance, that excesses had taken place and would no doubt continue to take place, but one needed to strike an intelligent balance between teaching techniques which are useful—the knowledge of which may create intelligent pressure for the provisions of additional data—and the other kind of things which it was felt it was important that people should know, economic history and matters connected with social, political and economic behaviour which were important. Mr. Cassen merely wished to make these remarks for the record and he hoped that Mr. Jackson and others who had made similar kinds of remarks would not feel that he had misinterpreted them.

The second thing he wanted to say something about was agriculture. Everybody talked about agriculture, but it was not really very clear to Mr. Cassen exactly what was to be done if economists were going to try to make some more intelligent remarks in their teaching, and the work they did, about agriculture in underdeveloped countries than they did at present. Very often he had the feeling that taking an interest in agriculture just means putting land and labour on the axes instead of capital and labour. The fact was that in many underdeveloped countries the system of agriculture that exists consists of a very delicately balanced, technologically well adapted, system of farming and what had to be done was to introduce some kind of changes to this system.

Understanding of how this agricultural system works made it much easier for us to appreciate why it is that the cultivator won't adopt changes. Very frequently a single change proposed by some foreign adviser was wholly inappropriate; take as a crude example the use of fertilizers. It may be that, for example, some cultivators cannot use fertilizers because fertilizers produce more weeds and more crops, and if they have a labour shortage at weeding and harvesting time they cannot cope. All he was saying was that economists do need to understand the system of agriculture that exists in these countries in order to make some headway in making suggestions for improving it, and he felt that the attention that had been given to certain aspects of this problem, such as the backward bending supply curve in agricultural production, was concentrated on the wrong things and what one should really wish to concentrate on was how it works, why it works, the way it does and what are the resistances to the introduction of change. In this kind of field there was a great deal of information; there were also certain techniques including linear programming which were extremely useful for changing these farm systems. He thought everybody would agree that the state of agricultural economics as practised by advisers in underdeveloped countries at the moment was pretty appalling. What passed on the whole for agricultural economics was people who went out and calculated the cost of improving the methods of production; they calculated, at the existing market prices, the value of yield which was going to be attained by the application of these techniques. Then they thought that the job was finished. The job was not finished, indeed it could hardly be said to have started. There were all kinds of things that must come in between, particularly the way in which new techniques interfere with old farming systems. The effects of this must be calculated. He was absolutely astounded to talk to the head of the F.A.O. Mission in Nigeria in which the Nigerian Government seemed to be laying a great deal of hope. When asked what kind of information he had collected about traditional farming systems, he replied, "They are terribly primitive, we didn't think it was worth while collecting any information at all". Mr. Cassen was not sure that the Head of the mission spoke for everybody in his team—he sincerely hoped not. Anyway his feeling was that quite a lot could be done about improving both the state of agriculture as practised in the field, and in what was taught.

Next Mr. Cassen wanted to move on to the subject of teaching. He only had a brief remark to make about this. He had sympathized very much with Dudley Seers's article on 'Why visiting economists fail', but he thought that perhaps one reason why visiting economists fail was that other visiting economists had been rather slow in imparting to those about to visit the benefits of their own experience. He had had on three occasions the problem of trying to design a course in economics for people who were going to be administrators or economists connected with underdeveloped countries. He wanted to say in parenthesis that he did not feel that there was all that much difference, apart from the provision of certain useful facilities, between the kind of economics one wished to teach to a planner in a number of underdeveloped countries and to anybody else who was going to have to do with the economics of underdeveloped countries. What he always felt—and he had been trying to do this—was, if only he could talk to people like Mr. Seers or read it somewhere and find out what parts of economics that he had learned had really been useful? What would he have liked to know more about before he went out? This kind of information would be terribly helpful and Mr. Cassen did not see why some attempt should not be made to get a body of information of this kind together.

The last thing he wanted to talk about was textbooks. Everyone had complained that the existing textbooks on the subject of economic development were unsatisfactory. He wanted to suggest that either a conference or something else should be held in which those interested might discuss what really ought to go into such a book. Because when one thought about it, it was not at all easy. He therefore proposed that anybody interested in making some kind of progress with a drawn-up table of contents for a textbook on economic development should make contact with him, either with a view to some kind of meeting in the future or with a view to just communicating ideas to him by mail. His feeling was that, when this Conference started off, there was a great deal of pessimism on the part of some people that the state of the subject was dreadful. There was also a great deal of optimism on the part of others that, although it was dreadful, there was also something useful that economists could do. Mr. Cassen said he sided with the latter, that while we were not yet on the road to having what had been described as a general theory, nevertheless the body of useful things that one could usefully teach to people who come from these countries was enormous, and he thought what was really difficult was making some kind of choice amongst these things. There was a very nice story which he had heard from an Egyptian. He said that a lot of Egyptian unemployed were sent to Syria to build roads, but when they got there they looked rather scruffy and the Syrians said to them: "What are all you people doing here, hanging about?" and they said: "We are not hanging about, we are visiting experts." Mr. Cassen didn't care what they were going to call themselves, visiting experts or anything else, but he was going to be very happy if they actually got some roads built.

MR. KALDOR

Mr. Kaldor said that he was wholly on the side of those who in the discussion had asserted the usefulness and importance of economic theory. The abstract or deductive method of analysing economic phenomena was extremely fruitful and powerful in giving an understanding of economic processes; such understanding was indispensable for sensible policy decisions. It was true, however, that the kind of economics now taught in our universities was not really suitable for people coming here from underdeveloped countries who wanted to get a background in economics in a short period of one or two years. He was not an assiduous reader of textbooks, but had certainly never come across a single textbook which was on the right lines for this purpose; this textbook was still lacking. Why was this so? he asked.

He thought that the answer was that the development of economic thought beginning with the physiocrats in the eighteenth century and leading through Adam Smith and Ricardo to Karl Marx and Mill had suffered a rather crude interruption with the growth of what Americans used to call "price economics", which concentrated on the implications of scarcity, the allocation of scarce means to different ends and the notion of market equilibrium as developed by Walras. This type of economics was not only not useful but often had a negative effect on all but those brilliant minds who could see their way through it and pick out from it those aspects that were illuminating. But brilliant minds were the exceptions, and for the rest this approach had a negative effect because it diverted attention from the important to the relatively unimportant things. It imparted a belief in the manner of operation of the market mechanism which was unrealistic in the case of economically developed countries and still more misleading in the analysis of underdeveloped economies. Neo-classical economics was almost entirely devoted to the study of individual behaviour as the key to an understanding of the economic mechanism. Earlier economists had a very different approach which, he thought, was more fruitful. They had concentrated on the nature of the economic circulation, had studied the circular flow of production and of money, and so on. Most of their doctrines were now obsolete and had never been properly rewritten. But we needed a textbook on these lines, incorporating the important contribution of Marx who had seen the development of social institutions in a dynamic setting, whereas all the other classical writers (except perhaps Adam Smith) had taken society more or less as they had found it, without realizing how any particular society fitted into a given stage of economic development.

Mr. Kaldor said that in recent years there had been a revival of classical theory. He referred to Mrs. Robinson's theoretical work and to his own and other people's work on growth economics which, starting from a Keynesian position, had close affinities with classical theory, joining it, as it were, from the other end. Even more important, however, from a basic theoretical point of view, than the line of thought coming from Keynes was v. Neumann's work published before the war. Von Neumann's model of general equilibrium was wholly in the classical tradition and in his view represented the ultimate resolution of the theory of value (or rather of the classical theory of the nature of general equilibrium), which Marx had attempted in the volume of *Das Kapital* but had never brought off. Sraffa had dealt with these classical problems more explicitly than v. Neumann and had independently reached the same conclusions, but it was v. Neumann, one of this century's great mathematicians, who had been able to provide a perfectly general proof.

Few students required elegant general proofs, however; what was needed was a stripped-down version of the v. Neumann model which, he thought, could be done more intelligently and simply than had been done so far. He was pleading for an economic text which, starting in the way in which the physiocrats had looked at the economy, would contain some general propositions valid for all kinds of societies and then go on to theories of special cases, using at each stage that amount of abstraction that was essential to make things intelligible. In other words, he was thinking of a textbook which would proceed from a general model of the v. Neumann type to a series of two-sector models, each designed to bring out a particular aspect of the economic problem as it presented itself in different situations. It would all be macro-economics, he said, and not micro-economics.

By macro-economics he did not mean general equilibrium in the sense of equilibrium of the whole economy, as against partial equilibrium of the individual consumer or firm. Walras's model of general equilibrium was in a sense micro-economics and not macro-economics. By the latter he meant the kind of economics that made use of the notion of strategic aggregates, a notion which neo-classical theory shunned. Ricardo had started from the existence of different classes in society: there were landowners, capitalist manufacturers, and workers, and he was interested in finding out what governed the distribution of income between them, because of the effect of changes in the relative position of different classes on the rate of growth of the economy. In contrast, neo-classical theory was formalized in a way that completely obscured these strategic relationships.

Moreover, when one was thinking in terms of strategic aggregates, the notion of economic sectors acquired an importance quite of its own and the relations between particular sectors of the economy were seen in a new light. There were important differences between agriculture and industry, for example, which in the neo-classical type of formalization were ignored. Food was the consumer good *par excellence* which could not be treated just like any other commodity. In the Ricardian analysis agriculture was viewed as the wage good industry and thus played a special role in the economy. To some extent this view was an exaggeration—classical writers, Mr. Kaldor said, had the courage to make assumptions which they knew were only broadly true—but it nevertheless had sufficient depth to illuminate an important controlling factor in economic development.

Another distinction drawn on different lines was used by Marx who had set up what we would nowadays call a two-sector model with a consumption industry and a capital goods industry. In some respects the investment sector had market powers which the consumption sector did not possess. An understanding of the strategic relations between these two sectors was in Mr. Kaldor's view essential for an understanding of the process of growth.

Coming back to what he had said at the beginning, Mr. Kaldor expressed his disagreement with Mr. Balogh who appeared to regard all rigorous deductive theory as useless, because it had to fall back on unrealistic and abstract assumptions. His answer was that any reasoning made use of abstract assumptions. We always had a theory or model in our mind when we made assertions; the only difference was that those who were deprecating a rigorous theoretical approach did not go through the mental discipline of clarifying to themselves on what assumptions their views were based.

When it came to econometric models the situation was different. Mr. Kaldor said that he agreed with Mr. Balogh's criticism of econometric models which tended to predict the course of events in a market economy from parameters derived from time series. For science to have the power of prediction it was necessary to be able to isolate the things that were really parameters (meaning that they were constant over time) and not just variables, whose behaviour could not be explained. He admitted that this was a difficult distinction to make, but the trouble with econometric models was that they assumed the future to be the same as the past, not just in all those respects where we had independent reasons for believing that things that are assumed to be constant really *were* constant, but in respect of all such factors which were not encompassed within the behavioural relationships of the model.

He was even more sceptical about the use of high-faluting techniques for the purpose of maximizing this or that objective. The advanced techniques of linear programming were subject to enormous limitations which, he said, were of two kinds. First, the input/output relationships were unknown and not stable in the sense usually postulated in linear programming models. Secondly, there were numerous factors limiting our choice or affecting the outcome which it was not possible to quantify and incorporate in a programming model. Thus the resistance of pressure groups often made it impossible to choose the obviously optimal method for obtaining a certain objective; but how could one quantify this?

He wondered whether all this tremendous work in linear programming had achieved any concrete results. He was often told that these techniques were employed to good effect in Soviet Russia, for instance, or by the big oil companies in the United States. But whenever he had had occasion to examine these claims, they had turned out to be very exaggerated. It was conceivable that linear programming had some application to planning in a completely socialist state, but it was ludicrous to suppose that it could be used by planners in Asia, Africa or Latin America, given the political structure of these countries and the nature of their economies. There was no government in any of these countries capable of allocating resources in accordance with an optimal plan. To suggest that young officials from Asia or Africa should come here to study these techniques in order to apply them later at home was naïvety in the extreme.

PROFESSOR HANSON

Professor Hanson said that the most consistent theme throughout the discussions had been the need for greater realism in the teaching of economic development. Referring to Professor Wilson's remarks on the need for managerial and administrative studies, he reported that at the University of Leeds they were just about to start a Diploma in Development Administration which would be a combination of economic and administrative studies focusing on the problems of public enterprise. This course should be of particular interest to those underdeveloped countries that were attempting to develop through various kinds of socialist patterns. Of the four major lecture courses which this Diploma would include, one would be devoted entirely to political and administrative problems.

Commenting on the place of political studies in such a programme, Professor Hanson said that the time had come when economists and political scientists ought to arrive at a closer understanding of what each side was endeavouring to do. Most political scientists had some idea of Keynesian economics but knew very little about later developments and controversies. On the side of the economists there was perhaps the feeling that political scientists were still primarily concerned with a rather arid and legalistic sort of institutional analysis, that is, with the kind of approach often associated with the great name of Lord Bryce. On both sides, he said, there was a cultural time-lag. Political scientists nowadays were interested just as much in analysing political behaviour as they were in analysing political institutions. A great deal of work had been done on the *interrelations* between political institutions and political behaviour, with special reference to underdeveloped countries, and he was not at all certain that the majority of economists had as yet taken note of this research, which had passed well beyond the stage of description and classification. He wanted to draw particular attention to the studies by David Apter (and especially to Apter's contribution to a symposium on Industrialization and Society) which, he said, was a serious effort to discover how far particular political systems were able, without destroying themselves, to initiate or accommodate economic and social changes. David Apter's analysis might still be insufficiently dynamic, but Professor Hanson said that he was looking with confidence to further developments in this field. He thought that these findings ought to be brought into courses on economic development, even at the expense perhaps of some of the more esoteric types of economic analysis, to which Mr. Kaldor and Mr. Balogh had referred.

Coming back to his debate with Mr. Kaldor on the role of economic advisers, Professor Hanson said that it was not his opinion that advisers ought to take the polical system for granted. There were circumstances when it was perfectly legitimate for an economic adviser to argue the case for a change in the political system and to put himself on the side of the opposition. It was clear, however, that no government was going to encompass or engineer its own destruction. The important thing was for everyone to realize what kind of economic changes a particular system could accomodate, and what kind it could not.

MR. STREETEN

Mr. Streeten said that there seemed to be general agreement that it was not the function of a teacher of economics to teach specific doctrines: as teachers, we should try to free people from doctrinal habits, cure them of intellectual cramps. In such "therapeutic economics" there was, in his view, an important place for models, and he did not think that there was disagreement on this matter between Mr. Balogh and Mr. Kaldor. Mr. Balogh had taught him that one of the functions of a model was to show up the limitations of other models, for models can never be refuted by facts—only by other models. Naturally, one would not want to waste one's time on completely useless models. He recalled an observation of Mr. Kaldor (at the Corfu Conference) on a model which he criticized, in which the deviations from the strategic variable were larger and more important than the variable itself: such a model was of little use. But one ought to introduce qualifications and change the assumptions even if one had a model that explained some features. For example, one might first take a growth model in which the savings ratio was considered independent of the capital-output ratio, and then proceed to a model where these two variables were considered interdependent. Only by using a variety of models was it possible to teach people to approach economic problems in a flexible way.

MR. BALOGH

Mr. Balogh replying to Mr. Kaldor said that he was not opposed to the deductive method or to rigour in economic analysis if they were used for purposes to which they were fit. These did however not seem to him interesting or applicable to reality. What was illegitimate was the kind of models that were constructed merely in order to get determinate answers. Such theories or models did not illuminate anything; variables and relationships were chosen for the sake of obtaining neat solutions, whether corresponding to reality or not. Up till now most econometric models were of this kind; illicit aggregation was the rule rather than the exception. By necessity the more complex the problems studied, the more simplified the assumptions underlying the basic relationships. They predicted nothing but the immediate past on which they were based.

PROFESSOR PARKINSON

Professor Parkinson reported that at Queen's University, Belfast, a paper on economic development had now been introduced as part of the Honours course in economics. But this affected only a small number of students and there was no prospect of introducing a special degree course for people interested in economic development. There might be other possibilities, however, of contributing to the training of people for jobs in developing countries. Speaking from his experience in Pakistan, Professor Parkinson said that the demand for professional economists who could serve on Planning Boards was small compared with the demand or need for people who knew something about management and business organization. A training in macro-economics or macro-planning was no doubt important for a limited number of people, but there was something to be said for putting more teaching effort into the micro-level and particularly, as Professor Wilson had stressed, into education for management. At Belfast, as well as in other universities, it should be possible to set up courses in industrial administration and introduce this topic into the syllabus for students of engineering who included a fair number of people from underdeveloped countries. The Conference had discussed at some length the advantage of combining several historical disciplines (or of combining the study of economics with that of languages) in the teaching of economic development. In his view at least as much emphasis should be given to the attempt to combine the engineer and the economist with a view to providing a better flow of personnel much lower down the chain than at the level of central planning.

PROFESSOR ZIMMERMAN

Professor Zimmerman, coming back to the question of textbooks in economic development, said that he had just written a new one where he had started in exactly the way Mr. Seers had suggested:

he had taken a view of the world economy as a whole and had tried to estimate the growth and geographical distribution of world income over the last hundred years. His central theme was how to explain the long-run tendency for the gap between rich and poor countries to widen. He had found it useful to distinguish between "growth", a situation where production and population were increasing *pari passu*; "progress", where production was increasing proportionately faster than population; and "development" which he defined as the transition from growth to progress. It seemed to him that while growth and progress lent themselves to a purely economic analysis, development processes called for a less abstract and more descriptive-historical treatment. He therefore agreed with Mr. Balogh and others who had expressed doubts about the relevance of highly abstract models in the analysis of economic development.

He also thought, however, that econometric decision models could be very useful when the problem was to assess the effects of alternative policies.

Mr. Worswick

Mr. Worswick said that he fully associated himself with those who had spoken out against extravagances in econometrics and programming, but he was sorry to hear the extreme statements of Mr. Kaldor, who had gone much too far in his criticism. There were many concrete problems—e.g. of joint products and costs in agriculture—which could be handled very satisfactorily with the aid of quite elementary programming methods; it took no more than a fortnight to learn them, and they were often more suitable than the methods described in the conventional textbooks. When new techniques were coming up, there was always the risk that nonsense was made of them by excessive use. But, as Mr. Cassen had pointed out, if there was to be change, there must be some people who in their particular fields were just a little ahead of their time, putting pressure on the rest. It was a perennial problem of education to train people to be that much ahead without getting lost in futile extravagance.

Index of Authors and Speakers in the Discussion

(*N.B.: references to Papers are shown in italics.*)